D1498311

THE GOSPELS RECONSIDERED

THE GOSPELS RECONSIDERED

A Selection of Papers
read at the International Congress on

THE FOUR GOSPELS
IN 1957

OXFORD

BASIL BLACKWELL

1960

Reprinted from
STUDIA EVANGELICA
(Texte und Untersuchungen zur Geschichte der altchristlichen Literatur
73. Band = V. Reihe, Band 18)

FOREWORD

This book contains a selection from a much larger collection of papers published under the title Studia Evangelica which were read at the International Congress of the ‚Four Gospels in 1957‘. This Congress met with a wide response not only from scholars in the more restricted sense, but also from the parish clergy, from ministers of Religion, teachers of divinity in the school and laymen with serious interests in the Gospels, and this explains to some extent the outward form of certain of the papers. Though written in entire independence and from very different backgrounds the papers suggest a remarkable convergence of view in contemporary studies in the Gospels.

It was felt that in addition to the volume Studia Evangelica, which was published in the celebrated series Texte und Untersuchungen, there was room for a more moderately priced volume which should be within the reach of many who were not able to obtain the original.

TABLE OF CONTENTS

The Present Position
of New Testament Textual Criticism

K. ALAND

Before I try to give an account of the present state of New Testament textual criticism, it seems to me desirable to preface my remarks by the following two caveats, to avoid possible disappointment of too high expectations.

I. My paper does not seek to add a new theory on the history of the New Testament text to the many already existing, nor do I intend to give a general survey of contemporary theories. What I have to say is rather the result of practical work. I shall try to give a picture of the present situation from my own experience of listing New Testament Mss. and from collaborating in the preparation of various editions of the New Testament text. It is necessary to examine the actual position dispassionately, for it is only too easily obscured both by the older and also by more recent publications on the theory of New Testament textual criticism. There is no doubt that these have greatly advanced our studies, but they have at the same time too easily induced, at least in my own experience, a feeling of false security in those who read or make use of them. Only viewing a fraction of the whole field, these publications do not present clearly enough either all that we do *not* know, or even how uncertain is much of what we believe we *do* know.

II. To treat my subject at all completely would require far more time than is at my disposal this afternoon, so I shall content myself with little more than a sketch.

If we look back over the history of the Greek text of the N. T. we see that for hundreds of years it lay under an unlucky star. When the art of printing was invented the West had only just begun to learn Greek again. Latin was the principal language.

1 The Gospels Reconsidered

The Bible was the first book to be printed, but it was a Latin Bible — the famous 42 line Gutenberg Bible. Up to the year 1500 about a hundred new editions of the Latin Bible were published. Meanwhile the Old Testament was printed several times in the original Hebrew, and many Greek editions of the Psalter appeared, but it was only in the 16th century that work began on the printing of the Greek text of the New Testament. How little trouble Erasmus took over his *editio princeps* is well known. All the same it was generally accepted, and deprived Cardinal Ximenez from reaping the fruits of his labours on the Compluten- sian Polyglot. From 1550 onwards the edition of Stephanus super- seded the edition of Erasmus, but nothing fundamental was changed. In both cases the *textus receptus* only was given in accor- dance with the tradition of the Greek speaking Church during the centuries before the invention of printing. In the 17th century the edition of Elzevier replaced the Stephanus text. Despite a number of minor differences as between the three editions of Erasmus, Stephanus and Elzevier, theologians and laymen alike read the text of the New Testament in its latest and worst form. The Reformation, also, based its Bible translations on the *textus receptus*, — we only have to think of the German New Testament of Martin Luther and the King James Version, — and theologians lent new authority to it with their teaching on verbal inspiration and inerrancy. As time went on the world became more and more flooded with editions of the *textus receptus*. In 1710 the Canstein- sche Bibelanstalt in Halle began to print it in large numbers and in 1810 the British and Foreign Bible Society followed suit; effective resistance seemed impossible.

It is one of the glories of scholarship that voices were raised against the primacy of the *textus receptus* as early as the 17th cen- tury, and it was all the more praiseworthy because anyone who criticised the *textus receptus* was suspected of deviating from the teaching of the Church. Englishmen came first: John Fell, John Mill, Edward Wells, Richard Bentley, William Mace. Germans follow them: Johann Albrecht Bengel, Johann Jakob Wettstein, Johann Jakob Griesbach. Nevertheless it was only in the 19th century that the dominance of the *textus receptus* was broken, and first in the realm of scholarship. In 1830—31 the Berlin philologist Carl Lachmann brought out an edition which paved the way for new developments. And in 1850 began the age of Tischendorf, Tregelles and Westcott-Hort with their great critical editions still used today. Energetic champions of the *textus receptus* still remained, however, — for example Burgon in England. The *coup de grâce* was given to the *textus receptus* in the life of the church by Eberhard Nestle's edition, which drew its conclusions from the large editions. In 1898 this text was published by the Württembergische Bibelanstalt in Stuttgart. In 1904 the British and Foreign Bible Society adopted it. From that time it has circulated in hundreds of thousands of copies. Nowadays we only see the *textus receptus* in official use in the Russian Orthodox Church which but recently gave it new official support and defended it with great vigour against the form of the text represented by Nestle.

It is well known that the edition of Nestle, which is today by far the most widely used, gives the average text resulting from the editions of Westcott-Hort, Tischendorf and Weiss, and is substantially the nineteenth century text. What about the editions which have been published in the last decades in competition with Nestle? For example those of Souter, Vogels, Merk and Bover? They each claim that their own form of text is independent of Nestle. If we wish to establish what the text of the Greek New Testament as used nowadays looks like — and this must be our first question — we have to begin with an analysis of these editions including that of Nestle. The edition of von Soden may be excluded, but we shall have something to say about it later.

The relationship which these modern small editions bear to the *textus receptus* has been investigated by Dr. Greenlee. On the basis of eleven sample chapters from all types of New Testament literature he arrives at the following results:

> Nestle differs from the *textus receptus* in 233 cases,
> Merk differs in 160 cases,
> Bover in 111 cases,
> Vogels in 67 cases, and
> Souter in 47 cases.

This result is astonishing. Worked out in percentages it means that Nestle differs from the *textus receptus* 496% in comparison with Souter, 348% in comparison with Vogels, 210% in comparison with Bover, 147% in comparison with Merk. Souter is nearest to the *textus receptus*, Vogels follows closely on his heels,

1*

but even Bover is not far behind. How near the three still are to
the text which it was the main endeavour of the last generations
to supersede becomes even clearer when we realize that the eleven
investigated sample chapters amount in all to about 37 pages in
the Nestle edition of the Greek New Testament. This means that
Souter has on three printed pages an average of only about 4
variants from the *textus receptus* and Vogels about 9 on 5 printed pages; everything else agrees with the *textus receptus*.

At this juncture I should like to say something about Souter's
edition. It is well known that it contains Palmer's reconstruction
of the Greek text, used as basis for the English Revised Version of
1881. This adequately explains its closeness to the *textus receptus*,
which despite Westcott-Hort still retained no small respect at
that time. How far this reconstruction does justice to the English
translation will not and cannot here be decided. That it does not do
justice to the Greek text of the New Testament, however, seems
certain. It is indeed impossible subsequently to reconstruct,
from a translation in a modern language which obeys quite other
laws than Greek, the Greek text on which the translation is based.
Every translation must preserve in numberless instances its own
freedom of construction. It does so in order to reproduce with its
own means of expression the sense of the original, thereby making an accurate reconstruction of the original from it impossible.
If one places any value on such a reconstruction, the only
possibility is to establish the intended Greek text line by line
while the translation is still being made. Every other mode of
procedure must inevitably lead to errors and false conclusions.
Such a reconstruction is an interesting experiment, but as
a printed edition it can only do harm in practical use, for example
among students.

Without doubt Souter's edition is of value because of its critical
apparatus, but for our purpose it must be excluded from further
consideration. We now turn to the important question: what
is the relationship between the texts now in use and the text of
Westcott-Hort. The result is very interesting. To make quite sure
the whole of St. Mark's Gospel has been examined; this amounts
to 53 pages in the Nestle edition — in other words 1/12th to
1/13th of the whole New Testament. If all the variants are first
counted, the number is surprisingly high. The differences from
Westcott-Hort are as follows:

Merk 613,

Nestle 423,

Vogels 362,

Bover 303.

This seems to indicate a remarkable advance beyond Westcott-Hort. But here all *orthographica* are included, for example changes in capitals and small letters etc. If variants of this kind are subtracted, the picture is considerably altered. When every alteration in the position of a word, or similar instances, have been included there remain in Merk 128 differences,

in Nestle 65,

in Vogels 239,

in Bover 160 differences;

that is to say only a small part of the original number. If we take into account that the entire Gospel of Mark contains about 12,000 to 13,000 words, then it becomes clear how small the percentage of these variants is, even though a number of them include more than one word.

It should be noticed, by the way, that the relative diminishing order in the number of variants, namely first Vogels, next Bover, then Merk and lastly Nestle, corresponds inversely to the relative order given earlier of proximity to the *textus receptus*. But we can go one step further in the analysis. Let us now take the text of the edition of von Soden and compare it in respect of the cases in which the modern editions have variants from Westcott-Hort. We obtain the astonishing result that of Vogels' 239 variants only 13 are not to be found in von Soden, of Bover's 160 only 15 are not found in von Soden and of Merk's 128 variants only 10 are not found in von Soden. Naturally this does not mean that these editions take over their variants automatically from von Soden, for we have here 117 other variants which do not appear in the above mentioned small editions. Yet it remains surprising that, as in the other examples mentioned, none of the variants which von Soden's edition lacks is found in any one of the other editions alone, but rather are the variants always found in at least two editions.

What does this finally amount to? Simply that even the modern editions which claim to break new ground still in general present the text of Westcott-Hort, although this is now 75 years old, although since then a mass of new and in part revolutionary discoveries have been made — I would only recall for example the Papyri — and although the principles of New Testament textual criticism have been remarkably developed. The era of Westcott-Hort, Tischendorf and their contemporaries is not over: we are still within it, as far as the practical establishment of the New Testament text is concerned. Where our present-day texts differ from those of 75 and more years ago, the influence of von Soden is marked and results in a closer resemblance to the *textus receptus*.

This situation is alarming. And if we take into account our present position regarding the material which forms the basis of these texts we all use, then our alarm and scepticism can only increase. We know today, including list No. VI recently published, altogether 4680 Greek Mss. of the New Testament: 68 Papyri (in fact there are about 75, but 7 are not yet officially published), 241 Uncials, 2533 Cursives and 1838 Lectionaries. This number is steadily rising. In view of the fact that the list of Mss. published since the 5th instalment in 1954, from which time I have been responsible for it, has increased by not less than 448 numbers, it is not too optimistic — or pessimistic if you like — to estimate that the next few years will see a rise to about 5000 numbers. No one in the whole world has a comprehensive picture of the extant Mss. Even the Kommission für spätantike Religionsgeschichte of the Deutsche Akademie der Wissenschaften, for which the list of Greek New Testament Mss. is compiled and which possesses the most extensive collection of material, knows nothing more of many Mss. than that they exist and roughly what they contain. In recent years American expeditions to Sinai, Jerusalem and Mount Athos have made conveniently available, by large-scale microfilming, manuscript collections otherwise difficult of access. But, apart from some regrettable gaps which still remain, we need not go as far as the Orient or Mount Athos; there exist in many places, particularly in small, but sometimes also in larger European libraries, New Testament Mss. which it is almost impossible to photograph. A particularly regrettable gap could now be closed; it has been possible for us (when I say "us" I always mean the above-mentioned Kommission für spätantike Religionsgeschichte, of which I am chairman) to photograph almost all the approximately 370 Greek Manuscripts and fragments of the New Testament in the libraries of the

USSR which have been practically inaccessible for the last 50 years. A full report on these is in preparation. But a vast amount of work still remains to be done before we can say that we really have access to all the 4680 Mss. now known to us.

What, however, is the position regarding Mss. to which we do have access? Has sufficient work been done on them and have they been used for the editions which have so far appeared? The answer can quickly be ascertained from the facts to hand, and I shall include in the field of investigation all editions since Tischendorf, that is to say all the scholarly editions of the New Testament — both large and small — which have appeared in approximately the last 100 years. To start with the Lectionaries: these have been almost 100% ignored. Particularly in America serious efforts have recently been made to master this very difficult material. But reliance is generally placed on collations of Mss. chosen more or less at random. We ourselves are at present working on the approximately 180 Lectionaries in Soviet libraries. Yet this does not remedy the situation either. One can say no more than that a beginning has been made. In the editions we find readings from Lectionaries only rarely and incidentally. As to the Minuscules with which the history of the printed text of the New Testament begins, we are better placed regarding the investigation of Manuscripts thanks to the work of von Soden. But in the critical apparatuses of all editions, including the one of von Soden, no fewer than 1938, or 77% of this Ms. total, have remained unused. It is likely that the majority of them belong to a late stratum immediately preceding the *textus receptus*, but apart from the fact that this has in general been taken for granted and not really proved, a closer investigation shows that 735 of these Cursives which have not been used in the editions of the last hundred years were written earlier than the 12th century. The main work of the 19th century was on the Uncials. It is well known that Tischendorf alone discovered, first edited and used about 40 of them. Nevertheless, even here the position is not too rosy. The maximum number of Uncials used in the large editions is only a little more than 50% of the total known to us, and not fewer than 75, that is to say over 30% of the total, have not been used in any edition. 53 others — over 20% — are found only in the apparatus of one or two editions. In the case of the Papyri the position is quite different. The Papyri were almost

completely unknown to the editions of the 19th century. By far
the greater number of them have first come to light again in our
generation. Even von Soden knew only 17 Papyri, all the others
becoming known later. But what use has been made of the Papyri
in the modern editions? The recently published 23rd edition of
Nestle, edited by Erwin Nestle and Kurt Aland, has made use of
55 Papyri. In this respect it stands alone. Bover follows next with
31 Papyri. Then comes Merk with 29 Papyri, Legg with 6 and
Vogels with 1 which he mentions having used. That Vogels uses
only one Papyrus is at least as surprising as the fact that Legg
uses six The Papyri — I would recall only the Chester Beatty
Papyri and the Papyrus Bodmer II — represent the outstanding contribution of our generation to the textual criticism
of the New Testament, and they, at any rate, should have been
used in modern editions as extensively as possible.

That this has only been done in the case of Nestle's edition
indicates that even with this limited and surveyable material
some unsolved problems still remain. I cannot here enter into
particulars, but I should like to refer to my article entitled "Neue
neutestamentliche Papyri" published in the last number of
New Testament Studies[1], and to the 6th instalment of the Mss.
list in the *Zeitschrift für die neutestamentliche Wissenschaft*, where
these questions have been dealt with at length. Regarding the
dating and classification of the contents and even the publication
of the texts, much more remains to be done than it is possible to
realize from the importance accorded to the Papyri and the
frequent discussion of them in scholarly literature.

If we now examine the question, on what basis the variants are
actually given in the apparatuses of the editions now used, we
find a new, and also somewhat disturbing situation. Let us take
as evidence for our investigation the two modern editions which
claim to have used the highest percentage of Mss.: I refer to those
of Merk and Bover. Merk lists as used 121 Uncials and 372 Minuscules, Bover lists 120 Uncials and 361 Cursives. These figures
themselves reveal how "used" is to be understood. Both are
pocket editions, the critical apparatuses of which take up about
a quarter to a third of a small octavo printed page. It is indeed
possible to cram into such an apparatus the most important

---

[1] New Testament Studies 3 (1957) 261—286.

readings of the principal Papyri, but it is quite impossible to mention there even a fraction of these Uncials and Cursives with a reasonably satisfactory percentage of their readings. Right from the start it is clear that both Merk and Bover — whom I only take as examples for which others would serve equally well — can only have referred occasionally to the greater percentage of the Mss. I would go so far as to say that the majority of them have been mentioned in fewer than ten places of the apparatus. That is one point. The other is of equal moment. Taking a synoptic compilation of the Mss. used in present editions, we see immediately how seldom a Ms. is used in but one edition; as a rule a Ms. is used in several editions. Practically speaking this means that an edition takes over its variants in general from other previously published editions. Certainly, every editor makes his own collations; in the normal course, however, he evidently uses other editions as a quarry out of which he takes those stones that appeal to him in order to construct his own building. In the case of the Uncials I have already said that Bover lists as used 120 and Merk 121. Of these we find that Merk uses not a single one on his own and Bover one only, while both together they are four times the sole users of a Ms. Obviously one cannot altogether deny that they have made their own collations of some, perhaps many manuscripts. The probability is, however, that they have taken over their citations from Tischendorf, von Soden or others. In the case of Merk this is very probable, because he works with the sigla and classification system of von Soden. As to the Cursives the details are as follows: Bover is sole user 12 times, Merk 26 times, and both together 36 times. The above conclusion holds therefore for the 372 Cursives listed as used by Merk and for Bover's list of 361 Cursives used.

This sample completes the picture. I could go on and make it even darker. One need only give the conclusions of Parvis following his investigation of the critical apparatus of the texts brought out by Tischendorf, von Soden and Legg in relation to their use of the most important Mss. of the Beta-Type, the so-called Hesychius-Recension. One could mention that most of the collations which Parvis uses for his article in the *Journal of Biblical Literature*, 1946, as a control of the editions, are themselves almost without exception of venerable age. The earliest is 120 years old, 3 come from the period between 1900 and 1914

and only two are of more recent date. One could further say that
Tischendorf, the main source of most modern editions, has not
used 171, that is to say 75%, of the 241 Uncials that we know.
Further, almost all critical editions of the old translations,
which are of extraordinary importance, only appeared long after
his edition, and these editions of the translations have been nothing like sufficiently used even in the other editions of the New
Testament since Tischendorf. Subsequent to the appearance of
these editions numberless Mss. have become known which,
therefore, have not at all yet been systematically used by anyone. But I think I have said enough to make clear the situation
in which we find ourselves regarding the Greek text of the New
Testament. I would now like to say something, even if only
briefly, about what is at present being done to improve the situation, in other words, about the editions which are actually in
course of preparation.

The most important undertaking is undoubtedly the International Project to Establish a New Critical Apparatus of the Greek
New Testament. Unfortunately the work on the first volume
containing the Gospel of St. Luke is not yet ready so that a real
evaluation of it is impossible. According to Colwell, Parvis and
Clark this edition will give with the *textus receptus* as basis a
complete collation of all the Mss. written up to the year 900,
that is to say of all Papyri and Uncials. There will also be included
some 300 Minuscules, a "considerable block" of Lectionaries and
all translations made before the year 1000. Patristic quotations
are to be added as well. Many questions arise in this connexion:
for instance regarding the suitability of the *textus receptus* as a
foundation, the arrangement of the apparatus, and the citation of
translations and of the Fathers. Difficult as all these matters are,
the main difficulty of the undertaking would appear to be the
attempt to achieve a complete reproduction of all Mss. earlier
than 900 on the basis of collations of the originals or of micro-
films. When the edition of the volume devoted to Luke's Gospel
appears we shall learn whether these problems have been solved.
Until then we must postpone all other comments beyond expressing our admiration for the courage shown in beginning such
a great undertaking, our hope that the appearance of the first
volume will not be long delayed, and our best wishes for the further
progress of the work. Even the first volume alone will be of

fundamental importance. Nevertheless, when this volume is ready new work will have to begin. For the chief hope of the undertaking is that it will enable us to obtain a new and more complete understanding of the history of the text than has hitherto been possible.

The other undertakings of which I now propose to give a brief account have a different character. One should, perhaps, begin with the latest of them, the Project of the American Bible Society. After preliminary discussions the editorial committee met for its first working session in the autumn of last year. It includes three Americans: Bruce M. Metzger (Princeton), Arthur Vööbus (Maywood), Allan F. Wikgren (Chicago), one British scholar: Matthew Black (St. Andrews), and one German: Kurt Aland (Halle-Berlin). This year they have had a second session and it is planned to hold further sessions at least during the next four years. By the beginning of 1958 we may hope to see in print a booklet explaining the aims and giving details of the work. In accordance with the first draft of this booklet I may already give you the following preliminary information: starting from the text of Westcott-Hort and examining the recent small editions it is hoped to obtain a text which will correspond to the present state of our knowledge. The critical apparatus will concentrate on passages of special importance for exegetes and translators for whom this edition is primarily intended. The number of variants mentioned will be confined to about two to three thousand (in comparison with the 10,000 in Nestle). The number of textual witnesses consulted will on the other hand be increased so that in each case relatively complete evidence for and against every reading will be available. In special supplementary volumes exegetes and translators will be given the reason for the decision taken in each case, and also additional material for their own particular purposes. Naturally, concerning the establishment of the text nothing definite can yet be said. But it seems obvious that the new edition will diverge in a good many places from the text now generally used, even where the editions up to now have found themselves in agreement with one another. Although this new edition arises immediately out of practical requirements, nevertheless it will indirectly further the work of textual criticism, because where an apparatus is provided it will be far more complete than in other modern editions. It is obvious on the other hand that the edition cannot contain sufficient material for a study of the textual tradition. A case without importance for the translator and sometimes even for the exegete can be of great importance for the history of the text, and vice versa. In the Papyri one can study this in many instances.

So much in brief for the new undertakings. Regarding the existing editions, all we know about the one of Bover is that it will be continued by one of his pupils. It is safe to say, however, that much less work is being done on the New Testament text in Spain than on the text of the Old Testament. The edition of Merk is to have a simplified apparatus and this is to be welcomed. The employment hitherto of the sigla system of von Soden makes it very difficult to use the existing apparatus. Concerning the plans of Professor Vogels for a fourth edition I cannot say anything. More information is available about the progress of the Greek New Testament which has continued to be published in England during the last 50 years. It is well known that the British and Foreign Bible Society adopted in 1904 the text established by Eberhard Nestle for the Württembergische Bibelanstalt and has circulated it with a very short critical apparatus in repeated editions. Nestle's own apparatus was 50 years ago still in an embryonic state, but the English edition has remained unchanged even yet, while the German edition, thanks largely to Erwin Nestle with the cooperation of German New Testament scholars, has improved from decade to decade. It was clear that the English apparatus was in no way sufficient to meet even modest critical requirements. So the British and Foreign Bible Society began preparations for a second revised edition, and the work was entrusted to Professor G. D. Kilpatrick of Oxford, and made its appearance in May 1958. [Meanwhile Professor Kilpatrick is engaged on a third edition which is due to appear in some eight years' time. It will contain a moderate revision of the New Testament text and this revised text is being used in connection with a new translation of the New Testament into English of which fascicles containing Matthew and Mark have already appeared.]

For a number of years there have also been new developments in the German Nestle. It finds its outer expression in the fact that Kurt Aland is named as collaborator on the title-page of the 22nd edition of 1956, while he is named as co-editor in the recently published 23rd edition. The 24th edition is in course of preparation. The 23rd edition differs from the previous editions in the way already mentioned: it makes extensive use of the Papyri, including the Papyrus Bodmer II. The 24th edition will appear in an entirely new form, with new types and different make-up. We shall complete what has been begun in the 21st edition with the help of a larger number of collaborators. Every sufficiently important reading of the great Mss. including the Papyri will in future be mentioned in the critical apparatus provided on the basis of new collations, and the apparatus will be more easily usable. The old translations and the Fathers also will be utilized in greater measure. Above all, the hitherto mechanically followed "majority text" will be in principle abandoned. To attain these objects one has to walk with great circumspection, for in the course of the last fifty years or so Nestle has developed from the private work of a single scholar to become to some extent the modern *textus receptus*, with which one must not experiment. The order in which textual alterations should be made seems clear. In very many more cases, perhaps, than necessary, owing to the mechanical system of comparison, square brackets are employed to indicate doubt as to the authenticity of a word or passage. One has to decide in such cases whether the word or passage is a true part of the text or rather belongs to the critical apparatus. Further, in a number of cases the derivation of the text from Westcott-Hort or Tischendorf can be clearly seen, in so far as it goes back in these cases only to the Codex Vaticanus or Sinaiticus or to both of them, supported sometimes by a few other witnesses. All these instances have to be examined, but not by the editor alone. Rather must he submit his proposals to his colleagues, and act according to their counsel. In this way the Nestle of the future will correspond as closely as in the past or even more so to the consensus of international New Testament scholarship.

At the same time a Greek Synopsis is in preparation and I must now briefly say something about it. The Synopsis is to be published, like the Nestle edition, by the Württembergische Bibelanstalt in Stuttgart. Its title is "Synopsis Quattuor Evangeliorum". It will include for the first time the complete Gospel of St. John and so will facilitate a study of the synoptics in relation to the fourth Gospel and vice versa. Not only the main parallels but also all secondary parallels are given in full and exactly side by side. To each section the whole material from the New Testament Apocrypha and the early Fathers is added. One must mention in this connexion that Professor Greeven of Kiel is also preparing a new Synopsis which is likewise designed to replace the synopsis of Huck-Lietzmann. Professor Greeven will, I believe, very much expand the critical apparatus and will submit his own recension of the text. This is to be welcomed, as everything else is to be welcomed which is calculated to overcome the stagnation of the last decades in regard to the practical establishment of the New Testament text.

Our present position is paradoxical. We are by and large in the same position with our text as our great-grandfathers were, although we have gone behind and replaced their fundamental basis, the "neutral text", through the establishment of the so-called "Mischtext" which was dominant in the 2nd and 3rd centuries. But this expression (Mischtext) is in itself already false, because a "Mischtext" follows previously compiled recensions while, in the case of the New Testament, recensions were first made in the 4th century. Be this as it may: the establishment of the textual character of the New Testament in the 2nd and 3rd centuries has taken away the firm basis for the form of text which the 19th century possessed or believed itself to possess. We cannot return to the principles of Westcott-Hort any more than to those of von Soden, who, with his homogeneous I—H—K text which according to him preceded the recensions, likewise chased a phantom. The question remains for us what we should do in this situation. A mass of discoveries have been made, numberless dazzling individual investigations and studies have been published. But nowhere have we a full picture, sufficiently convincing to enable us to construct a complete edition. The only edition which at the present day issues from a homogeneous conception is that of Vogels which is surely mistaken in its one-sided extreme character.

Shall we in this situation lapse into complete subjectivism or a state of resignation? This is the great danger and not a few New Testament scholars are threatened by it. It is certainly true that every passage of the New Testament has its own problems. Nevertheless, now as in the past, textual criticism without a history of the text is not possible. We must pursue our investigations into the history of the text if we really wish to make progress, not as hitherto at a few isolated points, but over the broadest possible field. Von Soden's abortive effort seems to have resulted in our losing courage. Only if we press forward from a similarly broad basis can real progress be effected. Perhaps the International Project provides us with such a basis. In any case we are at the present day in Berlin seeking to elaborate a new system which combines the classification of the extra-textual equipment of the Mss. with selected collations. We have begun to use, on the one hand, 200 hitherto unused Minuscules of the ninth to the twelfth centuries, and, on the other hand, the block of 370 Mss. in Russian libraries. It is still too early to assess the results of this work. At all events, — and I would conclude with this statement, for as I have said it is not my intention to become involved in theories concerning the history of the text, — it is clear that the situation with which our present-day method of establishing the New Testament text confronts us is most unsatisfactory. It is not at all the case that, as some seem to think, everything has been done in this field and we can for practical purposes rest satisfied with the text in use. On the contrary, the decisive task still lies ahead.

Literary Forms
and Contents of a Normal *Εὐχαριστία*
in the First Century

J. P. AUDET O. P., Montreal

It seems to have been long since agreed, among lexicographers, that the first, and principal, meaning of εὐχαριστέω, in New Testament language, is identical with one of the basic meanings of classical Greek and *koine* as well: εὐχαριστέω is, first of all, "give, or, return thanks", "rendre grâce, remercier", "Dank sagen", "gratias agere". Correlatively, we are told, εὐχαριστία is "thanksgiving", the "action de grâce", as an expression of acknowledgment and gratitude for a gift received ("Danksagung"), which links up with another classical meaning of εὐχαριστέω, "bestow a favour on", "accorder une faveur à quelqu'un", "Gunst schenken, erweisen". Save for a few nuances, all the rest of the lexicographical analysis is then subordinated, as is natural, to this basic premise. It goes without saying, moreover, that commentators, in their literary and theological analysis of the texts concerned, follow a line which coincides with that of the lexicographers. But, as a matter of fact, what more are they doing, in this, than to take back from the latter what was their own? The psychological pattern according to which the texts are analysed, and finally take on their theological significance, is that of gratitude: the gift received (χάρις, χάρισμα) calls for the acknowledgment of that gift (εὐχαριστέω), in turn, through a corresponding expression of gratitude inwardly felt as such (εὐχαριστία). So, according to this analysis, the εὐχαριστία becomes normally a returned offering (προσφορά, ἀναφορά) of actions and words of gratitude, or, better still, in a fuller form, an offering of a gift considered beforehand as acceptable to God (bread and wine, body and blood of the Lord) — a gift which is, on the part of the one who offers it, spontaneously accompanied by words and gestures primarily expressing gratitude[1].

Is this construction as solid as the universal favour it enjoys would have us believe? I have no time here to undertake a piecemeal examination of it, nor to pass judgment on the foundations on which it is supposed to be grounded. I shall satisfy myself with a remark of a more general, and partially negative, character, which will lead me to the positive considerations with which I am mainly concerned for the moment.

Indeed, it is true, first, that the verb *εὐχαριστέω* and the substantive *εὐχαριστία* do have, here and there, in Greek-speaking Judaism, and especially in New Testament Greek, a meaning identical with that which the rest of the Greek world has made familiar to us. For *εὐχαριστέω*, such is the case, for example, in 2 Makk. 12, 31, where we see Judah and his men "returning thanks" (*εὐχαριστήσαντες*) to the Scythopolitans for having graciously welcomed their oppressed fellow-countrymen (comp. Lk. 17, 16; Rom. 16, 4). It is more than probable, moreover, that it is again the simple meaning of "gratitude" which is supposed by *εὐχαριστία*, when, at Paul's trial, Tertullus the barrister takes it upon himself to express to the Roman Procurator, Felix, by way of flattery, the feelings with which the nation welcomes the good turn of his government (Act. 24, 3; comp. Sir. 37, 11; Esth. 8, 12 d = 16, 4; 2 Makk. 2, 27).

But, starting from examples like these, are we allowed to make broad generalizations? Are we permitted, in particular, to bypass the suggestion implied in a number of other cases by the proximity, and the recognized equivalence, of *εὐλογέω* and *εὐχαριστέω*? Moreover, do we have to neglect completely, as is usually done, the positive semantic relationship, manifest in many cases, of *ἐξομολογέομαι* with the group *εὐχαριστέω-εὐχαριστία*? Do we have — what would be much more decisive — to close our eyes to the evident fact that, in most of their uses,

---

[1] Almost endless references could be given here, among the ancients, from the latter half of the second century at least, as well as among the moderns. I shall content myself with three: among lexicographers, W. Bauer, Wörterbuch zu den Schriften des N. T., Berlin, 4 th ed., 1952, s. v.; among commentators and historians of the liturgy: M.-J. Lagrange, Evangile selon s. Luc, Paris, 6 th ed., 1941, p. 544; J. A. Jungmann, Missarum sollemnia (Fr. tr.), Paris 1954, III, pp. 14, 21—25, on the Preface.

εὐλογέω, εὐχαριστέω and ἐξομολογέομαι, with their corresponding substantives, are connected, in Septuagint as well as in
New Testament Greek, with a literary genre, or forms, the
normal function of which, from our present point of view, would
be to determine their meaning in one way or another? Or,
conversely, would we have to maintain around these words the
kind of artificial void in which our standard lexicons still keep on
presenting them? Have these words really been like wandering
stars, in the sky of Jewish and Christian consciousness also, at the
period with which we are concerned — or, on the contrary, did
they cluster, thanks to their meeting in common and definite
literary forms, to make up true constellations?

If due attention is paid to the laws which govern these things,
I believe we will favour the latter hypothesis. We shall give up,
then, consciously and resolutely, presupposing that words wish
only to exist in the "lived" language, as orderly units busying
themselves in the easy task of keeping their proper place in
alphabetical order as they are presented to us by our dictionaries.
In return, we shall presuppose — which seems sheer common
sense — that, if the words with which we have to deal at present
have shared the conditions of existence of definite literary genres
or forms, it is impossible that nothing could now be gathered
from these conditions in order to determine their real meaning.

The essential task which analysis would have to take upon
itself, is therefore to observe the effect, not only of the proximate
context, but of the literary genre as a whole, on the meaning of
the related words εὐχαριστέω — εὐχαριστία, εὐλογέω — εὐλογία,
ἐξομολογέομαι — ἐξομολόγησις. Some rather unexpected light
may very well come out of it.

I must, however, keep my present ambitions within certain
limits. Ideally, to give full strength to my further remarks, I
would have to trace back, in the first place, the origins and
development of the literary genre of the εὐχαριστία in Jewish
tradition, before entering upon the problems directly connected
with the records of the first Christian generations. But even a
brief sketch of the evidence would far exceed in itself the limits
assigned to this paper. I must content myself here with declaring,
rather bluntly, I am afraid, the literary categories, which, in my
mind, can be drawn from a careful examination of examples such

as are provided by the ancient Jewish tradition in the particular
field of the εὐχαριστία. These categories I shall have to use, later,
all through our analysis of the early Christian documents on the
same subject. For the Christian εὐχαριστία, as a literary genre,
has been a natural heiress to the older Jewish εὐχαριστία, which
had created the forms and attached to them very definite
meanings and equally specific worship values.

The Jewish "benediction" (*berâkhâh*), which has been, from
our point of view, the true parent of the Christian εὐχαριστία,
was twofold: first, there was the spontaneous original "benediction", essentially made up of two literary elements. The former I
call the "benediction" proper, which gives its name to the
literary genre as a whole; the latter I call the motive of the
"benediction", expressing the reason why God is actually praised
on a particular occasion. This reason, moreover, is always a
divine "wonder" as such, or a *mirabile Dei*, and accordingly, the
psychological pattern underlying the spontaneous "benediction"
is above all that of admiration and joy, not of gratitude, which
remains subordinated, in fact, to the fundamental feeling of
admiration, and is therefore secondary.

But there was also, as a somewhat later development of the
spontaneous "benediction" just described, another form within
the same literary genre, which I have ventured to call the cultual
"benediction", for lack of a better name, and in spite of a real
danger of equivocation. At the end of the process of its evolution,
this cultual "benediction" included essentially, no longer two but
three basic literary elements, which I would briefly describe in
the following way: a) the "benediction" proper, always rather
short, more or less stereotyped in its form, leaning towards the
invitatory genre, an enthusiastic call to divine praise; b) a
central element which I would call the anamnesis of the *mirabilia
Dei*; this second element is nothing else than a more or less
protracted development of the motive as it already existed in
the original spontaneous "benediction"; its proper object, thus,
is much less the transient "wonder" of a particular circumstance
as perceived by the individual conscience, than the permanent
and universal "wonders" as perceived and remembered (hence
the name of anamnesis) above all by the conscience of the
community itself; these "wonders", again, are of two kinds: on
the one hand, there are the "wonders" displayed by the power

and kindness of God in His creation, as they are set before the
eyes of all men; on the other hand, there are the "wonders"
especially intended by God's power and lovingkindness for the
enhancing of the destiny of His chosen people, as they are ever
shining in the collective memory of traditions; c) lastly, the
return of the initial "benediction" by way of *inclusio*, or doxology,
oftentimes coloured in different shades according to the particular theme which prevails in the anamnesis. In the use which I
shall hereafter make of these literary categories: "benediction"
proper, anamnesis and doxology, one will do well to keep in mind
that it is again the "benediction" proper, or, initial "benediction",
which lends its name to the literary genre as a whole.

With the help of these categories: spontaneous "benediction",
with its "benediction" proper and its motive; cultual "benediction", with its "benediction" proper, anamnesis and doxology, —
I come now to the "eucharistic" records of the first Christian
generations. Within the limits of this paper, however, I cannot
take upon myself to consider this documentation under all its
aspects. I would ask you, then, to allow me to retain for my
present consideration, as is natural, those texts only which have
a direct bearing on my subject, I mean, the few passages around
which a problem of literary forms can be profitably discussed.

To begin with, it will not be superfluous, perhaps, to dispel a
certain feeling of preliminary uneasiness, which could later
unconsciously foster some objections. It is necessary to state, in
effect, without ambiguity, that, in spite of the fact that it had
already gone a long way in the matter of expressing the religious
conscience of Israel, the literary genre of the "benediction"
(*berâkhâh*: εὐλογία — ἐξομολόγησις — εὐχαριστία) was still very
much alive at the time of Jesus, as is clear from the practice
and the creations of that period[1]. Let us say, in addition, to
make everybody at once feel secure, that, at least in Judaism, the

---

[1] Witness, in particular, the practice of the recitation of both the
Shemone 'esre and the Birkat ha-mazon, and the significant developments
which such traditional forms underwent in or around the first century
A. D. We can think also of the rich background of practices, still very
healthy, which the codification of tractate Berakhoth of the Mishna
presupposes in the following century. Furthermore, it would be relevant
here to draw from the global testimony of Qumran's Hodayoth, although
these last seem to belong to a somewhat different tradition.

old *berâkhâh* has remained alive down to the present day. So, through the centuries, the "benediction" has proved to be one of the most deep-rooted literary forms to which the religion of the patriarchs, of Moses and of the prophets gave birth. What we have to suppose on this point, at the outset, is therefore an unbroken and perfect continuity, not only of expression but also of conscience, between Jesus and his first disciples on the one hand, and the older tradition on the other. Besides, one can hardly think that a partial transposition into Greek of literary forms sanctioned by so constant a practice had already implied a perceptible alteration of their fundamental meaning, in Christian communities still dominated by their Jewish component. To be precise, the risk of alteration will not appear, and the alteration will not actually take place, before the time when the communities born from the gospel will begin to be dominated by Gentile converts.

Yet, it is a fact: from Jesus himself the gospel tradition has preserved for us, in actual terms, hardly more than one "benediction", or *εὐχαριστία*[1]. This *εὐχαριστία*, which is an *εὐλογία — ἐξομολόγησις* as well, takes on the primitive form of the spontaneous "benediction", with its two literary components: the "benediction" proper, and the motive of that "benediction", reflecting in the present a particular manifestation of the *mirabilia Dei*. The text is too well-known for me to linger on its analysis here. Suffice it to quote Mt. 11, 25 f.: "I praise thee, *ἐξομολογοῦμαί σοι*, Father, Lord of heaven and earth, that thou didst hide these things from the wise and experts, and didst reveal them unto little ones. Yea, Father, for so it was well pleasing in thy sight."

This is the classical form of the spontaneous "benediction", as we already know it. I would only like to note, in this respect, the normal persistence of the particular nuance of proclamation of the divine name implied in the "benediction" — a nuance which the Greek at least emphasizes here by using *ἐξομολογοῦμαι*. On the other hand, the motive of the "benediction" belongs, as we might have expected, to the realm of the *mirabilia Dei*, which Jesus sees on the way towards realization, through his action, in the very progress of the proclamation of the kingdom. The "wonder",

---

[1] To the example given below, add Jn. 11, 41 f., which is, however, somewhat special.

to him, is that, according to the good pleasure of the Father, the announcement of the coming of God's reign has found its way to the hearts of the little ones, that is, the simple, the meek and the "poor"[1].

In face of such a perfect example of "evangelical" εὐχαριστία, how could we avoid regretting the fact that the primitive tradition did not cling to more recollections of this quality[2]? But everyone knows that the earliest tradition, save for a few hints around the great event of the passion, is silent on the prayer of Jesus (Mt. 26, 26—44 and par.; Jn. 12, 27f.). At the most it takes care, here and there, to note the bare fact in passing (Lk. 3, 21; 5, 16; 6, 12; 9, 18. 28—29; 11, 1). Undoubtedly, however, the darkness into which we are thus thrown seems nowhere more regrettably palpable to us than around the εὐχαριστία.

Yet, the situation is not so desperate as we might perhaps think at first sight, if only we are prepared to remember the general laws of the literary genre of the εὐχαριστία, or "benediction", such as they can be gathered from elsewhere, to say nothing of the practice of Jesus himself, as we can see it in the example we have just examined. On the multiplication of the

---

[1] At the background of Jesus' marvelling and rejoicing, we should probably restore here something like the prophecy of Is. 61, 1—2, on the "good tidings" brought to the "poor" (quoted Lk. 4, 18f.). Thus, the "good pleasure" of the Father would appear, in reality, as a faithfulness to His promises. Such a relationship between the *mirabilia Dei* and God's faithfulness shows up fairly often in the literary genre of the "benediction". It is one of the most remarkable and constant theological aspects of the feelings which subtend it. Hence, around the "benediction" (εὐχαριστία), a natural atmosphere of attention to prophecies as indications of God's design, and as anticipated declarations of His favours [see, in this respect the really wonderful "evangelical" εὐχαριστία of Eph. 1, 3—3, 21: note that the "eucharistic" motive of the extension of the gospel to the "poor" (Mt. 11, 25f.; Lk. 10, 21f.) is replaced here by that of the extension of the gospel to the Gentiles, the "wonder" *par excellence* among men, but, in God's mind, "mystery" (μυστήριον) of such magnitude that even the prophecies could not, to speak properly, bring it to the "knowledge" (γνῶσις) of the first heirs to the promise].

[2] See again, however, Jn. 11, 41: πάτερ, εὐχαριστῶ σοι ὅτι ἤκουσάς μου, before the rising of Lazarus from the dead, a specific sign of the "wonder" *par excellence* of "life" in the Fourth Gospel. The case of 17, 1—26 is special and must be considered in the light of the more general relationships of the Johannine tradition with the words and deeds of Jesus.

loaves and fishes (Mt. 14, 13—21 and par.; 15, 32—39 and par.; Jn. 6, 1—13), all the narratives are at one in noting the attitude and the actions of Jesus, especially his *εὐλογία*, or *εὐχαριστία* (*εὐλόγησεν*: Mt. 14, 19; Mk. 6, 41; 8, 7; Lk. 9, 16; *εὐχαριστήσας*: Mt. 15, 36; Mk. 8, 6; Jn. 6, 11). Of this *εὐλογία-εὐχαριστία* we shall never know the actual terms. It has been sometimes conjectured that they must have reproduced fairly closely the general wording of the "benediction" which used to accompany the "breaking of bread" in the table liturgy of contemporary Judaism. This is possible. But if we take into account the consciousness of Jesus as regards his proclamation of the coming of God's reign, as well as of the links which connected, within his action, the "signs and prodigies" with the word, not to mention a relative, though certain, fluidity of the forms then in use, it is much more likely that the anamnesis of his *εὐχαριστία*, on such occasions at least, must have included an evocation of the "wonders" performed by God in the gospel, besides the usual recalling of the "wonders" of creation. The literary mobility of the anamnesis was precisely, in the tradition of the *εὐχαριστία*, or "benediction", the character which secured the constant adaptation of this to the variability of circumstances, individual and collective.

In short, from the point of view of forms, the mobility of the anamnesis was that which had always made, and was still making, the extraordinary vitality of the literary genre of the "benediction". It is hard to think, in these conditions, that Jesus might have satisfied himself, for his *εὐχαριστία*, with a mere repetition of a fixed formula of anamnesis, more or less common in his days, independent of the "good tidings" of the coming of the kingdom of God, at the very moment when, through him, as a "sign" of these "good tidings", God was about to revive on behalf of the crowds the "wonders" which had of old cast such a radiance of divine power, faithfulness and loving-kindness on the people's march across the desert.

Besides, the alternative conjecture of a true "evangelical" anamnesis would enable us to give a perfectly natural meaning to an important detail of the "breaking of bread" at Emmaus after the resurrection. The narrative of Luke tells us specifically that it is at the "breaking of bread" that the disciples recognized him whom they had till then taken for a stranger (Lk. 24, 35). What does it mean? The distinctive element of a "breaking of bread", actions and words together, as well as of an εὐχαριστία more generally, is in the first place its anamnesis[1]. All we would have to suppose, then, to explain the fact that the disciples recognized their master "at the breaking of bread" (ἐν τῇ κλάσει τοῦ ἄρτου), is that his personal anamnesis at the "breaking of bread" must have ordinarily taken on, at least towards the latter period of his ministry, a definite "evangelical" colour[2], obviously distinctive, which besides would have been very well known by all who had been close enough to him to be reckoned among his disciples.

As you would have already surmised, it is along the same line of observations and hypotheses that a certain number of particularly hard difficulties can be solved, so it seems to me, around the major "eucharist" (Mt. 26, 26—29; Mk. 14, 22—25; Lk. 22, 19—20; 1 Cor. 11, 23—25). Ancient, as well as modern, interpretation has always directed the best part, if not the totality, of its attention towards two elements of the texts from which the origins of the εὐχαριστία par excellence of Christian worship are first known to us. The former — and the one which has contributed more by far to the development of a "eucharistic" theology, especially in the West — is represented, as is well known, by the words with which Jesus has accompanied the distribution of the bread and the presentation of the cup to his disciples on the evening of the last Passover he was to celebrate among them. The latter — to which modern commentators seem to have paid even greater attention than the ancient – is to be found, as a matter of fact, only in the narratives of Paul and Luke: it is what critics are more or less agreed to call the "reiteration command".

---

[1] It has been a mistake, certainly, to look for the distinctive character of Jesus' "breaking of bread" in the mere action of the "breaking" itself. Everything is put back in the right order when due attention is paid to the literary genre of the εὐχαριστία, the sensitive point of which is its anamnesis.

[2] "Evangelical": in the limited and precise meaning already defined, of the "wonders" performed by God in Jesus (deeds and words) towards the establishment and progress of the promised "kingdom". Comp., in this respect, the "evangelical" colouring of the Pater in its relations with contemporary Jewish prayer, and also, its value as a distinctive sign in the piety of Jesus' disciples. Christians could recognize each other at the Pater, as Jesus himself, at the "breaking of bread", had become recognizable through the anamnesis of his εὐχαριστία.

But did this attention, however, apportioned as it was, keep as perfectly as one seems to suppose the inner balance of the most important cultual event to the understanding of which it was expected to lead? One would like to say that it did. But there are some serious reasons to doubt it.

First, the fact that the liturgical name which the "Lord's supper" has finally been given preferably to any other, has been taken from that *εὐχαριστήσας* (— *εὐλογήσας*) of the narratives, to which critical and theological reflexion indeed do not appear to have devoted an effort proportional to that which was actually displayed, with so much insistence and complacency, around the three short sentences: "This is my body", "This is my blood", and "Do this in remembrance of me". Next, this other fact, scarcely less significant, of the way in which, from very early times, the eucharist has been linked up liturgically with the day of the resurrection ("Lord's day"), rather than either the night when Jesus was arrested, or the day of his death on the cross. Moreover, is it very likely that the imperative *τοῦτο ποιεῖτε εἰς τὴν ἐμὴν ἀνάμνησιν*, however it might have presented itself in the beginning, should have to be so deeply dissociated as is usually implied, from the initial attitude, actions and words by which Jesus chose to relate the breaking of the bread, its distribution and the presentation of the cup to the company of the disciples, to the mysterious design of God? Now, since from the point of view of literary forms we are concerned here with an *εὐχαριστία*, it is clear that, in reality, such a relation was in the first place established in the mind of Jesus by an *εὐχαριστῶ σοι, πάτερ*, or its equivalent, followed by the development of an appropriate motive, or anamnesis.

It is not difficult to see, however, what has altered the inner equilibrium of the attention which commentators have devoted to these narratives. There is the fact, on the one hand, that, if we have every reason to believe that we possess a fairly close account of the words with which Jesus accompanied his breaking of the bread, its distribution and the passing of the cup to his disciples, we do not know the actual terms in which the initial *εὐχαριστία* was moulded. On the other hand, the silence of the gospel tradition on this point would have caused less damage to our understanding, if the received forms of the literary genre of the *εὐχαριστία*, and their proper meaning, had not themselves been more or less obscured fairly early in the liturgical practice of the ancient church. This twofold negative factor, to be sure, has very heavily influenced later theological reflexion, such as developed around the "eucharist".

But, at least in itself, the situation thus created was certainly not hopeless in all respects. A recovery of the ancient literary forms of the εὐχαριστία, of their inner arrangement and of their exact meaning, remained always possible. It seems to me that we are now in a position to begin to realize the gain that such a recovery could bring about. Shall I appear too optimistic if I say that this recovery already enables us to understand in a more correct way the relations which must have obtained in the beginning between the τοῦτο ποιεῖτε εἰς τὴν ἐμὴν ἀνάμνησιν of Paul and Luke, and the εὐχαριστία?

Every cultual εὐχαριστία included, in those times, an anamnesis. It belonged to its nature, so much so that its very existence would have been unthinkable without it. Now, we know, on the other hand, that the proper object of the anamnesis, in the literary genre of the ancient εὐχαριστία, as well as of the simpler motive of the spontaneous "benediction", was the *mirabilia Dei*, as such. What then remains for our supposition in the particular case of the εὐχαριστία which Jesus left for his disciples at his last Passover with them? Simply this, that its anamnesis, according to the laws of the literary genre and the practice of Jesus himself, as we were already able to see elsewhere, had been a properly "evangelical" anamnesis, that is, a last and plenary "proclamation" (ἐξομολόγησις), in marvelling and joyful praise (εὐλογία), of the many "wonders" that God had performed in Jesus, as the Messiah, all along in the development of the "gospel" (εὐαγγέλιον), and more especially, of the "wonder" *par excellence* which was about to crown it, that of Jesus' death already consummated in the "glory" of his resurrection, by anticipation of hope and certainty[1].

---

[1] Comp. the motive of the anticipated εὐχαριστία uttered by Jesus just before bringing his friend Lazarus back to life: πάτερ, εὐχαριστῶ σοι ὅτι ἤκουσάς μου (aorist!) (Jn. 11, 41); see, in the following verse, the reappearance of the ἐξομολόγησις value of the εὐχαριστία. Comp. also the feelings of admiration for God's design, and the deep joy which permeates the last conversations of Jesus with his disciples in the Fourth Gospel, especially the final prayer, very close, in fact, to the literary forms of the εὐχαριστία (Jn. 13—17).

It is in this profound sense that, on the lips, or, at any rate, in the mind of Jesus, an invitation to perpetuate his actions about the bread and the cup must necessarily have been at the same time an invitation to do it "in remembrance" of him (εἰς τὴν ἐμὴν ἀνάμνησιν). The distinctive element of any εὐχαριστία being its motive, or its anamnesis, it was simply normal that, within the "gospel", or rather, to be exact, at its summit, the anamnesis of the εὐχαριστία left by Jesus for his disciples should have been properly "evangelical". In short, Jesus' inviting his own to take over his εὐχαριστία in their turn was equivalently, within the limits of the "gospel", an attempt to awaken for ever their insight into the decisive order of values of his death and resurrection; as likewise an attempt to relate their faith and hope, through the ἐξομολόγησις function belonging to any anamnesis, into that which he knew to be, in the loving purpose of the Father's power, the completion, the ultimate consummation and the fullness of the εὐαγγέλιον, the "gospel".

This interpretation suggests, it seems to me, two particular propositions, which I should like to make, though briefly, before passing on to a text of Paul which is very significant from our present point of view. For the natural links of the anamnesis with the "gospel", εὐαγγέλιον, at the very heart of the εὐχαριστία, if we did not fail to describe them correctly, bring to full light, not only the actual indissolubility of the κήρυγμα and the Christian εὐχαριστία, but also the ideal balance of relations which κήρυγμα, baptism and εὐχαριστία must preserve within the general frame of pastoral action, Christian life and worship: κήρυγμα as a call to hope and faith in an order of "wonders" which God, in all lovingkindness, has performed in Jesus; baptism as the actual entering into that order of "wonders" of the "gospel", which appears to be the very fullness of the "wonders" of the creation, and at the same time the fullness of all the prefigurative "wonders" which had accompanied earlier human history, especially that of Abraham's lineage; εὐχαριστία as the consummation in marvelling and joyful praise, through freely received forgiveness, of faith and hope in the "gospel", in the individuals and the community as well, "till the Lord comes".

In this light — and let this be my second proposition — we perceive too, it seems, what has really been in the mind of Jesus and his first disciples the inner balance of the εὐχαριστία both as a "sacrifice of praise" and as a sacrifice of expiation, intended to bring to an end, some day, all the prior sacrificial patterns. In this respect, we should say in the first place that the εὐχαριστία does nothing else than to reflect, quite exactly, the general equilibrium of the "evangelical" event itself. In the course of his public action, and before laying down his own life, Jesus had not simply forgiven sins; and when he happened to do it, we should remember he did it with an authority and open-handedness which seemed precisely a thing of "wonder" in the eyes of those who believed that God was carrying out through him the plan of His benevolence towards men[1].

So, in the "good tidings", it was the "wonder" of the progress in the fulfilment of God's design that always remained pre-eminent. When, after that, we remember the links which originally connected the εὐχαριστία to the εὐαγγέλιον, we easily understand, so it seems to me, that the εὐχαριστία should have appeared, in the first place, very exactly as is suggested by the name it has finally retained: a "sacrifice of praise", a θυσία αἰνέσεως, or, as Aquila's translation will put it later, an εὐχαριστία (so Ps. 50, 14), the most beautiful "fruit of the lips" (καρπὸν χειλέων) proclaiming the "name of God" in the "wonders" *par excellence* of the "gospel": the death and resurrection of Jesus,

---

[1] In this respect, it is important to note, in the Synoptic tradition, the coincidence of the first remission of sins with one of the most signal healings which has been recorded. After that, it is all the more interesting to see the unanimity with which this same tradition has emphasized the "ecstatic" attitude of marvelling and praise of the witnesses, of those at least whom the cure had led to faith and hope: καὶ ἔκστασις ἔλαβεν ἅπαντας, καὶ ἐδόξαζον τὸν θεόν, καὶ ἐπλήσθησαν φόβου λέγοντες ὅτι εἴδομεν παράδοξα σήμερον (Lk. 5, 26; equivalently Mt. 9, 8 and Mk. 2, 12; note the motive of the "benediction"-εὐχαριστία, probably still recognizable behind the λέγοντες clause). These are the feelings primarily underlying the εὐχαριστία: a magnificent and candid prefiguration of the manner in which the "wonder" of the remission of sins by means of Jesus' death, and the concomitant "wonder" of this same death consummated in the resurrection, as the crowning of the "gospel", were to make up together the inner balance of the great εὐχαριστία! In the same line, see the enthusiastic, and fundamentally "eucharistic", tone with which Paul spontaneously speaks of our redemption freely acquired in Christ; especially Rom. 3, 21—26; 5, 1—11, etc., but above all perhaps, Eph. 1, 4—8, in the anamnesis of a true εὐχαριστία, precisely; also 2, 4—10, in the resumption of the anamnesis after the προσευχή of 1, 15—23.

Christ and Lord[1]. But, in an *εὐχαριστία* thus conceived, it goes
almost without saying that the free remission of sins, thanks to
the Lord's body "delivered up", and to his blood "shed", for the
"multitude" of men, is considered itself as a "wonder" for which
it is only just that praise should be made heard. The inner
unity of the *εὐχαριστία* seems to be, then, as strict as it is
harmonious. Everything, gratitude included, on the part of man,
is finally resolved in a marvelling and rejoicing admiration, as, on
the part of God, everything centers in the loving design which He
has revealed through Jesus in the "gospel". Besides, it is such
an understanding of the inner balance of the *εὐχαριστία* in its
relations to the *εὐαγγέλιον* which seems in part to have brought
about, as early as the first generation, the liturgical transference
of its celebration from the night of Jesus' arrest to the day which
saw him victoriously coming out of the tomb.

On the other hand, I cannot omit to say a few more words here
about one particular text of Paul, the true implications of which
do not appear to have been generally understood. The difficulty
is essentially connected with the general problem of the literary
forms of the *εὐχαριστία*. In his instruction (*διδαχή*) on the
eucharist, 1 Cor. 11, 26, Paul writes: "For as often as you shall
eat this bread and drink the cup, you proclaim the death of the
Lord, till he comes, *τὸν θάνατον τοῦ κυρίου καταγγέλλετε, ἄχρι οὗ
ἔλθῃ*." How do we have to interpret such a "proclaiming" of
the Lord's death (*καταγγέλλω*)? The wise among commentators
have most of the time preferred to leave us in vagueness. Those
who have ventured to propose definite suggestions, would like
to have us think of an actual "preaching", which would have
accompanied the celebration of the eucharist at Corinth.

In reality, we see at once what it is all about, in Paul's mind,
as soon as we refer ourselves to the function of "proclamation"
of God's name assumed by the Christian *εὐχαριστία* as well as
by the Jewish "benediction". As far as it is *ἐξομολόγησις*, the

---

[1] On this idea of the "sacrifice of praise" in its relations to the literary
genre of the *εὐχαριστία*, it will be to the purpose to recall here the very
significant phrasing of Hebr. 13, 15: *δι' αὐτοῦ* (Christ) *οὖν ἀναφέρωμεν θυσίαν
αἰνέσεως διὰ παντὸς τῷ θεῷ, τοῦτ' ἔστιν καρπὸν χειλέων ὁμολογούντων τῷ
ὀνόματι αὐτοῦ* (comp. what we have said elsewhere about the constant
mutual relationships of the *ἐξομολόγησις* and the *εὐχαριστία*, as a
proclamation of the divine "name").

εὐχαριστία left by Jesus for his disciples can only be, in fact, a "proclamation" of the "Lord's death, till he comes". It is the primary object of the anamnesis. One should note, however, to keep all things in their proper balance, that the death thus "proclaimed" in the εὐχαριστία, both by words and actions, is not only the death of Jesus, but that of the Lord (τὸν θάνατον τοῦ κυρίου), which clearly implies, beyond death, resurrection. Besides, this implication of the resurrection in the very anamnesis of the "Lord's death" (greatest of the mirabilia Dei in the "gospel") can alone make possible for the community a normal opening of view, beyond the εὐχαριστία itself, on to a last hope, "till he comes".

The last piece of evidence around which I should like to make some remarks, before concluding this short review of the records of the Christian εὐχαριστία in the first century, is taken from the Didache. The literature which has developed in these last seventy-five years or so around its chs. 9—10 and 14, is almost boundless. Fortunately, I need not enter here into any discussion of the several hypotheses which have been put forward in order to explain these texts. It is, however, of no small importance for us to note that, in all this critical flood, the pertinent observations devoted to the literary genre of the εὐχαριστία in the Didache, hardly amount to more than a few drops. Critics and historians have spoken, more or less at random, of "fragments of Christological hymns", of "eucharistic prayers", of "prayers of thanksgiving", of "prayers before and after meals", of "graces", of "prayers intended for the agape", or "breaking of bread", of "consecration prayers", of "communion prayers", and quite recently, of "prayers during the mass" intended for the use of the faithful!

For my part, I can only state here briefly the main conclusions I have reached. Chs. 9—10 of the Didache are essentially an instruction (διδαχή) on the "breaking of bread", this last being distinct from the major "eucharist", on the one hand, as well as from the "agape" which will develop later in Gentile communities, on the other. This "breaking of bread", I propose to call minor "eucharist". The instruction of the Didache which concerns it, besides, ends in a short ritual of transition from the minor "eucharist" to the major one (10, 6), emphasizing thus their liturgical distinction together with their mutual relationships.

Lastly, the ritual of the "breaking of bread", in the form incorporated by the *Didache*, seems to me of Palestinian origin, if it does not reflect even more directly the liturgy of the mother church of Jerusalem, and of a time which cannot be much later than the middle of the first century.

But the point with which I am concerned here, is that of the literary forms of this minor "eucharist". Now, I believe, it is enough to read the relevant texts along the line of the different remarks which have just been made on the literary genre of the *εὐχαριστία* to be in a position to see unmistakably where we are. The "breaking of bread" of the *Didache* comprises a twofold "benediction", or *εὐχαριστία*, before and after the meal, followed on both sides by a "prayer", *προσευχή*. These "benedictions" are moulded in the purest and most classical forms of contemporary *εὐχαριστία*: "benediction" proper, anamnesis and doxology. As regards the object of these anamneses, it corresponds exactly to what we could have expected: the "wonders" which the Father has performed through Jesus, *διὰ 'Ιησοῦ*, in favour of those who believe. So, the anamneses of the "breaking of bread" seem to reflect, as a rule, the common consciousness of the "life" that can be hereafter hoped for in the resurrection of Jesus. They are therefore, at bottom, in a more or less direct way, so many anamneses of the resurrection: a fact which can hardly come as a surprise, at the point we have reached in our examination of the evidence. There is not much in this which is new to us now.

Nevertheless, there is a characteristic feature of the "breaking of bread" in the *Didache* to which it is important to draw attention. We remember that in the general arrangement of the rite the "benedictions", or *εὐχαριστίαι* (9, 2—3; 10, 2—4), are immediately followed, before and after the meal, by a "prayer" properly so called, or *προσευχή* (9, 4; 10, 5). This is perhaps a very simple fact in itself, but, in my opinion, critics have never paid sufficient attention to it, nor have they properly understood its implications. They have constantly been inclined to confuse the *προσευχαί* with the *εὐχαριστίαι* proper, or more precisely, to turn the *εὐχαριστίαι* into *προσευχαί*, as is clear from the various literary categories which their analysis has forced into the texts ("eucharistic prayers", etc.). It is of great consequence, on the contrary, to abide unambiguously by the distinction of forms. It

is the only way to recognize afterwards, from the point of view of
the contents, their mutual relations and their proper meaning.
We see, then, that the προσευχή is subordinated to the εὐχαριστία,
and not inversely, as most critics seem all too prone to believe[1].
Such a subordination, besides, is correlative in Christian as well
as in Jewish conscience to the inner order of hope: the *mirabilia*
of the past, as extended into the present (global object of the
"eucharistic" anamnesis), support the striving of hope towards
what remains to be expected for the eschatological future from
God's loving-kindness, power and fidelity (object of the προσευχή
following the εὐχαριστία). Hence, in the "breaking of bread",
the admirable prayer for the gathering of the sanctified church into
the kingdom which the Father has prepared for her through
Jesus.

We might be tempted to go deeper here into the implications of
the results of our analysis of the literary forms which the
Christian εὐχαριστία inherited from the Jewish "benediction",
and of the fundamental values which have constantly been
attached to them all through their long history. I shall not
conceal, however, the fact that these implications seem of great
consequence. They outline the essential characteristics of a certain
religious conscience; beyond this, they point towards a certain
way of worship. Shall we live primarily on admiration, or on

---

[1] Some relations of the προσευχή to the εὐχαριστία in Paul: μετὰ
εὐχαριστίας τὰ αἰτήματα ὑμῶν γνωριζἑσθω πρὸς τὸν θεόν (Phil. 4, 6);
πάντοτε χαίρετε, ἀδιαλείπτως προσεύχεσθε, ἐν παντὶ εὐχαριστεῖτε (Col. 4, 2;
comp. Act. 16, 25, Paul and Silas, imprisoned, προσευχόμενοι ὕμνουν
τὸν θεόν). Along the same line, note also how the εὐχαριστία and the
προσευχή succeed each other alternately, together with the subordination of the latter to the former, in the great "evangelical" εὐχαριστία
of Eph. 1, 3—3, 21. The "eucharistic" anamnesis is interrupted twice
(1, 17—22 and 3, 14—19) to let loose the impulse of hope in the προσευχή.
As regards this passage from the εὐχαριστία to the προσευχή, see 1 Kings
8, 15—21. 23—24 and 8, 25—53 respectively; also, on the same occasion,
8, 56 ("benediction"-εὐχαριστία) and 8, 57—61 ("benediction"-προσευχή).
It will not be superfluous to point out, too, that the small collection of
"benedictions" discovered at Qumran belongs entirely to the secondary
genre of the "benediction"-προσευχή: we might say, it is like 1 Kings 8,
57—61 severed from 8, 56 (see Barthelemy-Milik, Qumran Cave I [DJD, 1],
Oxford 1955, n. 28 b, pp. 118—130); see also Numb. 6, 22—27; Sir. 50,
22—24 (Hebr.).

gratitude, at the peak, as it were, of the theological impulse of faith and hope, or in the anthropocentric falling back of self-consciousness? It is not unreasonable to think, perhaps, that, one day or another, conscious choices of immense bearing will have to be made in this respect; unless it is thought more convenient to leave the decision to the blind forces ruling over the individual and collective subconscious—which would certainly not do much credit to theological insight nor to pastoral care.

But I must break off here. By way of conclusion, I should like rather to point out possibilities of new research. It is a law of literary genres, so it seems, that they are all the more stable, in a given human group, for being related, in the world of expression, to a more elementary and deeper state of conscience of the same group; and correlatively, it is also a law that the more closely they have been connected by specific links, along their history, with a certain state of conscience of the group which gave them birth and in which they have prospered, the less they are transferable from one group to another. In this respect, literary genres, which are nothing else than more or less differentiated forms of expression, behave very differently from the "archetypes" of Jungian psychology, for example, which are less differentiated and more common forms, belonging to a lower level of the unconscious, although there is continuity and communication between the former and the latter and *vice versa*.

It happens, however, that as a consequence of historical accidents, literary genres sometimes do cross the frontier of their original habitat. In this migration, and in the new psychological implantation following, lies precisely for them the peril as well as the chance of a new life. Crossing the border of their psychological native land, will they actually carry with them the whole treasure of human significations and values which till then had been their *raison d'être* and their functional destination? Or, on the contrary, will they leave behind a more or less important part of this inheritance, eventually making up for the loss by acquiring in their adoptive homeland new significance and value? That is the question.

Now, such has been the state of affairs in which the literary genre of the Jewish *εὐχαριστία* found itself, as a consequence of its psychological implantation in Christian communities which were apt to become more and more exclusively made up of

Gentile elements, as soon as the progressive and ever more complete severance of the church from the synagogue took place, towards the end of the first century. For centuries, the εὐχαριστία had been perhaps the most specific and distinctive literary genre of the religious conscience of Israel. What would become of it after its implantation in a human group arising, for the most part, from contemporary Greco-roman paganism? From this particular point of view, in fact, it is not quite the same thing to have reached the faith in a creation and a salvation before the word, and to have come to it, after the event, thanks to the word through which this faith had meanwhile expressed itself, or, to use Pauline phrasing, it is one thing to be the olive tree, and it is quite another thing to be the wild branch grafted on to it.

In fact, the consequences due to the psychological implantation of the old εὐχαριστία in a community henceforth almost exclusively made up of human elements drawn from the Gentile world, become perceptible as early as the end of the second century. At the beginning of the third, where the *Apostolic Tradition* of Hippolytus can be dated, we get a strong impression that things have changed rapidly. What was henceforth beginning to take place, was roughly some kind of an inner breaking and dissociation of the literary forms of the ancient εὐχαριστία, together with corresponding modifications in the balance of the significa e and values which the εὐχαριστία had originally been intended to serve. So did it happen that the "benediction" proper was progressively bent towards "thanksgiving" (hence our own use and interpretation of the key word εὐχαριστία), thus giving way, little by little, to literary forms from now on inspired by a psychological and cultual dominant of gratitude, at the expense of the more theological marvelling and rejoicing over the *mirabilia Dei*, on which it had lived essentially till then. At the same time, the functional relationships of the anamnesis to the "benediction", at the very heart of the εὐχαριστία, were showing a tendency to grow looser, while recalling, besides, less and less the *mirabilia Dei* as such, and more and more gifts and favours received from the kindness of God (*beneficia, dona Dei*). A few centuries later, the Roman "preface", which nevertheless preserves in the West, even in its name, the memory of the function of ἐξομολόγησις, or proclamation of God's name, of the ancient εὐχαριστία, will go so far as to lose, here and there, all traces of anamnesis without anybody wondering too much about its absence. By means of a rather verbal link, in return, the name "anamnesis" will acquire, one day, the narrow and more or less disarticulated meaning now known to us. In these conditions, would not the doxology, the literary function of which had been originally to re-echo the initial "benediction" by way of *inclusio*, have seen its own meaning obscured? If the "preface" is no more than a solemn prologue to the canon, this resolving itself, in turn, in the "words of consecration" for its "eucharistic" meaning proper, what wonder if the doxology (doubled and anticipated, besides, in some way, by the *Sanctus*) can only with the greatest difficulty keep, in practice, its normal articulation to the anamnesis and the initial "benediction" (εὐχαριστία)?

But this very deep dissociation and falling apart of the forms, with its corresponding modifications of their significations and cultual values, has been accompanied, as was almost inevitable, by a sort of compensating phenomenon. Naturally enough, this took the form of a slow overflowing of the προσευχή into the εὐχαριστία, to such a point that the old and most important subordination of the former to the latter was now in no small danger of being inverted. In my opinion, the origin and development of the so-called "epiclesis" are nothing else than particular episodes in this impressive rising of the προσευχή within the general equilibrium of the different values of the εὐχαριστία, as is already perceptible in the *Apostolic Tradition* of Hippolytus (anaphora).

But there is much more which could be said about all this. This heavy task I must leave to others. Perhaps, however, these simple suggestions might prove to be useful to them.

3*

The Fourfold Character of the Gospel

J. H. CREHAN S. J., London

Ceremonies at which one would like to have assisted certainly include the deposition, somewhere about the middle of the second century, of the priest of Asia who wrote the *Acta Pauli* and who defended himself on the ground that he had done it out of love for St. Paul (Tertullian, *de bapt.* 17). The Church in Asia was taking no chances with the documents entrusted to its care, and it might have echoed the sentiment which one finds in the perhaps contemporary *Letter to Diognetus* that "the reliability of gospels is firmly based". Tertullian, who tells us about the deposition, is also witness (*de praescriptione haer.* 38) to the fact that Valentinus used the complete gospel-corpus; *integro uti videtur instrumento*, i. e. the whole proof-document, as he, with legal phrase, is in the habit of calling the gospels. We know a little more now about Valentinus and the evidence of his recently-recovered work goes to show that in fact he did, as Tertullian says, use the whole gospel-corpus. Tertullian contrasts him favourably with Marcion, who tried to set up his system on the basis of one gospel, but when he is dealing with Marcion himself (*adv. Marc.* IV 4, PL 2, 365) he calls for a tug-of-war. "The issue must be decided by priority of time; Marcion says his gospel is the genuine one, I say mine is; what shall decide the issue save a comparison of dates, allowing by prescription authority to that which shall be found to be older?" If Tertullian was ready to make such a challenge, it must be that he was convinced that his "evangelic instrument" was more ancient than the new-fangled gospel of Marcion. In view of this evidence, it is really quite impossible to accept the picture drawn e. g., by O. Cullmann (*The Early Church*, 1956, 39—58, The Plurality of the Gospels as a Theological Problem in Antiquity), where some orthodox Christian communities are said to have subsisted on one gospel until the end of the second century.

When Valentinus began his chief work with the words: "The Gospel of Truth is joy to those who have knowledge ...", he was trying to launch a new gospel in competition with what already held the field. One might venture the paradox that no one would call a work true unless he knew it to be false, but, even without going to that length, it is not unreasonable to think that he put that word Truth in the forefront of his work because he knew it would be challenged. Now if one asks why it could be challenged, coming out as it did somewhere in the end of Hadrian's reign, or early in that of Antoninus, the answer would have to be that the orthodox Christian gospels were already in possession. "This is the Gospel", says Valentinus, "which He has reserved to the perfect" (XVIII 12), as if he would say: "Of course there are the other gospels, but they are only for beginners." His claim to have received Pauline traditions through an otherwise unknown Theudas, said by him to be a disciple of Paul, is on a par with his treatment of the gospel, for clearly the survival of such a well-known disciple of Paul as Luke to the early years of the second century[1] must have proved an embarrassment to would-be perverters of Pauline doctrine.

But beyond all these arguments of likelihood which the new-found *Gospel of Truth* might provoke, there is the long-neglected evidence of the *Acta Timothei* about the formation of the four-fold gospel which I must now set forth. The *Acta Timothei*[2] were written in Greek before A. D. 356, and probably, according to Usener, who published them in 1877, between the years 320 and

---

[1] The anti-Marcionite Prologue credits Luke with great longevity and to him is ascribed by Clement of Alexandria the authorship of the second-century Dialogue of Jason and Papiscus.

[2] The Acta Timothei were published at Bonn by H. Usener in a Festival-Programme for the birthday of the Kaiser (1877), a circumstance which has meant that very little notice was taken of the publication. There are copies of the brochure in Oxford and Cambridge but there is none in London. The topography of the Acta was appreciated by J. Keil in Jahreshefte des Österreichischen Archäologischen Institutes in Wien 29 (1935) 82—92. The Latin version is not very successful in turning some of the Greek phrases. The χάρται which are brought to John are certainly papyri, but the translator omitted the word, nor did he do very well with the word ἀπεγράψατο which is used for the "registering" or the fixing of the titles of the gospels by John. In Anatolian Studies presented to W. H. Buckler, 1939, 77—84, Père H. Delehaye attacked Keil's work but without bringing any new facts to light.

340. They are very short; they have no extravagances; their local knowledge of the topography of Ephesus — where the martyrdom took place — has been found by the Austrian archaeologists to be first-class. They purport to be by Polycrates of Ephesus, and a Latin version of them can be found in Migne under the works of that bishop, but they quote Irenaeus and therefore must be later than the second century. But, for their simplicity, they merit to be regarded as worthy of some credence where they cannot be shown to be narrating impossibilities. Of the formation of the fourfold gospel they say this:

"Some followers of the disciples of the Lord, not knowing how to put in order certain papyri which were written in different languages and put together in random fashion by these disciples and which dealt with the miracles of the Lord Jesus which had taken place in their time, came to the city of Ephesus and by common consent brought them (the papyri) to John the renowned theologian. He examined them thoroughly and taking his cue from them, after he had put in order the three gospel narratives and entitled them Gospel of Matthew, Gospel of Mark, Gospel of Luke, assigning their proper titles to the gospels, he himself theologized upon the things they had not narrated ..., filling up also the gaps they had left, in their accounts of the miracles especially, and then he set his own name to this compilation or gospel."

Usener was ready to consider this as being *inter antiquissimas Asianae ecclesiae fabulas* and not as a fourth-century invention, and he found one or two small items of supporting evidence for it. In the *Catena on John* printed by Corderius there was a fragment from Theodore of Mopsuestia which related how:

"there happened about this time the publication (ἔκδοσις) of the other gospels. The faithful of Asia brought the books to John wishing to learn from him what he thought about them, and he praised the writers for their truthfulness, but declared that they had failed to record some few facts."

Eusebius (*hist. eccl.* III 24, 7) gives an account of the formation of the gospel-corpus similar to this but not so detailed; he has nothing about the papyri nor the affixing of titles. He says he is following a tradition to the effect that John received the other three gospels and witnessed to their truth, going on to write his own gospel as a supplement to theirs. The idea that the "spiritual" gospel of John was to supplement the "corporeal" gospels of the other three is found in Clement (cited by Eusebius, *hist. eccl.* VI 14, 7), but the source of the rest of Eusebius's story has not been noticed. It seems to come from Origen, an otherwise unknown fragment of whose first *Homily on Luke* (GCS, Origenes, vol. 9, p. 5) has been preserved in a Catena at Vienna. This tells, for what it is worth, how:

> "there is a story that must be told in outline that John, who was still surviving in Nero's time, gathered together the gospels that were written, recognizing some of them as genuine and accepting them ... but rejecting and condemning those which he was aware did not keep within the truth."

When R. A. Lipsius (*Die apokryphen Apostelgeschichten* II, 2, 377) somewhat hastily rejected the evidence of the *Acta Timothei* as being merely a dressing-up of what was in Eusebius, he was not aware (in 1886) of the papyri that were to come to light so soon after and to throw so much new light on the early history of the gospels, and he therefore does not attach due importance to the circumstantial account in the *Acta* of the papyri and of their titling by John, an account which it would have been difficult for a forger in the days of the big vellum codices (after 320) to make up for himself. It is far more difficult to-day to set aside the story of the *Acta* than it was for Lipsius. Even the word χάρται for papyri, itself frequently used in the documents themselves, would not have had quite the same meaning for Lipsius in 1886. Even in 1939 Père Delehaye, preferring the Latin version of the *Acta* to the Greek original, did not realise that this word meant more than a few bits of papyrus, though its use for a *libellus* or codex is now clear. Fr. Delehaye seemed determined at all costs to reject the *Acta Timothei*, for he supposed, without any evidence, that the cult of Timothy had arisen in Ephesus only after the townspeople were deprived of the body, which was translated to Constantinople in 356. This was directly contrary to the obvious principle (which he had himself set forth in *Sanctus*, 1927, p. 123) that wherever possible it was the tomb of the martyr that was the focal point of the cult, and it would require very strong evidence to set aside this principle. The cult of Polycarp in the rival town of Smyrna, and the fact that in the Greek calendars the date of the feast, January 22, is the same as that of the local pagan feast of the καταγωγία on which according to these *Acta* he met his death, make the rejection of the tradition still more difficult. It would be hard to imagine why the people of Constantinople should want the body of a man to whom no cult was paid in his own town.

There is one small feature of the gospel manuscripts which seems to support the tradition of the *Acta Timothei*. In the big codices the titles are given simply as κατὰ Ματθαῖον, κατὰ Λουκᾶν etc., and the word for gospel is not added. Now this word was in process of changing its meaning in the early second century. It had meant "the proclamation of good news" even to the pagans and was appropriated by the Christians in that sense from the days of St. Paul, but it had not come to mean "a written book concerned with that proclamation" until about the time of Justin. He uses it in the plural to refer to the four gospels in the well-known passage of his first *Apology* (I 66). Justin (*dial.* 10 and 100) also uses the word in the singular, saying: "As it is written in the gospel", and he must consequently be taken as referring to some kind of *Diatessaron*, as the late Dr. Blunt suggested[1], or else to be using the word in its old sense of "the good-news proclaimed". It had that sense still in Clement of Rome's letter (47), while some of the passages in Ignatius where the word is found are really transitional. Such being the evidence of language-usage, it seems reasonable to suggest that if someone had at the close of the first century assigned the titles κατὰ Ματθαῖον etc. to the four writings in which the good news was enshrined, it would be natural for the word εὐαγγέλιον to pass from meaning "the good-news proclaimed" to meaning "a writing in which this good-news is reported" in the early part of the second century, which is exactly what we do find. Thus the primitive usage would be to have κατὰ Ματθαῖον as title in the colophon of the codex, while later and more developed usage would write εὐαγγέλιον κατὰ Ματθαῖον etc., and this usage is found in the new Bodmer papyrus of St. John. Before the term εὐαγγέλιον was available to describe one of the writings, it seems to have been the practice to refer to them collectively as "the apostles" or in the singular as "an apostle". Athenagoras towards the end of the second century seems to have been the first to use "the apostle" as a term that designates St. Paul only[2]. If we had no tradition about the activity of John in forming the fourfold gospel, it would be indicated to us by these linguistic phenomena that some such labelling activity had taken

---

[1] See the note ad loc. in his edition of Justin, Apologia, 1911.

[2] Athenagoras, de resurrectione 18.

place just about the turn of the first century or early in the second.

The Muratori fragment has a confused story about John and the gospels which can be brought into line with what has been hitherto set forth, if carefully considered. The story is that John orders a three-day fast and that on the first night it is revealed to Andrew the Apostle that *recognoscentibus cunctis Iohannes suo nomine cuncta describeret*. This at first sight means that all should revise, but that John should write all down on his own account. If however the Latin translator of the Greek original had mistaken a passive for an active or middle participle when he put down *recognoscentibus*, the sense would be that, as in the *Acta Timothei*, John should make a thorough examination of all the papyri that were brought to him and then write on his own what he thought necessary for completeness. The moral drawn by the writer of the fragment supports such a view, for he goes on to say at once that although the gospels all have different beginnings, that is no matter, since one and the same Spirit set forth *omnia in omnibus*, all things in all of them, about the essential facts of the life of Christ. That the tradition should put the accent on the adequacy of the gospel-story in the face of the clear declaration in the end of the fourth gospel that myriads of books could be written about it, is perhaps a sign that the Church was very early aware of the danger that might arise from apocryphal gospels, elements of which we now know from the papyri to have been circulating as early as A. D. 130.

In a brief review of this kind one cannot enter into all the problems of the *Diatessaron*, but it is worth remarking that the present current of opinion is setting strongly in the direction of admitting that Tatian had the *Diatessaron* worked out in Greek before he left Rome and that a Latin version of it was in circulation there at once, somewhere about 170. It must have been about the same time that the collection of 114 sayings of Jesus, some fifty of which are parallel with the canonical gospels, was compiled by the heretics who entitled it *The Gospel of Thomas*[1].

---

[1] This is a matter of cumulative argument. One of the new Sayings is cited in II Clement; the Oxyrrhynchus papyri, which give some twelve of them, date from the third century; the new Coptic version of the whole work seems to be early. The work was used by Tatian, but he did not regard it as a fifth source, since his work is not called Diapente.

If heretics did so much, could not an orthodox Christian enter-
tain the idea of breaking up the four gospels into small pieces and
then reassembling them in his own way? That he should do so in
the seventh decade of the second century suggests that for him
it was obvious that these four gospels and only these had authority in the Church. That he should think of them as somehow one
is not surprising if we think of that strange animal the Tetramorph under which they were symbolized.

In Apocalypse 4, 7 the fourfold animal was described with
terms that are borrowed from Ezechiel 1, 10. It is not really
possible to depict how the four were joined together, but the
Christian artists tried. There is a carving of the late fourth or
early fifth century in the Cilician church of Alahan which attempts
this impossible task, and no doubt others attempted the same
before the miniaturists broke up the figure in order to set the
four separate creatures at the head of each gospel in their codices[1]. It is not of course a peremptory matter to interpret the
Apocalypse text in terms of the four gospels, for Oecumenius
takes it to refer to the four elements, but it is safe to say that the
interpretation which does so goes back to Papias. It appears in
Irenaeus and in Victorinus of Pettau, who are linked by no more
than by the fact that they both used Papias[2]. The other Greek
Father whose debt to Papias is large, Anastasius of Sinai[3], has
the same interpretation in spite of the fact that before his day,
a rival version (common to Jerome and Epiphanius) had assigned
the eagle to John and the lion to Mark. Papias, who regarded the
Apocalypse as inspired scripture, may therefore be suggested as
the author of this evangelistic interpretation of the fourfold beast.
But he is also responsible for something else about the gospels.

The brief sentences which Papias reports about Mark are introduced by the rubric that this is what the Presbyter said. It is

---

[1] An account of this church at Alahan was published by my friend,
M. R. E. Gough, in Byzantinoslavica 16 (1955) 201—211.

[2] The independence of Victorinus from Irenaeus was shown by Loofs
in his discussion of the sources of Irenaeus (TU 46, 2 [1930] 232, 333, and
337).

[3] Anastasius of Sinai, Quaest. 144 (PG 89, 797), Andrew of Crete
(PG 106, 257) and Arethas (PG 106, 572) follow him, though Andrew
knows of the view of Oecumenius that the four animals stand for the four
elements.

significant that these remarks reappear in Victorinus, in the passage where he is discussing the Tetramorph and its relation to the four evangelists. What Papias has to say about Matthew is not ascribed so clearly to the Presbyter, but it might be argued from the context that he meant to attribute that information also to him[1]. Now if the Presbyter is John himself[2], wearing the title of Presbyter or Elder much as Hillel did before him, forasmuch as he was the last surviving member of the apostolic college, it would be most reasonable to suppose that he had put together some few facts about the other evangelists when he was engaged in adding the titles to their gospels in the manner in which the *Acta Timothei* describe. Luke's gospel, which had a preface of its own, was less in need of this kind of illustration than the other two, and it may have been left alone. But it need not be thought that John left the work of Luke entirely without any notice by himself.

In an article which I am publishing shortly[3] in Theological Studies (U.S.A.) I argue that the variants found in the Western text of Acts are chiefly concerned to give additional importance to the position of Peter in the story, or else to add some local information about Ephesus. Since the textual critics desire a date early in the period 100—150 for the origin of the Western text and consider that the author of the changes was a Greek-speaking Christian with some knowledge of Hebrew[4], it does not seem quite impossible to attribute such changes to the activity of John at Ephesus in the period when he is said by the *Acta Timothei* to have "registered" the gospels under the titles of their authors.

---

[1] The remark of Westcott is still worth considering, where he says "The form of the sentence (with its μὲν οὖν) would seem to introduce this statement as the result of some inquiry, and it may refer to John the Presbyter." History of the Canon, p. 74.

[2] The use of Presbyter as a title is discussed by Archbishop Carrington in an appendix to his book The Primitive Christian Catechism, Cambridge 1940, pp. 69—70.

[3] Theological Studies 18 (1957) 596—603.

[4] It was J. H. Ropes who in The Beginnings of Christianity (III, CCXLIV and CCXXXIII) laid down these requirements for the date of the origin of the Western text. It is noteworthy that the latest editor of Acts, E. Haenchen, in Zeitschrift für Theologie und Kirche 54 (1957) 22—55, prefers to regard the Western version of Acts as secondary and not as the original of that work.

This is a more conjectural matter, as must be all that has to do with the Western text, but it would at least supply an explanation of the curious silence of Papias about Luke. One might add that the only major change in the Western text of Acts that has nothing to do either with Peter or with Ephesus is the variation in the regulations of the Council of Jerusalem, and here it must have required the authority of some considerable person to liquidate the older prescriptions about forbidden foods and to substitute a set of rules about morality. This business cannot have been done in a corner.

John himself may not have seen the significance of his vision of the fourfold animal of Ezechiel, but when he had put the three gospels together into a *corpus* and had added his own, it was open to his disciple Papias to interpret the vision in that sense. The mysteries of the Apocalypse certainly exercised that Chiliast, and something of his speculation about the number of the beast and the descent of the new Jerusalem has filtered down to Victorinus of Pettau. We are also assured by one writer who had access to his works that in considering the six days' work of creation he interpreted it all in terms of Christ and the Church. The fourfold river of Paradise may have given him his cue. As Victorinus wrote: *Hae ergo praedicationes quamvis quattuor sint, una tamen praedicatio est, quia de uno ore processit, sicut fluvius in paradiso de uno fonte in quattuor partes divisus est.* Although these proclamations of the good news are four, yet it is one proclamation, since it came from the one mouth, just as the fourfold river of Eden flowed from a single fount.

There are other signs of an awareness in the second century that John had been active editorially with regard to the gospels. The reading *scripsimus* (for the received *scribimus*) in 1. John 1, 4 is found in the Muratori fragment and must therefore have a Greek forerunner in the second century. It implies that the opening paragraph of the First Epistle of John has reference to some other writing of his which gave his disciples knowledge of Christ. It may not be what was in the text as it left its author, but it does give us a second century belief about John. Quite apart from the phrase in Clement (cited by Eusebius *hist. eccl.* VI 14) about John undertaking to supplement the other gospels at the instance of his friends and the words of the Prologue in the Toledo Ms. of the Vulgate that he wrote *postulantibus Asiae episcopis*, there is the elaborate account in Victorinus on Apoc. 11, 1 where the measuring of the temple is thus explained:

"He means the power which afterwards when freed from prison he manifested to the Churches. It was afterwards indeed that he wrote the gospel. Valentinus, Cerinthus and Ebion and the rest of the crew had scattered through the world and all the bishops from neighbouring regions came to him and compelled him to put in writing his own testimony to the Lord."[1]

One may discount the mention of Valentinus as an expansion of the story that is due to Victorinus himself, whose chronology was not his strong suit, but the substance of the tale is itself sound. The canon-building activity of John could hardly be better indicated than by the measuring rod which this passage of the Apocalypse is speaking of, the use of which Victorinus seems to have understood as referring to John's activity in adding his testimony about Christ to what existed already. Victorinus knew Greek better than he did Latin, as Jerome rather unkindly said of him, and his use of the word *potestas* here is probably meant to convey what ἐξουσία would mean in Greek, implying some authoritative action.

In view of all that has been argued, some of it more persuasive in fact than the rest may have been, it does not seem unjustified if one takes the last two verses of the fourth gospel as the conclusion not only of that work but also of the *corpus* of the four gospels. "John is prone to use οἴδαμεν when he wishes to express the common belief and assurance of the Christian community", wrote Archbishop Bernard[2]. Hoskyns supports this: "*We* has a perfectly definite meaning throughout the gospel which is entirely suitable here. It means the original apostles of the Lord, of whom the Beloved Disciple was one."[3] "This is that disciple who beareth witness concerning these things and who wrote these things." Are "these" the same things in both cases? If so, how does the "having written" differ from the "present witness"? But if the author has written his own gospel and is

---

[1] Potestatem dicit, quam dimissus postea exhibuit ecclesiis. Nam et evangelium postea conscripsit. cum essent enim Valentinus et Cerinthus et Ebion et cetera scola sparsa per orbem, convenerunt ad illum de finitimis civitatibus episcopi et compulerunt eum, ut ipse testimonium conscriberet in dominum (CSEL 49, 94—96).

[2] Commentary to John, II, Edinburgh 1928, 713.

[3] The Fourth Gospel, London 1947, 559.

bearing witness to the other three, could he possibly be content with the same indifferent pronoun for the two different objects? Some of the minuscules have felt trouble in the repetitiveness of the phrase and have changed to "who beareth witness about this man Jesus", but that does not seem to be the way out. But if the four gospels have now been put into order, the remark might be thought suitable that these three gospels are vouched for, this other one is written by (or dictated by) the Beloved Disciple, and though there might be many more books written about Jesus these must suffice. A survey of John's use of ταῦτα in the gospel shows that its reference can be sometimes quite vague, so that it is possible to take it here as pointing first to the collection of writings about Christ and then to the one in particular which John has written; it would be asking more of the language if one were to take the pronoun as referring first to the events and then to the writing about the events, for then there would be an antithesis rather than a vague general similarity of objects[1]. The difference of time, between present witness and past writing, would also be sufficiently accounted for on this view, while on other views it does present some difficulty, as Lagrange has noted.

So far then from the tradition that John was responsible for the fourfold character of the gospel having proved impossible to accept, it has been seen to be upheld by the testimony of converging evidence. The work of Valentinus supposes that something like it has already taken place; the *Acta Timothei* record it in detail, the titling of the gospels, the Tetramorph, the sayings of Papias, the ending of John's own gospel, all point to the same conclusion that the fourness of the gospel-makers was known and accepted by the Church in the early years of the second century.

---

[1] The distinction between corporeal and spiritual gospels is of importance here. Clement, who is the first one known to have held it, was a follower of the Stoics in his ethical theory, regarding body and soul as a harmony and not accepting the full Platonic theory that body imprisoned soul. Hence for him the fourth gospel is not the liberator of the message of Christ from the prison of the Synoptics, nor does it war with them as flesh warred against the spirit according to the Jews, but rather it is the regulative principle, giving by its Logos-doctrine a unity to the others which they do but haltingly anticipate, as Dr. Ramsey's paper at this Congress so ably showed [cf. this volume, p. 99—106].

The Fourfold Gospel as a Theological and Pastoral Problem for today

H. CUNLIFFE-JONES, Bradford

The purpose of this paper is to raise a question rather than to propound an answer. Let me first give the setting in which the question is raised. The literary and historical criticism of the Gospels has revealed wide differences between the first three Gospels — which from their similarity of view-point are known as Synoptic Gospels — and the Fourth Gospel. For many purposes of analytic study it is best to treat the first three Gospels by themselves, and to use the fourth Gospel not as forming a unit with them, but as belonging to one of the main distinctive groups of New Testament theology. This, of course, is a perfectly legitimate procedure, and such a procedure may well have its place in theology, in preaching and in the study of the Scriptures by the ordinary believer. I do not wish in any way to criticize this procedure.

The question that I want to raise is this: Has the conception of a fourfold Gospel — of four gospels which have a unity for thought and belief — of four gospels which taken together are all rightly thought of as synoptic, i. e. as all contributing to the one vision of the one Christ — has the conception of a fourfold Gospel any place in theological and pastoral work which has integrated into itself the continuing discipline of literary and historical criticism?

In this paper I am more concerned to attempt to start other people propounding answers to a question that I think of urgent importance, than to promulgate my own views. But it would be pusillanimous of me not to give some indication of the tendency of my own mind. I very much hope that an affirmative answer can be given to the question. And that for two reasons. One is the

Christological issue. Behind the classical Christological affirmations of the early centuries that Jesus Christ is very God and very man, there lies the use of the four Gospels as contributing to a common understanding of the meaning of our Lord Jesus Christ. I do not myself regard these classical formulations as necessarily binding upon the thought of the continuing church, or as ruling out *a priori*, alterations due to new evidence and to the continuing patient investigation of God's truth; and it seems plain to me that Christological affirmations of the late twentieth century must be based not upon the Patristic interpretation of the Bible, but upon the Bible as we now think it right to use it. At the same time, I do not believe that any modern Christological affirmation which radically repudiates the ancient Christological perspective will ever satisfy the Christian mind or content the Christian conscience. It may be that the Fourth Gospel considered as theology rather than forming a class with the other three Gospels can help to provide the basis for a completely satisfying Christology, but to my own mind it would be a happier and a sounder thing if we could still continue to find in the four Gospels the basis of a common testimony.

My second reason is a still more subjective one. If the only way to think about the Gospels with integrity of mind is to separate the first three from the fourth, then we must carry this through not only in scholarly, but also in theological and pastoral work, whatever painful breach of habits and prejudices this requires. But if this is not necessary, then for the ordinary believer it will be much easier to continue to think of the four Gospels as in some sense belonging together. We ought, I believe, to try to think of the four Gospels together unless this is clearly an offence against reason.

I fully recognize that the price to be paid may in fact be too high. In the volume of essays written in honour of Professor C. H. Dodd[1], the Dean of Sidney Sussex College, Cambridge, says in a footnote on page 74, "The most striking difference between the Synoptic and Johannine pictures of Jesus lies not in details but in their presentation of his personality as a whole. The Jesus of Mark and the Jesus of John are quite different persons." The last sentence to my mind strikes a chilling blow

[1] The Background of the New Testament and its Eschatology, ed. W. D. Davies and D. Daube, 1956.

both to my faith and to my thinking. I do not myself believe it, and I think that it should be accepted only after the most convincing demonstration and with very great reluctance. But if it did turn out to be true, then obviously we could not continue to think of the four gospels as a unit, because their unity would have been dissolved. But until that dissolution can be accepted as axiomatic, I hope that the possibility of thinking of a fourfold Gospel will be resolutely and confidently explored.

Let me ask then, What is the present practice among scholars concerning the integration of the testimony of the Gospels? I wish to make it plain that I do so in great respect and admiration, and with a full awareness that any attempt at closer integration may turn out to be a mirage, or at least a house built on an insecure foundation.

First let me turn to an article[1] by Professor R. H. Strachan. Professor Strachan divides his subject, after a preliminary study of the term "εὐαγγέλιον", into the Gospel in the Primitive Church, in the Gospels, in Paul and in the Johannine writings. He begins his study of "the Gospel in the Gospels" as follows: — "The Fourth Gospel, owing to its distinctive character, will receive separate treatment in the closing section of this article. At the same time it will be cited occasionally as a record and interpretation of the teaching of Jesus. It is assumed that all four evangelists have essentially the same purpose in writing as is expressed by the Johannine author: 'These [things] are written that you may believe that Jesus is the Christ, the Son of God, and that believing you may have life in his name' (John 20, 31)." This means that apart from occasional help from the Johannine narrative, the first three Gospels are to be treated by themselves. And this represents, substantially, the general practice of scholars.

What such occasional help can mean has been given striking expression in Professor T. W. Manson's treatment of the *Feeding of the Five Thousand*[2]. "This crowd", he says, "according to Mark, consisted of men. It was not just five thousand persons, but five thousand grown men. Along with this goes the fact that they were able to travel faster than the boat and get to the desti-

---

[1] The Gospel in the New Testament, The Interpreter's Bible 7 (1951), pp. 3—31.

[2] Cp. Jesus Christ: History, Interpretation and Faith, S. P. C. K. 1956, pp. 31—32.

nation first. This surely means that it was not a crowd of cripples or sick folk on stretchers coming for treatment, but fit and active men coming for — what? In the end they were talked to, they had a meal, and they were sent back home. If you go on with Mark's narrative to the next section (verses 45—52) you will see what pains Jesus took to get both the Twelve and the crowd away. He seems anxious to be clear of them all. Why was all this?" "I think", says Professor Manson, "the answer is given quite simply in John 6, 15: 'Jesus saw that they meant to come and take him by force in order to make him King, so he withdrew again into the hills entirely alone.' What we are given in the Gospels is the story of an abortive attempt at a popular rising, an attempt which miscarried because Jesus, who was expected to lead it, would not have anything to do with it. It is all the more significant, therefore, that John tells us (6, 66) that at this time many of his followers deserted and would have nothing more to do with him." Our comment on this must surely be: This is both legitimate in principle and illuminating in fact; but does this represent the main way in which the Gospels are to be brought into harmony with one another, and, in particular, does it represent the limits of integration?

We are at the moment without the benefit of the publication of the lectures which Professor C. H. Dodd has given at Oxford on the historical value of the Fourth Gospel. We are, therefore, limited for his views on the subject to the appendix to his book *The Interpretation of the Fourth Gospel* (1953), where he speaks in a guarded but hopeful sense. Though he says (p. 452) "a detailed examination of Johannine thought such as we have here essayed is an indispensable preliminary to any estimate of the historical element in the gospel", he has also said (p. 446) "I believe that the course which was taken by *Leben-Jesu-Forschung* ("The quest of the Historical Jesus" according to the English title of the most important record of that "quest") during the nineteenth century proves that a severe concentration on the Synoptic record, to the exclusion of the Johannine contribution, leads to an impoverished, a one-sided, and finally an incredible view of the facts — I mean, of the facts, as part of history."

To this may be added Dr. Vincent Taylor's later comment[1]: "What, then, are we to say of the historical value of the Fourth

[1] The Life and Ministry of Jesus, 1954, pp. 23—24.

Gospel? Little indeed, if we will have it that the historical is the purely factual, but much if we believe that interpretation is a valid form of historical writing, and that the Evangelist's work is legitimate interpretation. That his interpretation is legitimate, as compared, say, with the fantastic developments in the Apocryphal Gospels is shown by three things: (1) our knowledge of the Synoptic sayings with which he so often begins; (2) the many points of contact between the picture of the Johannine Christ and that presented by the Synoptists, and (3) the response his interpretation has evoked throughout the centuries, so that many Christians find themselves peculiarly "at home" with John, while appreciative of the worth of the Synoptics and the Pauline Epistles as a whole. To these considerations we may add the special Johannine traditions which historians of the calibre of Goguel believe to be historical, such as the tradition concerning a pre-Galilean ministry, the extended treatment given to the Jerusalem ministry, the reference to Annas, the date of the Last Supper, and the strong emphasis laid upon the reality of the humanity of Jesus, the divine Word who became flesh. "One cannot hesitate", says Dr. Taylor, "to affirm that the Fourth Gospel contributes to a fuller appreciation of Jesus and his teaching than can be gained from the Synoptic Gospels read in isolation."

Both Dr. Dodd and Dr. Taylor seem to be moving in the direction of a fourfold Gospel. (To them should perhaps be added Dr. C. K. Barrett. In his recent commentary on the Fourth Gospel[1] while he insists that [pp. 44, 117] "it is for interpretation not for accurate historical data, that we must look in the fourth gospel", yet he insists that [p. 117] "at every point history underlies what John wrote".) But it is not yet clear that any of these scholars have moved very far, or entered very fully into the possibility of a new understanding that the Gospel is fourfold. Can any further steps be taken?

Let me turn back here to Professor Dodd's remarkable Inaugural Lecture as Norris-Hulse Professor of Divinity in the University of Cambridge given in 1936. In this, as you will remember, he stressed the necessity of supplementing analysis with interpretation. "The kind of interpretation I have in mind", he said,

---

[1] C. K. Barrett, The Gospel according to St. John, 1955.

4*

"will in one sense reverse the main direction in which New Testament studies moved for a century. Our principal aim has hitherto been to discriminate as clearly as possible between various books and strata, so as to isolate for intensive study the special problems connected with each separate part; for example, the Pauline Epistles, the Fourth Gospel, the Synoptic Gospels, and within these the Marcan stratum, the 'Q' stratum, and so forth. This process of analysis should now be balanced by a movement in the opposite direction. I will not call it synthesis, for that term might imply the imposition of unity upon originally disparate material. But the unity of the New Testament is original, underlying the diversity of the individual writings. These writings have come down to us in the form of a Canon, representing the judgment of the early Church — of those best qualified to judge — that in them the Christian religion as a whole received authoritative expression, under a diversity of manifestations, but by the same Spirit. This fact is of primary significance for the interpreter of the Canon."

If we apply this thought of Professor Dodd's to the Fourfold Gospel as a theological and pastoral problem for today, there is a distinction which we are bound to make. Professor Dodd said that the New Testament scholar is not seeking to impose unity upon originally disparate material, and that is true also for the theologian and the pastor. But there is a distinction between the two types of activity. The New Testament scholar, though he stands in and is influenced by the thought processes of his own century, is seeking to penetrate ever more closely to the original meaning of the documents in their century. The theologian and pastor, though utterly dependent on that continuing study, is asking how the truth in the documents is available for today. So for the theologian and pastor, while he must be loyal to the given unity of the Gospels, must in addition ask himself what kind of unity of the Gospels he can rightly construct, in view of all the discussion about the Gospels that has taken place from then till now.

The title of this paper is an adaptation of the essay by Professor Oscar Cullmann[1]. I am not here concerned with the ade-

---

[1] 'The Plurality of the Gospels as a Theological Problem in Antiquity' E. T. in: The Early Church, 1956, pp. 39—54.

quacy of Professor Cullmann's historical study, which is a separate subject. I am only concerned with his theological conclusion (p. 54). "Four biographies of the same life", he says, "could not be set alongside one another as of equal value, but would have to be harmonized and reduced to a single biography in some way or other. Four Gospels, that is, four books dealing with the content of a faith cannot be harmonized, but require by their very nature to be set alongside one another." "And", he adds, "in any case the faith cries out for manifold witness." (This last sentence I find an unconvincing distraction from Professor Cullmann's main affirmation. It refers to an earlier remark (p. 50): "The plurality of the Gospels, the fact that there are four Gospels, is simply an expression of the human way in which the Gospels originated. That the revelation is clothed in this completely human garb; that the unity, the one divine εὐαγγέλιον of Christ resides within the human multiplicity of the four Gospels: this is just what the New Testament means by faith." Of course, the faith does cry out for manifold witness, but not necessarily in the foundation testimony to revelation. If the Gospel records had been gathered into one Gospel the disparity between the human record and the divine Lord would still be there.)

But Professor Cullmann's main point is: if they were biographies they could be harmonized; as they are Gospels they must be set alongside one another. This is in agreement with a saying of Bishop Westcott[1]. "The real harmony of the Gospels" said Bishop Westcott, "is essentially moral and not mechanical. It is not to be found in an ingenious mosaic composed of their disjointed fragments, but in the contemplation of each narrative from its proper point of view." But the question remains: What does it mean for the four Gospels to be set alongside one another? What is the moral harmony of the four Gospels?

If the Gospels represented simple unanalysable units, then it is true that we could unify their impact upon us only by turning from one to the other, and letting the resultant total effect be what it may. But the Gospels are not such. We can isolate elements in each Gospel which have a unity in their own right and which can be thought about in other contexts than as an expression of the point of view of the evangelist.

---

[1] This I find quoted as one of the frontispieces to Professor R. V. G. Tasker's study of The Nature and Purpose of the Gospels, 1944.

Also, while research is rightly concerned with the point of view from which each evangelist wrote for the illumination which this throws upon the meaning of the Gospel, the aim is not that we should have a clearer conception of the Markan, Matthaean, Lukan, and Johannine styles of Gospel writing, as if that were the primary thing, but that through better understanding of the evangelists' approach we should come to a better understanding of our Lord Jesus Christ in His life, death and resurrection.

In point of fact, we cannot share all the assumptions of any of the evangelists, if only because they lived in a different century from our own. We must criticize the standpoints from which they write, and such criticism, so far from being necessarily destructive of our understanding of the Gospels, can be a means of our penetrating nearer to the reality to which the Gospels are testifying.

Certainly, we must not think that the fact that each Gospel is written from a different point of view is a hindrance to a real unification (as opposed to a detailed harmonizing) of the contents of the Gospels. Such unification, if it is possible, must be a unification for thinking as well as for belief. The two must go together. What we cannot think about seriously and responsibly cannot have a true place in our praying. Unless there is a proper place for a fourfold Gospel in our thinking, it can have no fruitful impact on our devotion.

What is implied if we proceed to a unification of the Gospels is an honest integration of the results of critical studies with thinking and devotion. If such integration promotes divergences, it cannot be supposed that such divergences are likely to be any greater than the variety of standpoints that we have at present. There is a possibility of a fourfold Gospel on the basis of a literal or near-literal acceptance of the Gospels as all containing simple accurate factual information. There may also be a possibility of a fourfold Gospel — and this is the concern of my paper — on the basis of a full acceptance of the continuing discipline of historical scholarship, in its analysis of the mixture of memory compilation, witness and interpretation which is in all four Gospels. We cannot hope to move towards an integration of the Gospel records without the courage to make decisions about the most profitable handling of the material, even if alternative decisions are entirely possible, and legitimate.

Let me, then, take my courage in both hands and make a brief survey of the problem, focussing it afterwards in one particular illustration, and then conclude.

Let us think of the possibility of unifying the four Gospels on the lines of the main divisions of the fourth Gospel. We may divide the Gospel of John broadly into four sections: chapter 1 — the Introduction to the Gospel; chapters 2—12 — the rejection of the witness of Jesus; chapters 13—17 — the acceptance of the witness of Jesus; chapters 18—20 — the Passion.

How different are the Gospels in their introductions, and yet all of them are introductions to the one Gospel. The introductions cannot be harmonized, and yet perhaps we need to give more time than we have done to the question of how we learn from all of them when they are taken together. The common conviction of all four Gospels is more important than their divergences.

The presentation of the ministry of Jesus in the Fourth Gospel is markedly different from that in the other three, and yet it leads to the same result. If the right way to think of the Fourth Gospel is to think of it as an interpretation rather than a simple narrative, and that the independent factual historical traditions which it may contain are to be discerned through that interpretation rather than picked out from it as plums from a cake, can we not go on from there to ask whether we agree with the interpretation, and whether that interpretation expresses something that was true of the life and death and resurrection of Jesus as it happened? If our answer is in any way positive to these questions, then it should be possible to think together what we have accepted as true of the ministry in all four Gospels.

For example, in John 5, 30—47 we are taught that the authority of Jesus consists in his complete dedication to the Father's will, that those who oppose him might have known better if they had been prepared to learn from John the Baptist, or from the works which Jesus is doing, or from the Scriptures of the Old Testament, but their essential wrong-doing comes from resisting the testimony which comes from God the Father himself, and by their action in so doing they shut themselves out of the love of God. If we believe that that is a true interpretation of what was actually happening in the ministry of Jesus, can we not use it to illuminate the records of the first three Gospels?

That such a kind of thinking is to be reckoned as history is a different question and depends upon the precise connotation that we give to the term history. My suggestion is not to claim this as "historical" thinking, still less as the only type of thinking proper to the study of the Gospels, but simply that, provided it can be pursued with integrity of mind, it is a type of thinking that is desirable for the theologian and pastor, and that precisely because belief tends to follow the way we think.

Professor Dodd in his analysis of the Farewell Discourses in the Fourth Gospel (cp. pp. 390—399) has stressed the extent to which they correspond to material which is to be found in the Synoptic Gospels. If this is so, then the possibility of integrating together the teaching of Jesus in all four Gospels is not so remote as it might at first sight seem. If the teaching of Jesus as given to us in the Fourth Gospel is in fact in large measure a true interpretation of the actual historic teaching of our Lord, then while for other purposes we need to stress the analysis of the differences between the different traditions as to the teaching of our Lord, for many theological and pastoral purposes the unity and coherence of the teaching in all four Gospels is a stress of enormous practical importance.

It is in the Passion narratives that the four Gospels come closest together — yet, of course, even here the difference in point of view is important and considerable. Is it possible, not to minimize the differences in point of view so as to come to a pre-critical harmony, but to rejoice in all the differences which devoted Christian scholarship has brought to light and yet to ask how all four Gospels taken together contribute to a richer picture of the meaning of the Passion than each contributes separately? How can we have at the popular level a profound and far-reaching response to the meaning of the Passion unless at the teaching level there is hard thinking about how the different presentations of the Passion in the four Gospels cohere together?

Let me seek to focus this general survey in one particular illustration. What relation should hold in theological and pastoral work between Mark 14, 32—42, the prayer of our Lord in the Garden of Gethsemane, and John 17, 1—5, that part of the high-priestly prayer which speaks of our Lord's own relation to the Cross? The passages, of course, have different intellectual backgrounds. The one testifies to the cost of Jesus' subordination of

Himself to the Father's will, the other is a precious testimony to the glory that was manifest not only through but in that humiliation. Must we choose between these ways of understanding the mind of our Lord as he went to his death, appreciating what they have to give us in their separate settings, but not in any way trying to relate them? Or would we be right in thinking that they are complementary and that each is incomplete unless we relate it to the testimony of the other?

I realize that in raising this question of the fourfold Gospel as a theological and pastoral problem for today, I may be pursuing a will-o'-the-wisp. If so, I humbly ask pardon from my readers.

It may be that, for any who accepts the continuing discipline of historical criticism, the conception of a fourfold Gospel can no longer be pursued with integrity. But even if so, it would be valuable to have that established, and established in relation to theological and pastoral problems, which are in many ways different from the problems peculiar to the New Testament scholar as such. But I hope that the conception of a fourfold Gospel is a valid concept for the twentieth century, and that others abler than I am may show how with continuing research into the differences between the four Gospels, we may still, with complete integrity, think together their witness in a way that is fruitful for theology, preaching, and private devotion.

So I leave with you my question. Ought we, because of the continuing discipline of historical criticism, to think at the theological and pastoral level as well as in the work of New Testament scholarship that we have three Synoptic Gospels, and a fourth Gospel which stands apart as a reflective interpretation and is to be treated separately? Or can we think with full integrity of mind, and without diminishing the persistent analytic study of the New Testament documents, that whatever the intimacy of relation between the first three Gospels, and, even though we realize that it is quite impossible to compose a formal harmony between the Gospels, can we think that we have in fact for our thinking as well as for our devotion, four synoptic Gospels, because all four contribute to a common understanding of a common Lord?

The New Testament and the Theology of History

J. DANIÉLOU S. J., Paris

The essence of the Christian message is concerned less with doctrines in the abstract sense of the term than with bearing witness to events, to the work of God in history: the covenant with Abraham, the crossing of the Red Sea, the birth and the resurrection of Jesus Christ, the future Coming, Pentecost. Hence the Christian sees things above all as a sequence of divine actions that constitute the sacred history, the true history. Many modern N. T. theologians have concentrated their attention on this point. If I have thought it useful to come back to it this evening, it was because each of them preferred to single out a particular aspect, the relationship of the Old and the New Testaments, or of the N. T. and the future Parousia, the N. T. and the Church. It seemed interesting to bring together these different results — not for the sake of opposing them to each other, but to show them as complementary.

The question is important, because some modern exegetes seem to reject this history of the Redemption as a totality. Their work really consists not in "disengaging the history of salvation from the mythical representations which are its ephemeral vehicle", but in disengaging "the essential Christian message" from a history of redemption treated unreservedly as myth. As Cullmann has well put it: "The historical element, characteristic of the faith of the first Christians, is not essential for Bultmann; it is no more than the 'mythical' expression of a non-historical and non-temporal truth, which is its real substance."[1] Yet this history of the Redemption is the essence of the specifically Christian Faith which has for its object, not simply to teach us that God exists, but that He has approached man in history to establish

---

[1] Le mythe dans les écrits du N. T., Numen 1 (1954) 125.

a vital communion with him. When this is rejected, Christianity itself as a Faith is rejected, and what remains is a philosophy, perhaps an existential philosophy, but only a philosophy.

Yet if we consider what were the thought and the philosophy of the world in which Christianity appeared we realize that they were in no way prepared to appreciate the Christian view of history, but that, on the contrary, they opposed it with all their might. We find ourselves in the presence of Greek thought, for which the divine is the realm of immobile and eternal ideas. The immutable laws of the cosmos and of the city-state are the visible reflection of the eternity of this intelligible world. Movement itself is but an imitation of this immobility. It is conceived as cyclical both in the regular motion of the stars and in the eternal return guiding the movement of history, according to which the same events will be reproduced for ever. Hence the phenomenon of repetition causes even movement to participate in the eternity of the world of ideas and precludes all novelty. No event can ever intervene to modify this eternal order.

This is radically opposed to the Christian faith in the unique and irrevocable value of the event (καιρός) of the Redemption. According to the Epistle to the Romans, "the death of Christ was a death once for all (ἐφάπαξ) to sin" (6, 10). And according to the Epistle to the Hebrews, "Christ has entered once and for all (ἐφάπαξ) into the Holy Place" (9, 12) that is to say into the sanctuary of the Holy Trinity, by His Ascension. By this event something has been irrevocably accomplished. Henceforth, nothing whatever will be able to separate human nature from the divine Nature. Humanity is saved in its very substance. Here we are presented with an event which has introduced a definitive, qualitative change into time of a kind that precludes the possibility of ever returning to the former state of affairs. There is, in the fullest sense of the terms, a past and a future. This faith in the irreversible character of the salvation achieved is the foundation of Christian hope, waiting to enter into the joy of an already acquired good, according to the Epistle to the Romans, (8, 16—17). And that is in direct contrast with the Greek melancholy resigned to the eternal repetition of things.

The Christian view of history has a second trait, that of being eschatological. The notion of the end (τὸ ἔσχατον) plays a decisive part in it. In the first place, history is not a matter of eternal progress. It has an end. It unrolls according to a definite and limited plan which the Epistle of Barnabas (15, 1—8) defined as the Cosmic Week, followed by the eighth day, which is the world to come. In the second place, and that the proper goal of the New Testament, Christianity is this end: Christ represents Himself as coming at the end of time and as inaugurating the final world.

The message of the New Testament is not to teach us that history has an end, but that the end has already come. It did not announce, like Israel, the future coming of Paradise. But what Christ says to the good thief is: "To-day you will be with me in Paradise" (Lc. 23, 43). This "to-day" is the whole Gospel. This is what John the Baptist has to say: "*Ecce Agnus Dei*". Not that a Lamb will be sacrificed, but that the Lamb is already there. The prophecies are fulfilled in Jesus Christ because they were warnings of what was to come about — judgement, resurrection, new creation, — and in Jesus Christ these things did come about. "I am the resurrection and the Life" (John 11, 25); "Whoever believes in me is already judged" (John 3, 18). Christ is really ὁ ἔσχατος Ἀδάμ (I Cor. 15, 45) not only as if he was — and in fact he is not — the end of time, but in the sense that there cannot exist anything beyond Him, because in Him the σκοπός of the world is accomplished: God is perfectly glorified and the human nature united to the divine.

It is the great merit of Cullmann to have emphatically stated in his "Christus und die Zeit"[1], that with the Resurrection of Christ the decisive event of history was accomplished and no possible event will ever possess as much importance as this. All evolutionary illusions are thus dissipated by one blow. Henceforth, no progress can carry us toward what we already possess in Christ, since in Him the goal beyond progress is already present, the last state already exists, though in sacramental form.

It results from this that in the Christian view of history the central event is not at the beginning, as in Hellenism, neither at the end, as in evolutionism: it is at the centre. Around this centre and relating to it, past and future acquire a new significance. That part of it which precedes Christ is a preparation, and therefore

---

[1] O. Cullmann, Christus und die Zeit, Zürich 1946, p. 35 f.

primarily constitutes a time of expectation. The very difficult problem of the unity and distinction of the two Testaments was solved in this fashion. There is a continuity between the two, both being parts of one and the same plan. One and the same God acts in one as well as in the other: their history constitutes a unique whole. At the same time, however, there is a radical difference between them. In the Old Testament, the Kingdom of God is only announced and prepared for. It is not yet an accomplished fact. It is true, the same reality is present in both, but it exists in each under different modes: prefigured in the Old Testament, it is present, though veiled in mystery, in the New, to be clearly manifested in the world to come. We can discern here the appearance of the characteristically Christian view of history as prophetic, that is to say a view in which the events and institutions of one epoch, of one "aeon" foreshadow those of the following "aeon". This is the basis of the typological interpretation of history.

Paul and the first Christian theologians discovered the deepest reason for this "economy" in an idea to which the most modern biblical theology is returning, namely, the idea of a pedagogical device[1]. Since man is a temporal being and humanity lives in time, in communicating His gifts God adapts Himself to the human condition. The Old Testament represents that slow process of education in which the Word, present to the creature made in His own image even from the beginning, progressively familiarized man with divine things from the very time when he had scarcely left his animal condition. For before the mystery of the redemptive Passion was revealed to him, man needed to be taught the meaning of suffering; before the mystery of the Triune God was revealed, a humanity always inclined to polytheism has to be made familiar with the idea that God is One.

Yet at the very heart of historic reality (which had seemed incapable of being reduced to symbolism) there appears a new dimension in which the symbol finds its place. God's successive actions in history are bound together by their common characteristic of being creative interventions. But over and above this, in proportion as the divine plan develops it becomes clear that these interventions are connected with each other by a relation-

---

[1] Gal. 3, 24—25; Irenaeus, Adv. haer. IV, 14, 2.

ship of correspondance. Such a correspondance clearly exists between, for example, the Flood, the Passion of Christ, Baptism and the Last Judgment. The judgment of God strikes a sinful world on different levels of the divine plan, and one man is spared by His mercy that he may become the principle of a new creation.

Thus a new symbolism makes its appearance, the symbolism of the Bible, the essential character of which is to be historic; that is to say, there is a correspondance between different moments of sacred history. This symbolism is designated by the term typology (with reference to a passage of the New Testament in which it is said of Adam that he is "the figure [τύπος] of Christ" [Rom. 5, 16] and of Baptism that it is "the antitype [ἀντίτυπος] of the Flood" [I Peter 3, 19]. This new symbolism has its foundation in the unity of the plan of God. It is a divine consistency which manifests itself on the different levels of history. It takes nothing away from the unique value of the divine events, but rather gives them an intelligibility of their own which raises them above merely factual level. Thus it has the value of an argument and takes on the form of prophecy; indeed it was in this form that Pascal recognized the essential proof of the truth of Christianity, as the Fathers of the Church had done before him.

It is important to determine the genesis of this typology. It has often been masked by discussions on the diverse senses of Scripture. But as St. Thomas saw quite clearly, typology is not a sense of Scripture, but a sense of the Scriptural events[1]. It has its origin in the Old Testament which reveals to us in the past events of the history of Israel the figure of what will come to pass at the end of time. Hence typology is essentially eschatological. In the New Testament the advent of eschatological realities is manifested in Christ, and this fact gives the figures of the Old Testament their value. These eschatological events are also contained in the sacraments of the Church which fill the interval that exists between the Ascension and the Parousia. They will ultimately be made manifest in the Judgment, the Resurrection and the advent of a new heaven and earth.

Such a typological interpretation is part of the common doctrine of the Church. It goes back to Apostolic times, and the

[1] W. Eichrodt, Ist die typologische Exegese sachgemäße Exegese?, ThLZ 81 (1956) 641—653.

New Testament affords many examples of it; it is the basis of the
patristic interpretation of Scripture; it is finally given an equal
place of honour in the liturgy. It is also because of their eschatological meaning that this typology rightly refers the texts of the
Psalms to Christ and the Church. But we must make a rigorous
distinction between such a typology — which is historical symbolism — and the kind of allegorism practised by Philo and
adopted by certain Fathers of the Church[1]. For the latter is
really a reappearance of a cosmic symbolism without an historical basis.

More difficult is the problem of the signification of time after
Christ. We said that with Christ the end of all things is already
given. Does this mean that there is nothing more to be done? It
would mean this if, after the event of the Redemption, no fundamental task remained to be accomplished. It is certain that once
Christ has appeared in the scene, the primary task is only that of
handing on (παράδοσις) a deposit no longer subject to change
since it represents the end already given. But what has been
acquired by it as a right for all humanity must in fact be transmitted to all men. This is the New Testament mystery of the
missions. Sacred history is the history of the present in which we
live, in which the task is to extend to all nations what Jesus
Christ brought to us.

In *Christ and Time* (p. 103) Cullmann observes that in war there
comes the day when the decisive battle is won, and after that
the day of the victory march under the triumphal arch. Between
these two events there is a certain lapse of time. The Resurrection
is the decisive battle of the Redemption, the day when the battle
was won. But Christ would allow us to participate in the victory —
and some battles remain to be fought. Total victory, however,
does not depend on them; it has already been won. Christian hope
is the certitude of this victory by which we ourselves expect to
come into possession of peace. Present history is the history of
the combats through which God deigns to associate us with His
work until Christ has taken on His full stature in breadth and
depth in all hearts (Eph. 6, 13). This is the content of present
sacred history.

---

[1] J. Daniélou, Sacramentum futuri, Etudes sur les origines de la
typologie biblique, Paris 1950, pp. 257—258.

The Sacraments are historical actions corresponding to the particular characteristics of the time that extends from the Ascension to the Last Judgment, that is to say, of the time in which we live. This time is characterized by the fact that it comes after the crucial event of Sacred History by which the world has already attained its end, and hence in one sense it can add nothing to time. Jesus Christ cannot be surpassed. On the other hand, His glory has not yet been visibly manifested. In the second place, therefore, this time is characterized by this non-manifestation, by this "hidden" aspect. And, finally, the proper content of time is the extension to all humanity of the reality acquired by Christ.

Now these are precisely the characteristics which the actions of sacramental structure present. On the one hand, they are never anything but "imitations", "representations" of the Death and Resurrection of Christ: "All we who are baptized in Christ Jesus are baptized in his death" (Rom. 6, 3). The sacraments simply reproduce the sacerdotal action of Christ by which all things have attained their end. Still, the sacraments have a hidden aspect. Only the sign appears; its reality remains invisible. For, indeed, the reality of the Resurrection is not yet visibly manifest. This is admirably explained by St. Paul (Col. 3, 1—4): "Risen, then, with Christ, you must lift your thoughts above, where Christ now sits at the right hand of God. You must be heavenly-minded, not earthly-minded; you have undergone death, and your life is hidden away now with Christ in God. Christ is your life, and when He is made manifest, you too will be made manifest in glory with Him."

Thus the sacraments are the events of a time which is in tension between the Resurrection and the Parousia. They are a "memorial" of the Resurrection and the permanent "prophecy" of its manifestation. The Eucharist, as a "document" of the "New Covenant" prevents us from forgetting the crucial event by which this Covenant was definitely concluded: the union, in the Person of Jesus, of the divine and human natures, by which human nature, purified by the Blood of the Cross, was introduced into the sphere of the Trinitarian life. And the Eucharist, as an eschatological meal, is the prefiguration of the heavenly banquet, by which Christ communicated the fullness of His goods to those who were His own in the house of His Father.

Thus, while the Parousia is still delayed, the Eucharist, as a foretaste of the heavenly food, prevents mankind from tiring of waiting and from returning to earthly food.

So far we have been looking at sacred history with its particular content. But this is only one aspect of total history. We have now to ask ourselves what relation history, in the usual meaning of the word, has with the history of salvation. Many questions arise here. And it is interesting to seek the elements of an answer in the New Testament. There is first the question of the relations between sacred history and cosmic history. Here the Bible is very decisive. The God of creation and the God of redemption are the same. The Christian view of history embraces the whole of reality. The sacred history begins with the creation of the world. And his end, according to Isaiah, is the creation of a new earth and a new heaven. St. Paul explains that "the earnest expectation of the creation waiteth for the manifestation of the sons of God" (Rom. 8, 19). And according to the Epistle to the Colossians (1, 17), "by Him were all things created, that are in heaven and that are in earth" and (1, 20) "by Him the Father reconciled all things unto Himself, whether they be things in earth or things in heaven". Here the cosmic character of sacred history is clearly marked[1].

Another question is the relation between history of religion and sacred history. That is a very difficult and essential question. Many people consider Christianity as one religion amongst others. For them Christianity is a part of the story of religions. For the New Testament the contrary is true. The notion of sacred history is more comprehensive than that of history of religions. For Paul, on the one hand, pagan religions correspond to the first covenant, the covenant with Noah. We read in the Acts of the Apostles (14, 15—17): "In times past God suffered all nations to walk in their own ways. Nevertheless he left not Himself without witness, in that he did good and gave us rain from heaven and fruitful seasons." But on the other hand, according to the Epistle to the Romans (1, 21—23) "although men had the knowledge of God, they glorified Him not as God, but changed the glory of the incorruptible God into an image made like to corruptible

---

[1] C. H. Dodd, History and the Gospel, London 1938, p. 168.

man". Pagan religions appear together as a survivance of cosmic
revelation and as a perversion of it.

The last problem concerns the relation of the sacred history and
history of civilization. Civilization cannot be considered as
essentially the work of the devil. In so far as the political and
cultural worlds are a part of creation they enter into the action
of God. They are part of a world which is, indeed, fallen, but
which is not intrinsically perverse. It is the merit of C. H. Rust
in his book: *Christian understanding of History*[1] to have pointed
out so clearly that the whole history of the world is integrated into
the Christian view. But all civilization is ambiguous. According
to Augustine, if the cities of the earth accept the Kingship of
Christ, they are integrated in the sacred history. But if they
reject this Kingship, they become the expression of the city of
Satan. And, in this sense, the history is the judgment of God on
the city of this world.

We can add (and here we have once again the historical criterion) that the world of secular civilizations in some sense has
already passed away. With Christ, the Kingdom of God has
come. To-day the true society is the people of God. The universal
and exclusive Kingship of Christ is already with us. But until the
end the world of civilizations benefits from a kind of reprieve.
This ambiguity is expressed in the tragic situation of the Christian.
He belongs simultaneously to a world which no longer exists and
to a world which is not yet[2]. This is why the relation between the
spiritual City and the temporal City can never be conceived only
as the harmonious juxtaposition of two societies, one crowning
the other, but as a dramatic tension between two successive
epochs of total history.

Thus we see how the New Testament view of history has been
formed. It was by no means a question of a systematic construction. It was, on the contrary, occasioned by questions that derived
from historical circumstances and led to define its conception of
the history of salvation. What I said is a very short account on
a very broad matter. But I think it was important to trace this
chief lines of the vision of History in the New Testament, because

---

[1] P. 127.

[2] T. Preiss, The Vision of History in the N. T., in: On the Meaning of
History (Papers of the Oecumenical Institute, V), p. 57—61.

it seems that the time has now come when it is possible to gather these fragmentary data into a theology of history. This seems to be one of the tasks of the present time, and one of the most obvious fields where the various Christian denominations can work in common.

La Session à la droite du Père

J. Daniélou S. J., Paris

Si nous cherchons dans la communauté chrétienne les éléments
qui ont constitué la tradition évangélique, il paraît certain qu'il
faut reconnaître parmi eux un choix de textes de l'Ancien Testament. Ces textes étaient-ils proprement groupés en recueils,
comme l'a prétendu Rendel Harris? Existaient-ils seulement à
l'état indépendant, comme C. H. Dodd le croit? La première
hypothèse trouve dans les découvertes de Qumrân une confirmation. En effet, parmi les textes trouvés, il y a des recueils
de textes de l'Ancien Testament — et qui recouvrent en partie
les citations que présente le christianisme primitif. Le fait n'a
donc pas besoin d'être établi. D'autre part, plusieurs auteurs, en
particulier Lucien Cerfaux et C. H. Dodd, ont reconnu son importance pour la théologie du Nouveau Testament. En effet ces
Testimonia ont fourni pour une très grande part les catégories
dans lesquelles les premiers chrétiens ont exprimé la signification
des événements de la vie de Jésus. Avant Platon et Aristote,
c'est l'Ancien Testament qui a offert les instruments de la première théologie néo-testamentaire, qui a été une théologie
biblique.

Ceci ouvre la voie à des recherches qui paraissent devoir
être très fécondes. L'objet de cette communication est d'essayer
de le montrer à propos d'un exemple, qui est particulièrement saisissant, celui des premiers versets du Psaume 109. Ces
versets se sont en effet à ce point incorporés à la tradition évangélique qu'ils en sont venus à constituer un des articles du *Symbole des Apôtres* et à exprimer ainsi un des aspects du mystère du
Christ. Je voudrais montrer que l'influence de ces versets est
plus grande encore qu'il n'apparaît d'abord dans la constitution
de certains ensembles du Nouveau Testament dont ils expliquent
la composition et qu'ils nous font atteindre ainsi un aspect

capital de la formation de la tradition évangélique. Ils sont, comme l'a écrit Cerfaux, «une pierre d'assise de la théologie apostolique»[1].

L'appartenance des versets 1 et 2 du Psaume 109 aux *Testimonia* primitifs est une évidence[2]. Si nous nous y arrêtons d'abord, c'est qu'au point de vue méthodologique, ceci nous permet de dégager quelques-uns des traits qui permettent d'affirmer l'appartenance d'un texte de l' Ancien Testament aux *Testimonia* primitifs, antérieurs à la rédaction des écrits du Nouveau Testament. En premier lieu, il y a le nombre. Le Nouveau Testament nous présente 7 citations explicites et 14 citations implicites du texte. Ces citations sont réparties entre l'ensemble des écrits néo-testamentaires, à l'exception de Saint Jean. Elles se rattachent donc à une tradition commune antérieure. Nous ajouterons que ces versets se trouvent dans tous les recueils de *Testimonia* ultérieurs, en particulier dans ceux qu'ont utilisés le Pseudo-Barnabé, Irénée et Justin.

En second lieu les contextes où les versets se trouvent cités montrent qu'ils se rattachent à la vie de la communauté. Nous noterons ici deux directions principales. D'abord Ps. 109, 1 —2 est cité dans des discussions avec les Juifs. Et ceci dans deux passages importants. D'une part il est cité par le Christ lui-même dans une discussion avec les Pharisiens, qui se trouve dans les trois synoptiques (Mc. 12, 35—37; Mth. 22, 41—46; Lc. 20, 41—44), de l'autre par Saint Pierre dans le premier discours des Actes (2, 33—36). Les versets faisaient donc partie d'un dossier apologétique. Par ailleurs dans Rom. 8, 34; I Petr. 3, 22, l'expression ὅς ἐστι ἐν δεξιᾷ τοῦ θεοῦ, qui vient du Psaume, fait partie de petits ensembles christologiques, qui constituent des professions de foi et sont le noyau du symbole. «This particular verse was one of the fundamental texts of the Kerygma», écrit Dodd[3]. Ceci nous fait atteindre un usage très archaïque dans la communauté, dans un ensemble non plus apologétique, mais catéchétique.

Nous ferons deux remarques à ce sujet. La première est que cette présence dans le symbole persistera, avec des modifications littéraires. Or cette mention de la session à la droite dès l'origine montre l'importance donnée à celle-ci et comme l'a noté Kelly,

[1] Le Christ dans la théologie de Saint Paul, p. 331.
[2] Voir C. H. Dodd, According to the Scriptures, p. 35.
[3] According to the Scriptures, p. 105.

«meant much more than might seem apparent on the surface»[1].
En second lieu, la distinction des deux usages, apologétique et
catéchétique, du Psaume persiste d'une manière étonnante.
Ainsi dans la *Démonstration de la Prédication apostolique*, Irénée
mentionne deux fois nos versets; une première fois au paragraphe 48, comme preuve de la messianité de Jésus: c'est l'usage
apologétique; une seconde fois, au paragraphe 85, comme
affirmation de l'ascension et de la session.

Troisièmement le texte apparaît comme ayant fait partie d'un
recueil de *Testimonia*. Nous le reconnaissons au fait qu'il est
souvent groupé avec les mêmes textes de l'Ancien Testament.
Nous relevons par exemple son rapprochement avec Ps. 8, 7:
«Il a tout mis sous ses pieds» dans Eph. 1, 20—22 et I Cor. 15, 27;
avec Is. 45, 1: «Le Seigneur a dit au Christ mon Seigneur[2]: Toi
que j'ai pris par la main droite» dans Barn. 12, 10; *Dem.* 48; Nyss.,
Test.[3]; avec Zach. 12, 10, dans Justin, *Dial.* 32, 2 et Théodote,
Excerpt. 38, 3. Mais il y a plus. Un des traits de la tradition primitive est la combinaison de plusieurs textes de l'Ancien Testament en une seule formule. M. Earle Ellis en a relevé des exemples
dans Saint Paul[4]; Barnabé en présente continuellement. Or on
a relevé des exemples qui intéressent notre texte et qui portent
un cachet d'archaïsme certain. Le premier, noté par C. H. Dodd[5],
est la combinaison avec Dan. 7, 13 dans Math. 26, 64: «Vous verrez
le Fils de l'homme assis à la droite de la puissance et venant sur
les nuées du ciel». La citation du Psaume est enchâssée dans la
citation de Daniel. Il en est de même dans Act. 7, 55: le Fils de
l'homme est debout à la droite et non assis. Ceci vient de Daniel.
Dans Act. 2, 34 et 5, 31, l'expression «exalté ($\dot{v}\psi\omega\vartheta\varepsilon\dot{\iota}\varsigma$) à la droite
de Dieu» peut contenir selon Cerfaux une fusion avec Is. 53.
J'ajouterai que dans Hebr. 1, 3 l'addition $\dot{\varepsilon}\nu$ $\dot{v}\psi\eta\lambda o\tilde{\iota}\varsigma$ peut venir
du Ps. 93, 4 et que dans Hebr. 8, 1 et 12, 2 l'allusion au trône
semble se référer à Is. 6, 1.

Enfin un dernier caractère des *Testimonia* primitifs est l'existence de modifications ou d'adjonctions destinées à accuser le
caractère christologique des textes. On connaît le plus célèbre de

---

[1] Early Christian Creeds, p. 151.
[2] On notera le remplacement de $K\tilde{v}\varrho o\varsigma$ par $\varkappa\acute{v}\varrho\iota o\varsigma$.
[3] Harris, loc. cit., I, p. 37, cite par erreur comme Ps. 110.
[4] Paul's use of the Old Testament, p. 49—51.
[5] According to the Scriptures, p. 67.

ces cas, celui du «Le Seigneur a régné du haut du bois» du Ps. 95, avec lequel Justin était si familiarisé qu'il défend contre Tryphon son authenticité (*Dial.* 73, 1). Notre texte présente à cet égard une forme intéressante dans plusieurs textes. Nous lisons dans Eph. 1, 20: «Dieu, l'ayant ressuscité des morts, l'a fait asseoir à sa droite dans les lieux supercélestes (ἐπουρανίοις) au dessus de toute principauté, de toute puissance, de toute domination et de tout pouvoir.» De même Hebr. 8, 1: «Il s'est assis à la droite du trône de la majesté (τῆς μεγαλωσύνης) dans les cieux (οὐρανίοις).» Et Hebr. 1, 3, dans une forme un peu différente: «Il s'est assis à la droite de la majesté dans les hauteurs (ὑψηλοῖς).» Nous remarquerons que l'expression ἐν δεξιᾷ τῆς μεγαλωσύνης est celle du symbole alexandrin.

Il est clair que ces diverses adjonctions sont en rapport avec l'application du texte à l'ascension. Le Psaume ne parle pas d'exaltation céleste, mais d'intronisation messianique. Mais dès lors que cette intronisation devenait l'expression de l'exaltation céleste du Christ, elle appelait des précisions. Ces précisions ne viennent pas ici de la combinaison avec des données évangéliques, mais d'un appel à l'imagerie apocalyptique qui est une autre source de la théologie de la communauté primitive. Nous en avons la preuve dans l'*Ascension d'Isaïe*, où nous voyons admirablement cette combinaison du Ps. 109 et de l'apocalyptique. Nous lisons d'abord en 10, 14: «Des lieux de la mort tu monteras de ciel en ciel et tu t'assieras à ma droite: alors les princes et les puissants de ce monde t'adoreront.» Plus frappant encore est 11, 32: «Et je vis comme il monta dans le septième ciel et tous les justes et tous les anges le glorifièrent. Et alors je le vis s'asseoir à droite de la Grande Gloire.»

Nous retrouvons ici les mêmes éléments que dans les textes d'Eph. et d'Hebr.: la conception des sept cieux, l'élévation au dessus des anges, la désignation de Dieu comme la Grande Gloire. Comme par ailleurs l'*Ascension d'Isaïe* ne dépend évidemment pas d'Hebr. ni d'Eph., il nous faut remonter à une source commune, qui est l'apocalyptique chrétienne primitive. Ceci nous conduit à un troisième milieu, qui n'est ni celui de l'apologétique, ni celui de la catéchétique, mais celui de la dogmatique, de la gnose des presbytres. Nous remarquerons aussi que cette élaboration théologique implique une autre conséquence capitale. Celui qui monte à travers les cieux était d'abord descendu du

ciel. Il est le Fils de Dieu. Dès lors le mot κύριος dans le verset 1:
Dixit Dominus Domino meo, qui ne désignait que la dignité
messianique dans l'interprétation primitive, va prendre le sens
de dignité divine. C'est ce que nous trouvons chez Barnabé 12,
10 et déjà dans Hebr. 1, 13.

Cette référence à l'apocalyptique nous conduit à une dernière
question: l'importance du Ps. 109 dans la communauté chrétienne primitive vient-elle de ce qu'il faisait déjà partie des
Testimonia messianiques juifs? Or ici l'enquête aboutit à un
résultat presque entièrement négatif. Billerbeck écrit que le
Psaume n'apparaît avec un sens messianique dans la littérature
rabbinique qu'après le IIe siècle après le Christ; les manuscrits de
Qumrân ne présentent pas nos versets parmi les textes messianiques; Tryphon, dans le *Dialogue* de Justin, l'applique à Ezéchias;
l'allusion à la droite de Dieu dans les Apocalypses juives relève
d'un tout autre terrain: ce n'est pas l'intronisation du Messie,
mais la présence de l'Ange de la droite; c'est dans les apocalypses
chrétiennes que ce thème se combine, comme nous l'avons vu,
avec le Ps. 109. Le seul passage en sens contraire est Mth. 22, 24,
où la question posée par le Christ aux Pharisiens semblait supposer
que ceux-ci interprétaient le Psaume messianiquement. Mais
cette évidence est peu de chose. Et il paraît qu'ici c'est la communauté primitive qui a donné au texte son importance. Et sans
doute, avant la communauté, Jésus lui-même, comme l'a montré
C. H. Dodd.

Une fois établie l'appartenance de nos versets à la couche la
plus ancienne de la tradition évangélique, nous avons à montrer la
place qu'ils ont tenue dans la constitution de la théologie apostolique. Nous laisserons de côté les textes où ils sont invoqués pour
prouver la messianité ou la divinité du Christ[1]. Nous n'aborderons
pas non plus les allusions que le Nouveau Testament fait à
d'autres versets du Psaume, en particulier le commentaire que
donne l'Epître aux Hébreux du verset 4: «Tu es prêtre pour
toujours selon l'ordre de Melchisedech». Nous nous concen-
trerons sur l'application, catéchétique et théologique, qui est
faite du Psaume à l'ascension. Il est clair en effet qu'il est une

---

[1] On peut remarquer avec C. H. Dodd (According to the Scriptures,
pp. 120—122) que c'est sans doute de Ps. 109, 1 que vient ce terme κύριος
appliqué à Jésus.

source essentielle de la théologie de celle-ci en tant qu'elle est l'instauration de l'humanité du Christ dans la gloire trinitaire.

En premier lieu le verset sert à expliquer le contenu de l'Ascension comme intronisation de Jésus dans la dignité messianique. C'est ce que montre Act. 2, 32—36: «Dieu a ressuscité Jésus, nous en sommes tous témoins. Et maintenant, exalté par la droite de Dieu, il a reçu du Père l'Esprit-Saint promis et l'a répandu. Car David, lui, n'est pas monté aux cieux. Or il dit lui-même: Le Seigneur a dit à mon Seigneur: Assieds-toi à ma droite jusqu'à ce que j'aie fait de tes ennemis l'escabeau de tes pieds. Que toute la maison d'Israël le sache donc: Dieu l'a fait Seigneur et Christ, celui que vous avez crucifié.» Comme l'a bien vu Cerfaux, Seigneur désigne ici la royauté messianique et est synonyme de Christ. La montée aux cieux signifie l'intronisation de Jésus comme Seigneur: la session à la droite est ascension elle-même.

C'est la même idée qui est développée dans Eph. 1, 20—22: «Dieu a déployé sa force en la personne du Christ, le ressuscitant d'entre les morts et le faisant siéger à sa droite, dans les cieux, au dessus de toute principauté, puissance, vertu, seigneurie. Il a tout mis sous ses pieds.» Nous avons ici d'une part un développement d'origine apocalyptique qui précise l'étendue cosmique de la Seigneurie du Christ montrant qu'elle s'étend à toute créature. C'est de façon analogue qu'Hebr. 1, 3; 1, 13; 8, 1 utilisent notre verset pour décrire l'ascension comme un fait passé, avec référence à la suprématie sur les anges.

Mais une seconde série de textes laisse apparaître une idée nouvelle. La session à la droite y est présentée non au passé, comme se référant à l'exaltation du Christ, mais au présent, comme désignant sa royauté actuelle. C'est ce qui apparaît dans les textes catéchétiques. Ainsi Rom. 8, 34: «Le Christ Jésus qui est mort et ressuscité ($\dot{\epsilon}\gamma\epsilon\varrho\vartheta\epsilon\acute{\iota}\varsigma$) est ($\dot{\epsilon}\sigma\tau\iota\nu$) à la droite de Dieu et intercède pour nous.» De même aussi dans Col. 3, 1: «Recherchez les choses d'en haut, où le Christ est assis à la droite du Dieu.» C'est également ce qui apparaît dans certains fragments apocalyptiques où les cieux ouverts laissent voir le sanctuaire céleste. Ainsi Etienne voit «la gloire de Dieu et Jésus debout à la droite de Dieu» (7, 55). Et au verset suivant: «Je vois les cieux ouverts et le Fils de l'homme debout à la droite de Dieu» (7, 56).

Mais à partir de ce moment, la session à la droite ne désigne plus l'instauration messianique, l'ascension, mais la royauté actuelle du Christ. Ainsi les deux mystères commencent-ils à se distinguer. C'est ce que nous trouvons dans un texte catéchétique qui marque une nouvelle étape, celui de la Iᵃ Petri. Il s'agit de la profession baptismale[1]. Or elle a pour objet «la Résurrection de Jésus-Christ, qui, monté au ciel, est à la droite de Dieu, après s'être soumis les anges, les dominations et les puissances» (3, 21—22). Les deux mystères sont ici bien distingués. Il y a d'abord l'ascension, qui est conçue en style apocalyptique comme exaltation au dessus des anges, comme dans l'Epître aux Romains ; et à celle-ci a succédé la session à la droite, qui dure encore. Nous avons la même séquence dans Marc 16, 19: «Il fut enlevé au ciel et s'est assis à la droite.» C'est cette séquence que nous retrouverons dans les symboles et qui constitue la session à la droite comme un mystère particulier.

Une seconde série de textes va nous montrer le Psaume non seulement servant à formuler un mystère particulier, mais commandant une séquence de mystères. D'abord la session à la droite est mise en rapport avec le temps qui va jusqu'à la Parousie. Nous partirons d'un texte de Justin, à cause de son caractère très explicite: «Dieu, le Père du monde, devait enlever le Christ au ciel, après la résurrection, et il doit l'y conserver jusqu'à ce qu'il ait frappé les démons ses ennemis et jusqu'à ce que soit complet le nombre des prédestinés, à cause desquels il n'a pas livré l'univers aux flammes. Ecoutez le prophète David prédire ces événements: Le Seigneur a dit à mon Seigneur: Asseyez-vous à ma droite, jusqu'à ce que j'aie fait de vos ennemis l'escabeau de vos pieds» (*Apol.* 45, 1—3). Ici c'est l'expression «jusqu'à ce que j'aie fait de vos ennemis l'escabeau de vos pieds» qui commande le développement[2].

Or ce thème se trouve déjà dans deux textes du Nouveau Testament. Le premier est I Cor. 15, 24—27: «Puis ce sera la fin, quand il remettra la royauté à son père, après avoir détruit toute principauté, domination et puissance. Car il faut qu'il règne jusqu'à ce qu'il ait placé tous ses ennemis sous ses pieds. Le dernier ennemi détruit, c'est la mort: car il a tout mis sous ses pieds.» Nous avons ici le même contexte d'expression que dans Eph., mais Paul présente ici la victoire sur les puissances comme

---

[1] Voir Bo Reicke, The disobedient Spirits and christian Baptism, p. 199.
[2] Voir aussi Irénée, Dem. 85.

un événement eschatologique, tandis que dans Eph., comme dans I Petr., la victoire sur les puissances coïncide avec l'ascension et précède la session à la droite. Or ceci apparaît bien en dépendance de Ps. 109, 1 comme dans Justin.

Nous avons un témoignage plus explicite dans Hébreux 10, 13: «Lui, ayant offert pour les péchés un unique sacrifice, il s'est assis à la droite de Dieu pour toujours, attendant désormais que ses ennemis soient placés comme un escabeau sous ses pieds.» Ici c'est le caractère unique de la Passion qui est opposé à la permanence de la session à la droite durant tout le temps de l'Eglise, jusqu'à l'achèvement de la victoire sur les puissances, comme aussi dans 12, 2. Ces puissances paraissent bien ici les démons. Et ceci vérifie l'interprétation de Justin. C'est une interprétation des «ennemis» du Psaume, mais dans le prolongement de son sens. Ainsi le thème de cette victoire eschatologique sur les puissances paraît amené par le Psaume, ou au moins est pensé dans le cadre de celui-ci.

Il est curieux de voir comment Théodote reprendra ce thème, mais le transportera dans la perspective de la gnose. La session à la droite désigne pour lui le séjour du Christ psychique auprès du démiurge dans le Lieu intermédiaire entre l'hebdomade et l'ogdoade: «Ainsi donc le Christ psychique est assis à la droite du Démiurge, selon la parole de David: Assieds-toi à ma droite etc. ... Il est assis jusqu'à la consommation finale (συντέλεια), afin qu'ils puissent voir celui qu'ils ont transpercé» (*Excerpt.* 72, 1—2). Le mouvement est le même. De plus on remarquera le rapprochement avec la prophétie de Zach. 12. Mais on pense aussi à la séquence du symbole: Il est monté aux cieux, il est assis à la droite, d'où il viendra juger les vivants et les morts. La structure est la même et elle est celle du Ps. 109. Non seulement celui-ci a fourni son expression au mystère de la session à droite, mais il donne son articulation au groupe des trois mystères de l'ascension, de la session et de la parousie.

Il faut remarquer toutefois qu'un autre verset du Psaume a orienté une série de textes dans une autre direction qui ne met pas la session à la droite en relation avec la Parousie, mais avec la Pentecôte; ou plus exactement qui met directement en relation la session à la droite et l'évangélisation. Ainsi nous lisons dans un passage que nous n'avons pas encore utilisé, Marc 16, 19: «Après leur avoir ainsi parlé, le Seigneur fut enlevé au ciel et s'assit à la droite de Dieu. Et eux s'en allèrent prêcher partout, le Seigneur travaillant avec eux et confirmant leur parole par des miracles qui l'accompagnaient.» Nous avons ici une nouvelle séquence: Ascension, Session, Mission.

Or ceci se retrouve ailleurs. Ainsi dans Act. 2, 33, nous lisons: «Ayant été élevé à la droite de Dieu et ayant reçu l'Esprit-Saint, il a répandu ce que vous voyez et entendez.» L'effusion de l'Esprit est ici attribuée au Christ et apparaît comme une suite de la session à la droite. Nous remarquerons le thème unique de la communication de l'Esprit au Fils par le Père en vue de son envoi. C'est encore une relation analogue que nous avons dans Eph. 1, 22: «Il a tout mis sous ses pieds et il l'a donné pour chef à son Eglise.» Ici la dépendance n'est pas littéraire, mais la suite des idées est la même et la présence de Ps. 109, 1 dans le voisinage autorise à reconnaître son influence, ainsi que dans Eph. 4, 10—11.

Or si nous reprenons le Psaume 109, nous constatons que le verset 2 dit ceci: «Le Seigneur fera sortir de Sion le sceptre de la puissance.» Reprenons maintenant la suite du commentaire du Psaume telle que nous la trouvons dans Justin, nous lisons: «Le Seigneur fera sortir de Jérusalem le sceptre de la puissance. Ces mots annoncent la parole puissante que, sortant de Jérusalem, les apôtres prêchèrent partout» (*Apol.* 45, 5). La suite des idées est exactement la même que dans les passages que nous avons cités. Plus encore les mots sont ceux mêmes de Marc. N'est-il pas légitime alors de se demander si la succession dans Ps. 109, 1 de la session à la droite et de l'envoi du sceptre, que Justin interprète de l'intronisation et de la mission, n'est pas déjà ce qui a commandé la séquence des deux mystères dans Marc et dans Actes?

Ainsi nous apparaît le rôle considérable de Ps. 109, 1 dans la tradition évangélique primitive. Il a servi à donner une formulation théologique à l'ascension, à exprimer un mystère propre, celui de la royauté actuelle du Christ, dont il reste l'expression autorisée, il a marqué également le lien de ce mystère avec la mission d'une part et avec la Parousie de l'autre. C'est donc tout un ensemble de conceptions théologiques fondamentales qui se sont constituées autour de lui. Ainsi les *Testimonia* nous apparaissent-ils comme ces noyaux actifs au sein de la pensée chrétienne primitive par lesquels les catégories bibliques essentielles ont servi d'expression au donné chrétien pour en dégager le contenu théologal. Et l'exemple que nous avons choisi est singulièrement important pour nous puisqu'il nous aide à comprendre qu'entre le dernier des mystères passés du Christ, qui est l'Ascension, et ce que nous attendons encore, qui est la Parousie, il y a un mystère et un seul dont nous sommes contemporains et qui est la Session à la droite — et qu'ainsi nous vivons toujours en pleine histoire sainte.

Lignes maîtresses de la prière johannique[1]

A. Hamman O. F. M., Besançon-Paris

Celui qui aborde l'étude johannique est frappé de l'infime place que la prière occupe dans une littérature par ailleurs abondante: Il n'existe pas une seule monographie qui lui soit consacrée. W. Bauer affirme même sans ambage que le Christ johannique ne saurait prier[2]. L'étude souvent compromise par des préjugés a singulièrement dévié de l'essentiel: l'authentique pensée johannique. De combien de savantes constructions les découvertes de Qumrân font un rapide procès?

Notre propos n'est point de reprendre ici l'étude critique de l'authenticité johannique des écrits qui lui sont attribués par la tradition. Nous nous bornerons ici à l'étude de l'évangile et des lettres johanniques que nous supposons l'œuvre de Jean l'Apôtre, tout en reconnaissant la part que des rédacteurs ont pu apporter à son œuvre littéraire. D'ailleurs notre recherche permettra de découvrir des parentés nouvelles entre les divers écrits qui sont attribués au disciple bien-aimé[3].

Derniers en date, les écrits johanniques permettent de mesurer à la fois la continuité doctrinale avec les Synoptiques et la théologie paulinienne, et le singulier approfondissement qu'imprime au message primitif le génie propre de l'auteur, tout en en demeurant le témoin fidèle, à la fin du premier siècle[4]. Notre

---

[1] Le présent aperçu de la prière johannique suppose nécessairement une analyse des textes essentiels que nous ne pouvons faire ici. Le lecteur la trouvera dans notre étude, La prière. I: Les origines chrétiennes (sous presse).

[2] W. Bauer, Das Johannesevangelium, 1933, 154.

[3] On trouvera les variations des exégètes sur ce point dans l'excellent cahier de Ph. Menoud, L'évangile de Jean, 1947, 73—74.

[4] Cerfaux écrit: «On pourrait montrer aisément dans son enseignement tel que Jean le rapporte les échos de la tradition évangélique primitive.» Recueil Cerfaux, II, 49—50. Même avis chez C. H. Dodd, The Interpretation of the Fourth Gospel, 1953, 445, note 1.

propos consistera donc à cerner les composantes de ce témoignage,
au sujet de la prière, située dans son contexte cultuel.

Nombreux sont les exégètes qui comparent Jean et Paul pour
discerner les influences qui les marquèrent dans leur pensée, pour
dégager les lignes maîtresses de leur théologie particulière ou
pour mettre en lumière, au delà des personnalités différentes,
leur confluence doctrinale. L'objet propre de cette étude nous
oblige d'analyser avant tout l'approfondissement très personnel
d'un kérygme qui est commun au quatrième évangile avec les
autres. L'évangile johannique commence où finissent les autres,
en respectant les lois d'une croissance organique, à partir d'un
même message.

Un demi siècle s'est écoulé entre les Synoptiques et le quatrième
évangile: une vie d'homme, une vie de méditation, illuminée de
visions, nourrie d'oraison, où tout enseignement est devenu
confession, toute méditation, prière, où chaque épisode, chaque
discours reflète la foi chrétienne tout entière, expérimentée dans
la communauté apostolique.

Le culte en esprit et en vérité

La doctrine johannique sur la prière jaillit d'une double expérience ecclésiale et personnelle, qui caractérisent de façon si
originale sa théologie. Cette double expérience s'appuie sur la vie
sacramentaire, qui constitue le cadre même de son évangile. Un
des traits saillants est l'importance accordée à la vie cultuelle[1].
La vie de Jésus se déroule dans le cadre de la vie spirituelle juive.
Elle est centrée sur Jérusalem, la capitale liturgique. Le Christ
opère ses miracles et prononce ses discours en liaison avec les
principales fêtes et souvent dans le Temple. Il se situe au centre
des institutions juives pour définir la religion en esprit et en
vérité (Jo. 4, 23).

L'évangile commence la vie publique de Jésus par l'expulsion
des vendeurs irrespectueux, qui profanaient le Temple (Jo. 2,
13—22). Là aussi il promet l'eau vivante, en pleine célébration
liturgique (7, 37—39). Les fêtes religieuses rythment le marche de
l'évangile. La pâque en est le pivot autour duquel s'articule
tout le récit. Les trois pâques commémorées par Jean seul sont

---

[1] D. Mollat a très bien mis en valeur cet aspect dans sa remarquable
introduction à l'évangile johannique, dans la Bible de Jérusalem, 1953,
32—33.

les articulations majeures qui commandent tout l'écrit. Toute la fin de l'évangile est encadré par la fête de la pâque (Jo. 11, 55; 12, 1. 12. 20; 13, 1; 18, 28. 39; 19, 14. 31. 42).

Les images chères au quatrième évangile ont une résonnance liturgique: agneau, temple, eau, pain, pasteur, cep, vigne. Il en est de même des paroles, et plus particulièrement de la prière sacerdotale de Jésus, qui prélude aux futures anaphores. Cette dernière prière a des analogies frappantes avec le Notre Père: Même adresse au Père, même préoccupation de la sainteté de Dieu, même prière pour être préservé du Malin (Jo. 17, 15 et Mt. 6, 13). Nous y trouvons aussi le procédé très personnel par lequel le rédacteur assimile et rapporte les paroles de son Maître. Loisy va plus loin même. Il écrit avec beaucoup de perspicacité: «Cette prière complète non seulement les leçons, mais la forme eucharistique du dernier repas: c'est comme l'action de grâces solennelle de la première agape et le mot suprême de la charité. L'attitude même de Jésus est eucharistique et l'on peut dire liturgique.»[1] La prière sacerdotale reprend les thèmes de tout le discours: promesse de retour, assistance permanente, unité et charité parmi les disciples. L'essence de la prière y apparaît la demande au Père que l'œuvre du salut soit achevée par les disciples, dans l'Eglise.

Jésus n'est pas prisonnier d'un rituel ou de fêtes juives. S'il se situe dans leur prolongement historique, c'est pour donner aux figures leur valeur, en les accomplissant. Il les habite, les fait siennes mais en les transcendant. Il les scrute en leur profondeur, parce qu'elles parlent de lui. Le caractère provisoire du culte et des institutions religieuses d'Israël apparait dans l'entretien avec la Samaritaine, le seul événement qui n'est pas lié à une fête, mais qui annonce le mystère qui éclaire de l'intérieur tous les signes comme toutes les figures, qui constituent les «temps nouveaux», où les vrais adorateurs «adoreront en esprit et en vérité» (Jo. 4, 23). Le culte nouveau n'est plus lié désormais ni réduit à un lieu, mais centré sur une personne, qui vient sauver le monde.

Le galbe liturgique du quatrième évangile lui imprime son rythme et son style très particuliers. Certains exégètes en ont conclu que l'évangile de Jean était purement et simplement une

---

[1] A. Loisy, Le quatrième évangile, 1927, 2, 441.

liturgie, servant aux célébrations eucharistiques. C'était aller vite en besogne.

Le caractère à la fois sacramentaire et catéchétique est indéniable. Jean part du mystère chrétien, vécu dans le culte, par les sacrements essentiels du baptême et de l'eucharistie, qui permettent à la foi de la communauté de rejoindre le Christ de l'histoire. Toute la religion chrétienne et la prière s'appuient sur la foi sacramentaire.

O. Cullmann[1] s'est efforcé d'aller plus loin et d'expliquer la structure de l'évangile johannique par le rapport qui unit l'histoire et le sacrement, les événements de la vie de Jésus et le culte de la communauté. S'il est possible de mettre en doute l'une ou l'autre application que l'éminent exégète de Bâle fait de ce principe, ce dernier lui-même semble hors de doute. Le point critiquable de la thèse de Cullmann est une certaine systématisation trop pressée. Jean n'est pas tellement préoccupé de prouver. Son exposé est d'instinct nourri d'une expérience sacramentaire, parce que le culte lui a permis d'approfondir le kérygme. Cette structure sacramentaire paraît plus une seconde nature qu'une démonstration intentionnelle.

Le caractère liturgique de la première lettre de Jean confirme cette affirmation[2]. Celle-ci apparaît comme une catéchèse mystagogique à partir de l'agapè eucharistique qui constitue le centre de l'assemblée liturgique. Nombreux sont les liens qui apparentent cette lettre au discours des adieux, et plus encore à la prière sacerdotale[3]. De part et d'autre nous retrouvons la même doctrine, la même expérience spirituelle et jusqu'au même rythme.

---

[1] O. Cullmann, Les sacrements dans l'Evangile johannique, 1931, 27—28.

[2] Le P. Braun la transcrit tout entière en versets rythmés, dans la Bible de Jérusalem.

[3] Il est suggestif de comparer la première lettre de Jean à la Prière sacerdotale:

I Lettre	Prière sacerdotale	I Lettre	Prière sacerdotale
1, 3	17, 21	3, 1	17, 23
1, 4	17, 13	3, 2	17, 24. 25
1, 7	17, 21	4, 14	17, 1
2, 14 cf. 5, 19	17, 15	4, 16	17, 6
2, 23	17, 6	5, 18—19	17, 15—16
3, 1—3	17, 4	5, 20—21	17, 3—4

Prière et foi

A première vue, Jean a parlé moins que Paul de la prière, et pourtant elle affleure partout, elle est plus inextricablement liée à tout l'enseignement de Jésus chez Jean que chez les Synoptiques. La prière johannique est expression de la foi, indissolublement unie à la contemplation du Verbe de vie.

Une longue méditation dans la foi a permis à Jean de pénétrer l'âme de Jésus et de saisir ce qu'a pu être la prière de Jésus. Ce qui nous est livré par les autres évangélistes à l'état brut est devenu chez Jean chair de son âme et âme de sa contemplation.

La prière de Jésus exprime nécessairement l'unité et la réciprocité qui existent entre le Fils et le Père. Jésus contemple et fait sienne la volonté de son Père : elle est l'agapè, qui le nourrit et le mène. Les œuvres de Jésus sont filles de sa prière comme elles sont l'expression de sa soumission filiale. Elles expriment la volonté et la mission que le Fils ne cesse de contempler dans la prière.

Il ne peut pas exister le moindre doute dans l'âme de Jésus sur l'exaucement du Père[1], le doute ne pouvant provenir que de l'homme qui ne discerne plus la volonté divine. La clarté avec laquelle Jésus voit l'œuvre que le Père lui a donné mission d'accomplir le met à l'abri de toute hésitation et lui garantit que «le Père l'exauce toujours» (Jean 11, 42). La prière de Jésus est exaucée nécessairement, puisqu'elle est au service de l'œuvre et de la glorification du Père.

C'est la raison pour laquelle toute demande, toute intercession de Jésus, chez Jean est en même temps action de grâces : son unité de vie, sa conformité avec le Père lui permettent d'anticiper sur le temps et lui donnent la certitude que le Père l'entend, puisque lui-même écoute le Père. Le temps fractionne en demande et en action de grâces ce qui en l'agapè de Dieu ne fait qu'un.

La prière de Jésus est inséparable de son activité comme de son être, elle est, comme ses œuvres, signe de l'irruption que Dieu a faite dans le monde. Aussi est-elle témoignage en face du monde. Elle confesse, c'est-à-dire, elle proclame la mission reçue. La prière de Jésus est parfois publique, afin d'amener les hommes à reconnaitre l'œuvre du Père qu'il accomplit, et de l'accueillir dans la foi. Le Christ au tombeau de Lazare place les hommes devant

---

[1] F. Büchsel, Das Evangelium nach Johannes, 1934, 129.

l'option fondamentale: refus ou accueil, incrédulité ou foi. L'évangile johannique montre d'ailleurs combien la résurrection de Lazare a provoqué des déterminations contraires (Jo. 11, 45 à 47).

La foi chez saint Jean est l'accueil du message du Père et du Messie, le messager incarnant le message: il est le Logos qui parle de Dieu au monde. La foi est donc une rencontre personnelle avec le Christ. Elle permet au chrétien comme à l'Eglise de rejoindre le Christ glorifié. Cette rencontre du Seigneur rend présent pour le croyant l'*eschaton*, elle réalise dans le temps l'éternité[1].

La prière chez saint Jean est l'expression même de cette foi: elle possède la même assise, la même παρρησία, au sens d'assurance et de certitude, selon le mot cher à Jean pour la caractériser. Comme la foi qui l'inspire et qu'elle orchestre, la prière est une extase, un exode, qui arrache le croyant de sa condition charnelle et lui permet de rencontrer Dieu et de baigner dans l'intimité ineffable de sa vie.

Le Christ a ouvert au fidèle l'accès auprès du Père, il a établi le dialogue de la prière, qui permet de mesurer à la fois la présence et la distance[2]. Dans la prière, le chrétien prend conscience qu'il est encore dans le monde et qu'il en est arraché, qu'il mène dans le provisoire une vie eschatologique, dans le temps une existence d'éternité. Toute prière est conditionnée par l'union au Christ que Jean appelle «demeurer en moi» (Jo. 6, 56; 15, 4. 5. 6; cf. I Jo. 3, 6. 24). La certitude de l'exaucement provient de la solidité de cette réciprocité mystique. «Si vous demeurez en moi et que mes paroles demeurent en vous, demandez ce que vous voudrez et vous l'aurez» (Jo. 15, 7).

La prière implique, de plus, une confession du Christ glorifié, elle est un témoignage rendu à la communion avec lui; ce que Jean appelle «prier en son nom» (Jo. 14, 13; 15, 16; 16, 23. 24. 26). Implorer la médiation du Christ glorifié pour atteindre le Père, c'est mettre Dieu en demeure de répondre. En exauçant la prière, le Père confesse à son tour le Fils invoqué[3].

Pour Jean il semble indifférent que l'on prie le Fils ou le Père, d'attribuer l'exaucement à l'un ou à l'autre, parce que la réponse exprime toujours un même et unique amour: «Je ne prierai pas

---

[1] R. Bultmann, Πίστις dans Th. W. z. N. T. VI, 228.
[2] R. Bultmann, Theologie des N. T., 1953, 433.
[3] Ibid. 433.

le Père pour vous, car le Père lui aussi vous aime, parce que vous m'aimez et vous croyez que je suis sorti de Dieu» (Jo. 16, 27).

La prière jaillit de l'existence chrétienne, elle élève le croyant au-dessus du monde vaincu, des désirs du monde et de la chair; elle demande ce que déjà elle possède (I Jo. 5, 15). La supplication est déjà exaucement et action de grâces, puisqu'elle est l'expression de la vie éternelle en nous et inspirée par l'Esprit.

La prière chrétienne, chez saint Jean, a vaincu le monde et ses désirs; elle immunise le chrétien contre toute angoisse; elle est confiance inébranlable et assurance absolue, parce que portée par la foi du Christ en gloire. Nous en trouvons le témoignage à la fois discret et ferme, tout au long des écrits johanniques.

Prière et expérience spirituelle

Il suffit de relire le début de la première lettre de saint Jean pour soupeser de quelle expérience spirituelle est chargée le message qu'il adresse aux églises d'Asie (I Jo. 1, 1—2):

«Celui que nous avons entendu,
celui que nous avons vu de nos yeux,
celui que nous avons contemplé,
celui que nos mains ont touché
— et cela concerne le Verbe de vie —
nous l'avons vu, nous en rendons témoignage.» [1]

Genèse de cette expérience [2]

Jean nous désoriente par l'ampleur même de son expérience spirituelle dont témoignent tous ses écrits. Ce tempérament bouillonnant, passionné, que Jésus appelait «enfant du tonnerre» (Mc. 3, 17) ne paraît plus à travers ses écrits que dans la sérénité d'une âme apaisée. Son évangile nous apparaît comme ces vieilles peintures dont toutes les couleurs sont effacées, il ne reste plus que le dessin gris, qu'il faut lire du dedans.

Il serait cependant grave de ne pas découvrir dans le ton de sa confidence la véhémence de son âme ou de se représenter cette nature virile et éruptive sous les traits doux et désincarnés que

---

[1] Notre traduction est inspirée par l'article de J. Héring, Y a-t-il des araméismes dans la manière épistolaire de Saint Jean?, dans Revue d'histoire et de philosophie religieuses 36 (1956) 114.

[2] Nous avons utilisé les études de J. Mouroux, L'expérience chrétienne, Paris 1952; R. Guardini, Jesus Christus, Würzburg 1940.

lui ont prêtés certains peintres. Ceux qui se laissent aller à de pareilles erreurs méconnaissent ce que l'existence de Jean renferme de plus profond et de plus fort.

Il a fallu à ce fils du tonnerre rencontrer le Christ pour quitter l'âme juive et naître à l'agapè de Dieu. Si cette rencontre a été moins brutale, moins fulgurante que celle dont Paul fut gratifié, aux portes de Damas, elle l'a marqué d'une empreinte peut-être encore plus forte. Jean n'a jamais oublié le premier contact que rien ne peut effacer. Quatre-vingt ans plus tard, en rédigeant son évangile, il situe encore l'événement et jusqu'à l'heure: «C'était environ la dixième heure» (Jo. 1, 39).

Il suffit pour s'en convaincre de relire sa première lettre où Jean, plus libre de son sujet que dans l'évangile, révèle le bouleversement opéré par le Seigneur dans sa vie, le changement intérieur qu'il lui a fallu opérer pour connaître l'amour vrai, celui de Dieu.

Cette âme contemplative, naturellement abîmée en Dieu, au point de s'abstraire des hommes, a cependant dit, avec moins de lyrisme peut-être que Paul, avec plus de profondeur et de densité combien se trompent et s'illusionnent ceux qui croient rencontrer Dieu sans voir leur frère. Il serait meurtrier de prendre pour une richesse de nature ce qui fut une victoire de la grâce.

Certains exégètes expliquent l'insistance de Jean à souligner le réalisme de l'incarnation de Verbe fait chair par les jeunes hérésies naissantes de l'époque qui mutilaient le mystère de Jésus. Jean combattit d'autant plus énergiquement l'hérésie naissante qu'elle aurait ou avait pu être une tentation pour sa tournure d'esprit. Pour l'avoir combattue et vaincue, il en connaissait mieux tout le danger.

Aussi trouvons-nous sans cesse des tournures concrètes, des termes comme ποιεῖν, ὁρᾶν, βλέπειν, θεωρεῖν, ἀκούειν. Son expérience spirituelle a besoin de s'exprimer en termes vécus. S'il emploie le mot Logos, il l'associe à celui d'un brutal réalisme, insupportable pour un esprit grec: σάρξ. L'expérience spirituelle parvient à Jean à travers une expérience sensible, le Verbe de Dieu lui est apparu à travers un corps. La divinité lui est demeurée unaccessible, parce qu'elle lui échappait du fait de sa transcendance. «Il n'y a pas eu saisie du Verbe de Dieu, écrit J. Mouroux, de la vie éternelle, mais communion à travers ce qui apparaissait, ce qu'on pouvait voir, entendre, palper, du Verbe

incarné, et participation corporelle et spirituelle à la saisie de la
vie éternelle, bref, union à Dieu à travers ce grand signe qu'est
l'Homme-Dieu.»[1]

Les expressions abstraites elles-mêmes prennent chez Jean
une signification concrète: la Vérité est une personne, son contraire n'est pas l'erreur mais le mensonge et derrière lui le Démon.
Vrai est l'épithète non pas d'une doctrine mais de Dieu. Les
exégètes qui ont voulu mettre l'historicité de l'évangile johannique en doute ont fait un contre-sens qui vicie toute leur interprétation. Si les autres évangélistes se contentent de narrer les récits
avec plus ou moins de pittoresque, de rapporter les paroles avec
fidélité, Jean commence où finissent les Synoptiques. Ce que les
autres entrevoyaient Jean le contemple et le décrit. Ce qui est
allusion chez les premiers, ici est médité, creusé et compose la
trame même de l'Evangile. Là où les autres ne voyaient que des
points, Jean découvre des étoiles. Il en est ainsi de Matthieu 11,
25, allusion passagère qui devient la structure même du quatrième évangile. Jean n'innove pas, mais il voit mieux et plus profond.

Jamais Jean ne s'arrête au pittoresque, au paysage qui
retient les distraits, parce qu'il n'écrit pas pour eux: il écrit
uniquement pour proclamer au monde, au nom de l'Eglise apostolique, le contenu de l'évènement, ce qu'il a vu, palpé du Verbe de
vie. Tout son évangile est une confession, au sens premier du
terme, qui est peut-être aussi celui du livre d'Augustin «Les
confessions», qui permettent, par leur parenté spirituelle, de
mieux comprendre la structure mentale de Jean.

Jean n'est pas un gnostique qui spécule sur les données de la
foi comme certaine théologie; ou du moins, il ne l'est plus. Il met
son esprit spéculatif au service de cette rencontre intérieure.
Il s'agit pour l'apôtre non de construire une somme mais de
rendre compte d'une rencontre qui fut une épiphanie. Sa pensée
méditative ne paraît se répéter qu'à ceux qui ne suivent pas sa
progression et qui voudraient trouver une gnose là où Jean
nous livre un témoignage. Il ne veut pas voir pour connaître
mais pour contempler, il écrit pour décrire, il pense en images.

Tout ce que Jean relate jaillit d'une expérience prolongée,
exprime ce qu'il a vécu et contemplé: la naissance à la vie de

---

[1] J. Mouroux, L'expérience chrétienne, 169.

Dieu qui se développe dans une communion spirituelle, l'action de l'Esprit, promis au moment des adieux, qui lui permet de se souvenir et donc de découvrir toute l'épaisseur des paroles de Jésus, toute leur portée spirituelle qui, chez lui, semble trop lourde pour se traduire en mots humains.

La parole de Dieu apparaît toujours à travers une confidence, qui exprime une réalité vécue, ce qui donne sa tournure particulière à l'exposé, son originalité à l'expression («demeurer» par exemple), la surcharge à une phrase, qui ne s'embarasse plus de grammaire, soucieuse uniquement de fidélité et de vérité.

Jean ne respecte pas une logique linéaire. Les discours de Jésus qu'il rapporte donnent apparemment une impression d'incohérence: Jésus n'y répond pas aux questions, mais à sa pensée. Jean ne connaît que la logique de la contemplation qui s'efforce d'exprimer l'Inexprimable, de traduire sans trahir.

Les évènements, les paroles ne valent plus pour eux-mêmes ni par eux-mêmes mais par la contemplation qui les sous-tend et l'expérience qui les a vues. Le discours après la Cène est chargé de toutes les harmoniques de la vie chrétienne. L'intensité même de la vision intérieure rend plus riche et plus difficile l'échange entre l'objet et le sujet. Le sujet s'abîme dans l'évènement, semble s'y perdre et en perçoit lentement la signification. L'objet se dévoile et lui dévoile des aspects sans cesse nouveaux, insoupçonnés, inexplorés.

Cette fidélité à une contemplation intérieure, complexe et unique à la fois, saisie et insaisissable, se traduit par la phrase johannique, qui s'avance en recommençant et s'organise dans une apparent désordre. Jean ne peut exprimer son expérience que par approches successives. Jean est un peintre, il travaille et progresse à force de retouches.

Le lecteur est obligé sans cesse de chercher le centre de sa pensée. Il est porté comme le flot de la mer, où les vagues successives se recouvrent et rythment le mouvement en avant.

Au cœur de sa contemplation Jean découvre en Dieu le monde, le drame du cosmos, la tension ontologique entre les antinomies, monde — Dieu, lumière — ténèbres, mort — vie, les mêmes qui s'étaient exprimées dans ses résistances et dans sa conversion. Il construit une économie, non de la gnose ou de la raison, mais de la révélation, de la vision: il discerne la dimension cosmique de l'évènement évangélique. Si l'universalisme paraît moins en

étendue chez Jean que chez Paul, elle s'y développe davantage
en profondeur. Jean voit sa mission en Dieu, Paul voit Dieu dans
sa mission; Paul découvre, en œuvrant, la cité de Dieu, Jean
contemple la Jérusalem céleste descendue sur terre et la décrit
aux hommes.

Jean écrit, non pas pour construire une synthèse, mais parce
qu'il se sait une mission, il est apôtre, il doit proclamer au monde
une découverte qu'il doit partager avec les autres. Ceux-ci peu-
plent sans cesse sa pensée comme ils hantent la prière de Jésus.
Jusque dans l'intimité de sa communion, Jean découvre l'Eglise.

Prière et expérience

L'expérience religieuse chez Jean est d'abord christique.
Elle s'enracine dans la révélation du Verbe de vie. L'incarnation
du Fils de Dieu est le point de départ et la voie d'accès au mystère
de Dieu. Par la foi au Christ, sa médiation nous est assurée.
Bien plus, par la foi nous pénétrons jusqu'à Dieu. Etre en Dieu,
en définitive, c'est «être dans le Véritable, dans le Fils, Jésus-
Christ, lui qui est le Véritable et la vie éternelle» (I Jo. 5, 20).
Rien d'étonnant dès lors que le Fils soit associé au culte du Père
et que l'âme mystique puisse perdre le sens de l'humanité, une
fois parvenue au terme.

Toute prière chrétienne est faite au nom du Christ, parce qu'il
est la voie d'accès nécessaire mais sûre à Dieu; elle est communion
à Dieu dans le Christ, par une immanence réciproque: «Celui qui
confesse le Fils confesse le Père» (I Jo. 2, 23). Il s'agit d'un état.
Pour cette raison Jean emploie de préférence le mot «demeurer»
(I Jo. 4, 12; 2, 28; 4, 16). Mais la réalité de la foi est dynamique,
elle se développe depuis les humbles commencements jusqu'aux
splendeurs de la contemplation. Le Père est au commencement
et au terme de cette longue ascension intérieure, qui n'est
jamais que perception plus profonde dans la foi, l'espérance et
dans l'amour de cette vie en Dieu.

Cette expérience spirituelle est pneumatique: elle est l'œuvre
de l'Esprit (Jo. 14, 16; I Jo. 5, 6). Jean donne toute son extension à une parole que Luc est seul à rapporter, quand il affirme
que Dieu répond à la prière des fidèles en leur envoyant l'Esprit:
«Combien plus le Père du ciel donnera-t-il à ceux qui le prient
l'Esprit-Saint» (Lc. 11, 13). Celui qui apparaît dans la prière de
Paul, à la pointe de l'âme, prolongeant les balbutiements humains

en «soupirs ineffables» (Rom. 8, 26), enseigne chez saint Jean du
dedans la vérité et le mystère de Dieu (I Jo. 2, 20—27). Il est
une source jaillissante qui permet au chrétien de recevoir l'enseignement et de le traduire en prière.

La dernière note caractéristique de l'expérience spirituelle de
Jean c'est qu'elle est ecclésiale. Certains exégètes ont parlé de
«l'individualisme de saint Jean». A y regarder de plus près, si le
quatrième évangile insiste fortement sur le rapport personnel du
croyant au Christ, dans la foi, toute expérience spirituelle a ses
racines dans la vie ecclésiale et sacramentaire. Il n'est pas exagéré
de dire, avec le P. Mollat, que «le quatrième évangile est un
évangile ecclésial»[1]. Toute vie spirituelle prend son point d'appui
dans les sacrements de la foi, le baptême et l'eucharistie qui
forgent la communauté. L'amour des frères est la garantie
que l'agapè de Dieu habite le cœur du chrétien. Hors de cette
dimension horizontale qui lie le fidèle à la communauté toute vie
de prière, toute expérience spirituelle serait un leurre[2]. Si Jésus
est la prière incarnée, la prière des siens ne peut être que la prière
des pampres de la vigne, qui accèdent au Père par la médiation du
Logos.

---

[1] Bible de Jérusalem, L'évangile de saint Jean, 23.
[2] J. Mouroux, L'expérience chrétienne, 191—198.

Topography and Archaeology in the Fourth Gospel

R. D. POTTER O. P., Oxford

This paper can be but a small contribution towards the total of considerations required in the exegesis of the gospel. Let me start with a plea for a more down-to-earth exegesis, a more realist attitude to the Fourth Gospel, and with it, a better and fuller use of the data of topography and archaeology. Such data have in fact been accumulating over half a century, and archaeology in Palestine has passed from early enthusiasms to a certain maturity. Now the present paper is not concerned with the newest finds, as for instance the Qumran Scrolls[1] or the Bodmer papyrus; but it does urge a fuller use of the data, laboriously and lovingly acquired by those who have lived long in Palestine, for the express purpose of knowing the gospels and their background better, and whose competence and scientific rigour in such matters none would question.

There have, for years, been Schools of Archaeology in Palestine. But Schools of Archaeology are not enough. We need archaeology, topography and much else to subserve exegesis. To arrive at a fuller and more realist exegesis of this sort, our ideal interpreter must synthesise what he can of topographical, archaeological and like data.

While urging "le réalisme historique de S. Jean"[2], there is no question of belittling the very plentiful and scholarly work which has been done on so many aspects of the Fourth Gospel in the last few years. We are very grateful for it, and it all has its due place. Let us simply say that a fuller chapter needs to be added

---

[1] Cf. the valuable article of Braun, in Revue Biblique 62 (1955) 5—44, "L'arrière-fond judaïque du quatrième Evangile et la Communauté de l'Alliance".

[2] Lagrange, S. Jean, 1925, p. CXXIV.

to our introduction to the Fourth Gospel, and its contents integrated into the commentary. Only then can we have the perfect commentary on the greatest Gospel.

Where the problem lies and what remains to be done can be shown by making a list of place-names which occur only in the Fourth Gospel. This should be easy enough. Yet while there are 12 names in Dr. Barrett's[1] list, there are 23 in Père Lagrange's[2]. The difference is because, obviously, there are two ways of assessing and appreciating topographical references. Or again, let us work through all the place-names in the commentary of Dr. Barrett. Then take the same names and references in Abel's *Géographie de la Palestine*, I, and (especially) II. The results are startlingly different. The significance and force of topographical and archaeological factors are varyingly estimated, perhaps sometimes unappreciated. Take an analogy from another domain. Grammar is not enough for the appreciation of a foreign literature. We need a *Sprachgefühl*. So too, we must need some sort of sixth or seventh sense for the proper appreciation of data from Palestine. And with it, of course, the enthusiasm of a Professor Sanday[3] who went off to Palestine in the very early days of Palestinian exploration.

Such a plea for a realist attitude, for the following of the findings of those who had known Palestine best is more consonant with the evangelist's purpose. All our interpretations must respect that purpose, and realise that he wrote a gospel which has the structure of a gospel and the purpose of a gospel. No other evangelist speaks so often of belief and unbelief, as also of the aural and visual witnesses to the deeds of Our Lord. "So that you may believe that Jesus is the Christ, the Son of God, and that believing you may have life eternal in His name" (20, 31) is what wholly interests our evangelist. Close-linked with "belief" is his notion of "witness" to the point that μάρτυς and μαρτυρεῖν are key words of this gospel.

With this realist attitude in mind, let us proceed to a survey of those points in the gospel which admit of some topographical or archaeological reference.

---

[1] C. K. Barrett, St. John, p. 102.

[2] Lagrange, S. Jean, 1925, p. CXXIV.

[3] Sacred Sites of the Gospels, 1903. This is of course outmoded, but we could do with a contemporary equivalent.

I propose briefly to note all the texts concerned, and to some extent to systematise the data. Much of what I have to say will be a suggestion of what needs to be surveyed and further investigated.

(a) Let us take as a first example, a passage whose topography can be fully appreciated and verified, I mean Jo. 4. Most of this chapter is taken up with the dialogue of Our Lord and the Samaritan woman. Let us remember the geographical details. He came from Judea; he had διέρχεσθαι διὰ τῆς Σαμαρείας (4, 4). This, the shortest way north, was sometimes used, despite the animosities of Jews and Samaritans (Josephus, Ant. Jud. 20, 6, 1). If Our Lord pursued the old road northward, He would arrive at Συχὰρ (4, 5), perhaps the modern "Askar"[1]. The Bordeaux pilgrim (Baldi, no. 270)[2] knew Sechar; and the Madaba map gives Sychora (... χωρα) besides Σικιμά. On the other hand St. Jerome identified Sychar and Sichem (Quaest. in Genes. 48, 22, PL 23, 1055), and if this identification can be accepted, then we can imagine Our Lord heading N. W. towards the valley of Nablus, through Sichem which is the site of Balata, and much nearer the Πηγὴ τοῦ Ἰακώβ which is a centuries old and certain site[3], unmistakable in a region of several water-points, in that it is the deepest well in Palestine, cf. 4, 11 τὸ φρέαρ ἐστὶ βαθύ. As we sit there we can get the full force of ἐν τούτῳ τῷ ὄρει (4, 20); we can picture the Samaritan woman's gesture towards Mount Gerizim, looming up behind. Further we can, at the right season, see from Jacob's Well τὰς χώρας ὅτι λευκαί εἰσι as we glance over the great level plain stretching south and east. No passage could show better that our author knew this bit of Samaria well[4]. Note too that all the setting of the chapter, its cadre, its place-names are not in Southern Palestine[5].

---

[1] Against this cf. Albright, The Background of the N. T. and its Eschatology, Cambridge 1956, p. 159.

[2] Enchiridion Locorum Sanctorum, 2nd ed., Jerusalem 1955. An indispensable handbook for this sort of study.

[3] Cf. Abel, Le puits de Jacob et l'église St. Sauveur, Revue Biblique 42 (1933) 384—402.

[4] Cf. Lagrange, S. Jean, 1925, pp. 102—103.

[5] Against a tendency in modern commentators cf. C. H. Dodd, The Interpretation of the Fourth Gospel, pp. 452—3, and C. K. Barrett, St. John, p. 102.

(b) Now for a particular text. St. John the Baptist was baptizing ἐν Βηϑανίᾳ πέραν τοῦ ᾿Ιορδάνου. Our author knew that there were two Bethanies, and distinguished this Bethany from ἡ κώμη τῆς Μαρίας (11, 1). Origen on the other hand, read Βηϑαβαρᾶ[1] while admitting that most Mss. had Βηϑανία, and mysteriously seemed unable to accept two Bethanies[2], and so took Βηϑαβαρᾶ, or like form, from the "maʿbroth" or fords of the Jordan, no doubt with Judges 7, 24 in mind. There is a difficulty[3]. How did the name disappear in 100 or 150 years? The answer is that Origen, despite his pious assertion about visiting the scenes of our Redemption, had never been there. He is reporting hearsay (δείκνυσϑαι δὲ λέγουσιν). He never discovered Bethany beyond Jordan because he never went to look. He did not even get to Bethabara on this side of Jordan. Subsequent tradition, manuscript and patristic, as we might expect, was much influenced by Origen. But now that Origen has been found wanting on a particular point let us expunge Βηϑαβαρᾶ from our texts, and so rid ourselves of weighty notes, and leave the Fourth Gospel to tell us that there was a Bethany beyond Jordan, and archaeologists to decide which of the several possible Tells might best correspond.

(c) Next in our survey, is a group which we will call the "Galilee" texts[4], mostly associated with Κανὰ τῆς Γαλιλαίας (2, 1; 2, 11; 4, 46) which may reasonably be Kefr Kenna of today; Καφαρναούμ or Καπερναούμ which is certainly known to archaeologists as Tell-Hum; and Βηϑσαϊδὰ τῆς Γαλιλαίας represented by Et-Tell with Kh. elʿAraj by the waterside. Here I will only dwell on one point. Careful reading of 4, 46—54 shows the author's familiarity with the topography. There is a marked stress on the descent from Cana to Capernaum (... ἵνα καταβῇ ... κατάβηϑι ... αὐτοῦ καταβαίνοντος vv. 47, 49, 51). The author knew and felt

---

[1] With some older Syriac Mss. (Cur, Sah).

[2] In Evang. Joan. 6, 40 (PG 14, 269).

[3] Put with force by C. K. Barrett, St. John, p. 146.

[4] Complete list: Cana 2, 1; 2, 11; 4, 46. Nazareth 1, 46. Capernaum 2, 12; 4, 46; 6, 17. 22. 24. 59. Bethsaida 1, 44 and 12, 21. Εἰς τὸ ὄρος (6, 3) or slopes on the far side of the Sea of Galilee. For all this Galilee section, cf. Dalman, Sacred Sites and Ways, S. P. C. K. 133—159; Abel, Géographie de la Palestine, II, 1938; Kopp, in Dominican Studies 2 (1949) 213—235; 3 (1950) 10—40, 275—284, 344—350; 4 (1951) 35—68; 5 (1952) 185—204.

the drop from well above sea-level to well below sea-level, which is so marked a feature of that region, then as nowadays. Our author is not basing himself on imaginative reconstruction or hearsay.

(d) Another particular locality associated with the ministry of the Baptist was Αἰνὼν ἐγγὺς τοῦ Σαλειμ (3, 23). This site is probably south of Beisan, in the extreme north-east corner of Samaria (once again, we note, not in southern Palestine). This identification of the site rests upon Eusebius' Onomasticon[1]; and the site certainly has πολλὰ ὕδατα welling up from a number of closely related points, and very impressive and noticeable for someone coming up from the Jordan depression. "De toute façon l'évangéliste donne ici une preuve de sa connaissance des lieux."[2] Albright[3] however prefers a "Salim" three miles east of Sychem, where the name still persists, but where we find no adequate explanation of the gospel's πολλὰ ὕδατα, which of course means much more than several wells around the countryside.

(e) Next let us note the pool of Bethesda (Jo. 5, 2) and the pool of Siloam (Jo. 9, 6). Both are referred to as κολυμβήθρα, both are eminently satisfactory archaeological finds. Being both below ground level they have both survived the passage of time, and to this day we can "see, touch, handle" the manifest remains of these pools. "It is the Jerusalem of Jesus with which one comes into contact in the depths under the ruins."[4] Few things could be more impressive and could better generate conviction, in the old city of Jerusalem of today.

(f) For the purpose of our quick survey, we can group together the "Temple" texts with their considerable topographical connotations. Thus He finds the healed man (5, 14) ἐν τῷ ἱερῷ and this introduces us to the regular term for the Temple, cf. 7, 14. 28; 11, 56; 18, 20. Two particular parts figure: ἐν τῷ γαζοφυλακίῳ (8, 20), and ἐν τῇ στοᾷ τοῦ Σολομῶνος (10, 23). This latter appears in Acts 3, 11, and 5, 12. There is no reason for doubting that this was the colonnaded portico which lined the eastern wall of the present day Haram area. With these passages we put the expulsion from the Temple (2, 13—25), and note that very signi-

---

[1] Klostermann 40. 41.
[2] Lagrange, S. Jean, pp. 92—3.
[3] Op. cit., p. 159.
[4] Dalman, Sacred Sites and Ways, 1935, p. 310.

ficantly we find ὁ ναός (2, 20), for the Temple and the Temple
that was His body. For the Temple and all its archaeological
history we now have the monumental work of Vincent and
Stève, *Jérusalem de l'Ancien Testament* (1955). More lowly, yet
scholarly and accessible is Parrot, *The Temple of Jerusalem*,
S. C. M. Press (1957).

(g) A large and important section I have labelled the "passion-
drama texts". Our Lord (11, 54) withdraws to the edge of the
desert εἰς τὴν Ἐφραιμ λεγομένην πόλιν, in fact to the highest
point of El-Taiyibeh with its amazing view over the Ghôr and
the desert of Judah. Ephraim which is the same as ʿOphra or
Apherema of later texts, is the classic example of a change of
name by "Taiyibetism". ʿAfr being an ill-boding root, it became
El-Tayibet-el-ism (good in name) to avert the evil eye.

Now the passion draws close, and He withdraws πέραν τοῦ
χειμάρρου τῶν Κέδρων (18, 1). Our author has used the very
exact term for this, the usual type of Palestinian torrent bed.
Notice too the κῆπος, a humble yet a big word in this part of the
gospel (yet not in Kittel's Wörterbuch). A garden there was at
Gethsemane and a garden for His tomb.

In 18, 28 we read how He was led εἰς τὸ πραιτώριον. At this
point let us pause to compare the narrative of Jo. 18—19 with
Mk. 14, 53—15, 15. A usual view is that Jo. is an expanded
narrative of Mk; that the action of Pilate ἐξῆλθεν, εἰσῆλθεν etc.
(18, 29. 33 etc.) are highly dramatized and "written-up" or an
artificial construction. We can however argue that now we know
the lay-out of the immense Antonia fortress, how it dominates the
Temple area, and was meant to, how roads led out to the new
suburbs such as Bezetha, and ramps led down to the Temple, how
there were courtyards and rooms in plenty. We are inclined to
think that our author knew all this too, and further, knew the
common name for the whole massive masonry that told of Roman
rule. It was Γαββαθᾶ, "up there", — as it still is, if you look
from the Temple area northwards towards the rock escarpment
that faces you. Further it was (19, 13) Λιθόστρωτος and certainly
the large and splendid paving of these Roman barracks has been
found[1]. One doubt remains. The Roman Procurator could have

---

[1] A brief summary of this in Albright, Archaeology of Palestine (Pen-
guin) pp. 245—247; classic loci are Vincent, Revue Biblique 42 (1933)
83—113; 46 (1937) 563 sqq.; 61 (1954) 87—107.

his πραιτώριον where he willed, and he may equally well in that
fatal spring time have had it at the Royal Palace of the Herods on
the high western hill[1]. That western hill would also be Γαββαθᾶ,
"up there", to someone in the Temple area. But there is no
Λιθόστρωτος on this other site, though there may have been.
And a "lithostrotos" which we can see and walk on, is always
more convincing than a hypothetical courtyard.

The topography of the Crucifixion appears in 19, 17 κρανίου
τόπον ... Γολγοθά and finally in 19, 20 ἐγγὺς ἦν ὁ τόπος. "Skull
place" still appears on a contour map of Old Jerusalem as
a flattened knoll, and the rās or skull-place still lingered on in the
speech of an Arab workman of fifty years ago. And this place was
near the city walls of those days. Our author had precise and
accurate information about the place of the Crucifixion, and
where it lay with respect to the then north wall of the city[2].

(h) Finally we have the "Burial and tomb" texts. Note 19, 41
ἦν δὲ ἐν τῷ τόπῳ ὅπου ἐσταυρώθη κῆπος καὶ ἐν τῷ κήπῳ μνημεῖον
καινόν. Every word in this passage is significant. The site of the
Crucifixion must have resembled the Moslem cemetery north of
the Damascus gate; an enclosed "garden" with hillocks and
tombs. In the garden was a new tomb, which in the light of our
knowledge of Jewish first-century tombs, tells us that it was a
two-chamber arcosolium type of tomb. Contrasting with this was
Lazarus' tomb 11, 38. This appears to have been more of the
khokim type.

This ends our rapid survey of the topographical and archaeological content of the gospel. The total is impressive, even when we
allow fully for the debatable and uncertain results. For the
moment it is another point which I would like to stress — time
and again, it will be found that those who have lived long in
Palestine are struck by the impression that our author did so.
He knew the Palestine that they have learned to know.

The last part of this paper is concerned with a particular site
about which we need have no hesitation, I mean the Pool of
Bethesda (Jo. 5, 2).

---

[1] Cf. Benoît, Revue Biblique 59 (1952) 531—550.
[2] For all this section we read: J. Jeremias, Golgotha, Leipzig 1926;
E. T. Richmond, The Sites of the Crucifixion and Resurrection, Jerusalem
1934; Dalman, Sacred Sites and Ways, S. P. C. K. 1935, pp. 346—381;
Parrot, Golgotha and the Church of the Holy Sepulchre, S. C. M. 1957.

In 1873, the architect Mauss, while restoring the Church of St. Anne, stumbled upon a portion of this now famous find — as the Franks had done in the twelfth century.

In 1878, the White Fathers, owners of the property, started excavations. These were pursued at intervals for fifty years, with the results that are known[1]. The results show that there were two all-but-square pools[2], cut deep into the rock, and girt about with porticoes of the Graeco-Roman type; a fifth portico formed the gangway between the pools. That this was the Pool of Bethesda or Bezatha is accepted almost unanimously[3].

Now let us re-read our texts in this new light. Our Lord visited a large and sumptuous lido or pool, with its five great colonnades. We need to note this, and that Herod's building left its mark on the Jerusalem of the time. Further the pool was deep (16 metres), a veritable κολυμβήθρα, without a shallow end. A cripple would have to be carried down the steps and held all the time, and thus was utterly dependent on others.

Whence the water for these vast tanks? It was certainly not rain-water (which would require a closed cistern and could not be changed); and there is no spring in that area, as some have supposed. As fragments of stone-piping have been found, it is reasonable to argue that the water was brought from the Temple area, or possibly by-passed the Temple and came directly from "Solomon's Pools" south of Bethlehem. A study of the contours of the city[4] shows the possibility of this. Then, the "moving of the water" would be the necessary renewals. We get some inkling of how this was from the evacuating tunnel found cut in the rock, deep under the southern pool.

---

[1] Vincent, Jérusalem, II, 1926, pp. 609—628; Van der Vliet, St. Marie, où elle est née et la Piscine Probatique, Jerusalem-Paris 1938; J. Jeremias, Die Wiederentdeckung von Bethesda, Göttingen 1949; Baldi, Enchiridion Locorum Sanctorum, 2nd ed., Jerusalem 1955 (for the history of the tradition).

[2] The measurements are: Northern pool $40 \times 55 \times 40 \times 50$ metres; southern pool $57.50 \times 49.50 \times 65.50 \times 48$. The pools were 6, 50 metres apart, at the transverse portico.

[3] Albright, The Background of the New Testament and its Eschatology, p. 160, seems to be alone in his hesitation.

[4] Cf. Vincent and Stève, Jérusalem de l'Ancien Testament, I, Plate 1.

An immense accumulation of rubble still lies over a great part of the site. Some day we may hear of yet more finds. These would, as all else in such investigations, confirm us in the opinion that we have in this gospel not only the Word of God, but also the narrative of a reliable witness, a Palestinian Jew.

The Gospel and the Gospels

A. M. RAMSEY, Archbishop of York

Meeting in Oxford for the study of the Gospels we recall some
of the great New Testament scholars with whose names Oxford
is linked. Among them none is more revered than William Sanday.
Throughout a life devoted to the study of the New Testament he
set before him the aim of writing a "Life of Christ", and he
regarded his various published books as preliminary studies towards the goal before him. The task was never completed. Today,
there is little doubt that the prevailing advice of New Testament
scholars would be that such a task ought not to be undertaken.
The Gospels, we are told, are theological works, and not biographies. Though the Gospels contain indeed the record of
historical events, the interest of the evangelists was not in the
events for their own sake but in the Gospel of God embodied in
them. The Apostolic Church was not interested in the life of
Jesus as such.

My aim in this lecture is to discuss the Gospel and the Gospels.
I shall suggest that if the quest of Dr. Sanday was mistaken, the
reaction from it today is leading us to positions which themselves
invite criticism.

The Prologue to S. Luke's Gospel will serve as an introduction
to the nature and background of the Gospels. S. Luke intends to
write a continuous account of the things which the excellent Theophilus had been taught. Before him, many had tried to compile
accounts, based upon what had been handed down by those who
were (1) eyewitnesses, and (2) servants of the Word. This twofold
description of them is a clue to the character of the traditions, and
to the motive in preserving them. "Eyewitnesses": there is the
concern for historic facts. "Servants of the Word": the historic
facts are important because God speaks through them a message
about salvation. We learn therefore that behind the writing of

7*

the Gospels there was in the Church a concern for history and a devotion to the "Word" which was uttered through it.

What is meant by "the Word"? We need to examine the theological use in the New Testament writings of the terms ὁ λόγος, ὁ λόγος τοῦ Θεοῦ, οἱ λόγοι, with some notice also of the word ῥῆμα.

1. There is ὁ λόγος in the sense of the message preached by Jesus in his ministry in Palestine: e. g. Mark 2, 2 "he preached the word to them", Mark 4, 14 "the sower soweth the word". It is also called the "word of God", e. g. Luke 5, 1 "the people pressed upon him to hear the word of God". The term was used not only of the content of the message, but also of the act of preaching, e. g. Mark 4, 32 "his word was with power". In the Fourth Gospel the phrase "my word" is used eight times, to denote the total message which Jesus brought from the Father.

2. There are the sayings of Jesus, οἱ λόγοι, or sometimes τὰ ῥήματα. To these is ascribed a dynamic character, proper to the Biblical conception of the Word of God. Instances are Mark 8, 38 "whosoever shall be ashamed of me and my words ... of him also shall the Son of Man be ashamed"; Mark 8, 31 "heaven and earth shall pass away, but my words shall not pass away". Luke described the words of Jesus as words of grace or graciousness (Luke 4, 22). The sayings of Jesus were treasured in the Church; and Form-Criticism has rendered the valuable service of bringing out the fact that many episodes in the tradition were remembered and recorded less for the sake of the story itself than for the sake of the sayings of Jesus which was its climax. In the Fourth Gospel we find a doctrine about the significance of the sayings of Jesus, with an emphasis upon their dynamic and quasi-sacramental character. They are to be heard and kept (12, 47), they are to abide in the disciples (15, 7), they are "spirit and life" (6, 63).

3. Thirdly, there is the Logos as the message concerning Jesus eprached by the apostles. The term is often so used in the Acts. It is still "the word of the Lord" (Acts 15, 35) and "the word of God" (Acts 6, 2; 11, 1). It goes not infrequently with the verb εὐαγγελίζεσθαι: the apostles "preach the good news of the word". That Jesus himself is the core of the message preached is seen from the expressions "to preach Jesus Christ" (Acts 5, 42; 11, 20), "to preach Jesus" (Acts 10, 36), "to preach Jesus and the

43780

resurrection" (Acts 17, 18). The content of this preaching is described in the speeches in Acts and in S. Paul's summary in 1. Corinthians 16, 3: the death and the resurrection of Christ are central. Allusions to the preaching in the Epistles shew that it is called "the word of God" (2. Corinthians 2, 17; 4, 2; Phil. 1, 14; 2. Timothy 2, 9) and also "the word of the Lord" (1. Thessalonians 1, 8; 4, 15; 2. Thessalonians 3, 1). And various aspects of this Gospel are brought out in particular descriptions of it: "the word of the Cross" (1. Corinthians 1, 18), "the word of reconciliation" (2. Corinthians 5, 19), "the word of truth" (Ephesians 1, 13), "the word of life" (Philippians 2, 16).

4. These three aspects of the Word were, then, the concern of those of who were "eyewitnesses, and ministers of the word". The message preached by Jesus, the sayings of Jesus, the Gospel concerning Jesus. But there is a fourth use of Logos which also comes in view: Logos as a description of the Person of Christ. S. John asserts in the prologue of his Gospel that "In the beginning was the Word ... and the Word became flesh and dwelt among us" (John 1, 1.14).

This is not the occasion for an examination of the complex background to the doctrine of the Johannine prologue. Suffice it to say that the background is in part Jewish and in part Hellenistic. It is in part Jewish, inasmuch as the language of the prologue is unmistakably reminiscent of Genesis. It is in part Hellenistic, inasmuch as the identification of Jesus with Logos would convey to readers with a smattering of popular philosophy that the principle of unity and rationality indwelling the world has now been disclosed in the coming of Jesus. But there is also the Christian background to the Johannine conception of Jesus as the Word. "The workshop in which the conception was forged ... is a Christian workshop; the tools are Christian tools" (E. C. Hoskyns). The clue lies less in any novel speculation of S. John than in the conviction, appearing already in many parts of the New Testament writings, that there is a very close connection between the Word of the Gospel and the Person of Jesus. The evidence, alike in the synoptic tradition and in the Epistles, has been set out fully by Hoskyns[1] and I need not repeat it here. It is from this background that the Johannine conception emer-

---

[1] The Fourth Gospel, vol. I, 1940, pp. 159—164.

ges. It is indeed a distinct, metaphysical conception. But there is
no substitution of a metaphysical conception for the conception
of the Word which has already been known in the Church.
Rather does John trace that conception back to its roots in
eternal Godhead: the final utterance of God the creator within
the created world is Jesus. Gospel and Person are one:

"The heavenly word proceeding forth,
yet leaving not the Father's side."

Such are the elements in the "Word", with which the early
Church was concerned on account of Jesus of Nazareth. The
servants of the word, whom S. Luke mentions as handing down
the traditions about Jesus, were concerned with the message of
Jesus, the individual sayings of Jesus, the apostolic gospel about
God's saving acts through Jesus and with Jesus as in Himself
the Word. To each of these elements there belonged that dynamic
character associated with "the word of the LORD" in the Old
Testament. To each of these elements there belonged promise,
command, gift, warning; to hear was to respond — by trusting
the promise, by obeying the command, by accepting the gift, by
trembling in the presence of the warning. There could be no
neutrality: "the word of God is living, and active, and sharper
than any two-edged sword, and piercing even to the dividing of
soul and spirit, of both joints and marrow, and quick to discern
the thoughts and intents of the heart" (Hebrews 4, 12).

It was in relation to these various aspects of the Word that the
traditions about Jesus were handed down within the Church.
What were the proportions of interest in the various parts of the
traditions: the life, the teaching, the Passion, the Resurrection?

So far as the preaching of the Church was concerned the
evidence suggests strongly that the Passion and Resurrection
were of primary interest. Dr. Dodd has shewn, both from the
speeches in the Acts and from the allusions to the preaching in
the Epistles, that there was a central core of *data* used in the
preaching and we are familiar with the description of this central
core as the *Kerygma*. Now if this group of *data* was predom-
inantly used in preaching to the unconverted, are we to conclude that it monopolised, or even dominated exclusively, the
interest of the early Church in Jesus? I submit that the evidence
suggests the answer "No". Let us collect what we know about

the life of Jesus, quite apart from the *Kerygma*, from some of the apostolic writers.

S. Paul (including the Pastorals)

He was born of woman, born under the law
He was seen of angels
He pleased not himself, and allowed reproaches to fall upon him
He said, "the labourer is worthy of his hire"
He said, "it is more blessed to give than to receive"
He shewed meekness and gentleness
He instituted the eucharist
He witnessed before Pilate a good confession
He became a curse for us in his death
He appeared to Cephas, to the twelve, to five hundred brethren at once, to James.

1. Peter

He left an example that we should follow in his steps:
    not reviling when reviled, not threatening when he suffered, but committing himself to God who judges aright.

Here indeed is evidence enough for the existence within the Church of a sort of interest in Jesus different from that of the *Kerygma*. But the most remarkable collection of such evidence is in the Epistle to the Hebrews. Dwelling as he does upon the heavenly priesthood of the exalted Jesus, the author tells us this:

When he came into the world he was worshipped by angels
When he came into the world he was from the first obedient, taking as his motive "I came to do thy will, O God"
He was tempted in all respects like us
He learned obedience by his sufferings
He was perfected by the range of his human experiences
He offered up strong crying and tears
He had godly fear: and was heard in virtue of it
He instituted a new covenant
He endured contradictions
He shewed faith, and endurance, looking for a reward of joy beyond his sufferings
He was totally destroyed outside the gate
He entered heaven, not as Son of God raised by the power of the Father, but as man our forerunner and pioneer.

Here indeed is a wealth of interest in the human life of Jesus, reaching far beyond the limits of the *Kerygma*. It is an interest in the experiences of Jesus on earth with a concern about two aspects of those experiences, (1) their completely human character, (2) their movement in a process whereby Jesus was "perfected", from the earliest acts of obedience until the consummation of his obedience in the Passion.

In short, we learn from the Pauline Epistles, from 1. Peter, and from Hebrews, that there was in the early Church considerable interest in the life of Jesus and a concern to know what Jesus was like. The concern had at least two motives, (1) to learn about the example which Christians had to follow, (2) to shew how far-reaching was the identification of Jesus with the human race. All this lies outside the *Kerygma*. But it lies within the traditions handled by those who were "eyewitnesses and ministers of the Word". It concerns history. It concerns Jesus. It concerns the Word wherewith Jesus is identified.

No less comprehensive than this was the background of knowledge and interest against which the Gospels were written. Within this background of knowledge and interest the *Kerygma* had its central place, and in the four Gospels it is clear that the motive of the *Kerygma* is strongly felt. Sayings and episodes again and again point forward to the Passion as the climax. The evangelists are theologians. They are writing not history for its own sake, but testimony to the coming of the Gospel of God through Jesus. But there are limits to the extent to which the motive of *Kerygma* controls the writing of the Gospels. (1) Is it true that the Church was not interested in the order of events, and that therefore it is idle to try to shew an order of events from any of the Gospels? (2) Is it true that the Church — and therefore the evangelists — had no interest in Jesus as a human figure?

The order of events. I make a plea that the question be not regarded as closed. As to S. Luke, it does not seem that the *Kerygma* was his sole interest. His second volume shews an interest in the march of events, from Jerusalem to Rome; and it is arbitrary to deny that he had a like interest in the case of his first volume. This is not to say that he had at his disposal the scientific means for providing an historical order; but it is to say that he probably wished to provide such an order, and thought in such terms. It is noteworthy that S. Luke shews an interest, akin to that of the Epistle to the Hebrews, in the growth of the human nature of Jesus from his early obedience, through many πειρασμοί, to its perfecting and assumption into glory.

As to the Marcan order, the question is keenly debated. It is not easy. There are arguments on either side. But I wish very strongly to urge that it is unscientific to use as an argument the presupposition that "the Church was not interested in the order of events in the life of Jesus". Rather did the Church's interest in the life of Jesus, if it was an intelligent interest at all, include inevitably some interest in the movement of the story. It does not seem too dogmatic to say that it would have been impossible to be interested in certain of the episodes without being interested in their relation in sequence to other episodes. Here are examples. If an episode is told of how Jesus scandalized the disciples by telling them of the necessity of his death, how is it possible not to relate this in the mind with earlier episodes where Jesus made or implied such claims that death and disaster would seem to the disciples inconceivable? If an episode is told of how the disciples confessed Jesus to be the Christ of God, does not this inevitably relate itself in the mind with episodes, earlier in the sequence, where Jesus so acted as to cause the confession to grow? If the Pharisees plot to destroy Jesus, there have at an earlier stage been actions of His which cause them to want to destroy him. It seems impossible for the Church to have had the interest in Jesus in his life on earth, which the evidence shews that it had, without a concomitant interest in the "before and after", the stages in the movement of the story. The onus of proof would seem to rest heavily on those who think otherwise.

An interest in Jesus as he was. We are rightly warned against psychologising. The "liberal" lives of Jesus contained imaginative psychologising, read between the lines of the documents. We do not indeed want that. But the documents themselves describe psychological traits. Mark tells us of compassion, anger, surprise, questioning, on the part of Jesus. Luke tells us also of grief, joy and the endurance of πειρασμός. Our critical analysis divides episodes into legends, stories of a deed done, and apothegmata, stories of a word spoken. But if the Church was interested in Jesus it matters how the deed was done, or the word spoken; and that is something which eludes the categorisation of Form-Criticism. It seems that Luke, in particular, was interested in that elusive thing, the character of Jesus, seen as it is in the contrasted traits of remoteness and nearness, austerity and gentleness, urgent impatience and patient tenderness. "It

is conceivable that he was no less interesting for his own sake
to people in the first century than to historians in the twentieth" (T. W. Manson).

If my contentions are true, it may follow that, though Dr. Sanday was on a hopeless quest in trying to write a "Life of Christ",
none the less partial outlines of the life of Christ as to its main
stages lie within what scholarship properly can achieve. Two
things have been allowed to cloud our view of the landscape of the
apostolic age. (1) There has been the idea that the *Kerygma*
exclusively dominated the Church's interest in Jesus. In query-
ing this, I am fortified by the recent article by C. F. Evans[1],
where criticism is brought to bear upon the view that the *Kerygma*
was one unit, substantially unvaried throughout the Apostolic
age. (2) There has been the idea, sometimes unconsciously or
half consciously accepted, that the Pauline theology represented
the central core of interest in Jesus and that the Epistle to the
Hebrews was a book of specialised, out-of-the-way concern. Here
I am fortified by Dr. William Manson's recent monograph on the
Epistle to the Hebrews[2] with its arguments for the view that this
Epistle was in one of the main streams of thought about Jesus
within the missionary Church.

It goes without saying that the Passion and the Resurrection
had their unique and dominant place in the Church's thought of
Jesus. To think of those events at all must have been to be over-
whelmed by their majestic and compelling significance. S. Paul,
it seems, remained throughout his life as an apostle dominated by
those two events as one who knew nought else, from the day
when the risen Jesus confronted him until the day when he went
to his death, fulfilling "what was left behind of the sufferings of
Christ". But that was not the whole of what the apostolic
Church was, by God's goodness, permitted to know and to care
about, concerning Jesus of Nazareth; and the Church was able
to carry, into the sub-apostolic age and after, the conviction that
the human life of the Lord had meaning indeed for the salvation
of mankind. Did not Clement of Rome write: "You see, dearly
beloved, what is the pattern that hath been given unto us" (ad
Cor. 1, 16), and did not Ignatius of Antioch bid his readers "take
refuge in the Gospel, as in the flesh of Jesus" (ad Philad. 5, 1)?

---

[1] Journal of Theological Studies N. S. 7 (1956) 46—52.
[2] The Epistle to the Hebrews, 1951.

Instruction and Discussion in the Travel Narrative

B. REICKE, Basel

I

The central part of the Third Gospel, Luke 9, 51—18, 14, which is also the central enigma of this Gospel, being a great interpolation as compared with Mark, is generally called the Travel Narrative. One gets the impression here that Jesus is moving from Galilee to Judaea. For on the one hand, we are told in 9, 51, where the setting is still Galilee, that the Lord decided to go up to Jerusalem. On the other hand, the context that follows after 18, 14 runs parallel with sections of Matthew and Mark which are expressly referred to Judaea; and in 19, 28, Jesus is described as being near Jerusalem[1]. But in reality it is evident that Luke has filled up the space between the Galilean and the Judean events with material that has in itself very little to do with this journey. There are only a few scattered passages in the whole narrative where the journey to Jerusalem is mentioned or even alluded to, and these are 13, 22. 33, and 17, 11. In addition, there are three passages where the verbs πορεύεσθαι and συμπορεύεσθαι occur, 9, 57; 10, 38, and 14, 25. But these words have here a quite neutral meaning, and only indicate that Jesus was moving

---

[1] Because of this notice in 19, 28, some scholars are inclined to make the Travel Narrative include not only 9, 51—18, 14, but also 18, 15—19, 27. With regard to its contents, the latter section is also in fact only a continuation of the former so that the Travel Narrative may in its actual state be said to run as far as 19, 27. Cf. below, § III. However, as we are primarily concerned with the Travel Narrative in so far as it is peculiar to Luke, we have to stop at 18, 14. Cf. J. Blinzler, Die literarische Eigenart des sogenannten Reiseberichts im Lukasevangelium, in: Synoptische Studien A. Wikenhauser ... dargebracht, 1935, p. 20; J. Schneider, Zur Analyse des lukanischen Reiseberichts: ibid., p. 211; H. Conzelmann, Die Mitte der Zeit. Studien zur Theologie des Lukas, 1954, p. 51f., 59f.

about, as he did continually, and not merely on his journey from
Galilee to Judaea. Furthermore, there is no place-name or any
other detail in the whole narrative that betrays any acquaintance
by the author with topographical circumstances. On the contrary,
he seems to have made a curious mistake in 17, 11 where he says
that Jesus passed on his journey to Jerusalem "between Samaria
and Galilee". Geographically this is difficult to understand[1], but
it may be regarded simply as an attempt to explain why one of
the ten lepers was a Samaritan[2]. We must conclude that Luke's
ideas of the topography of the journey in question were vague and
partly incorrect[3].

Doubtless the Lord did pass from Galilee to Judaea. For this is
unanimously reported by all the evangelists, and is also to be
presupposed from the whole structure of his life on this earth.
Luke was certainly right when he, in agreement with Matthew and
Mark, reckoned with a period during which Jesus passed from
Galilee to Judaea, Jerusalem and Golgotha. But evidently there
was nothing in the evangelical traditions, in so far as they have
been preserved by Matthew and Mark, to show what had happened during the interval between the Galilean and Judean mini-
stries of Our Lord; for in these Gospels there is only a sudden
transition from Galilee to Peraea and Judaea (as it says in Matt.
19, 1: "... he went from Galilee and came to the parts of Judaea
that are on the other side of the Jordan"). It is natural to presume
that Luke knew only that there was such a transition, as is indicated by Matthew and Mark, and that he felt a need of filling up
the gap he found here in the earlier traditions. For this reason he
produced the so-called Travel Narrative, and made it to look
like the relation of a journey by adding the two or three comments
about going to Jerusalem that were mentioned above.

This conclusion is confirmed by the following observation on
the origin of the material used in the Travel Narrative. With only
a few exceptions, we find here either traditions common to
Matthew and Luke, i. e. Q traditions, or traditions peculiar to
Luke. And the few exceptions to this rule are only apparent ex-

---

[1] Although it was regarded as quite natural by W. Gasse, Zum Reise-
bericht des Lukas, ZNW 34 (1935) 296.

[2] W. Manson, The Gospel of Luke, 1930, p. 195.

[3] H. Conzelmann (cf. above, p. 101, n. 1), pp. 48—60.

ceptions — they are found in 10, 25—28; 11, 14—23; 12, 1. 10;
13, 18—19; 13, 30; 14, 34; 16, 18, and 17, 2. 23. 31, which passages have also quite short parallels in Mark, sometimes confined
to single words. For in each case it is easily seen that Luke is
not parallel with the short narrative of Mark, but with the more
extensive one represented by Matthew; so in reality Luke has not
used Mark as a source at these points, but Q and other traditions[1].
Now if the many Q passages contained in the Travel Narrative
are compared with the corresponding passages in Matthew, it
is evident that none of them in Matthew refers to the Lord's
going up to Jerusalem. This fact makes it probable that it was
Luke, or a predecessor of his, who incorporated these Q traditions
into the Travel Narrative. Furthermore, the same would be the
case with the traditions found in this Narrative that are peculiar
to Luke, since they also have no individual relation to the Jerusalem journey.

So we may conclude that Luke, wishing to fill up the gap between the Galilean and the Judean periods, simply used material
available to him partly through the source called Q and partly
through peculiar traditions, and then gave this material a super-
ficial relation to the biographical framework by inserting a few
remarks on the Lord's going up to Jerusalem. This also gave Luke
the opportunity of conveniently accommodating here a mass of
traditions which Matthew has taken the trouble to distribute
throughout different sermons, e. g. the Sermon on the Mount.
It also provided a place for several peculiar traditions available
to Luke. In a similar way he conveniently got rid of some Q and
special traditions by means of the smaller insertion that is found
in Luke 6, 20—8, 3. Thus, Luke gained a double advantage by
including the material in question in the Travel Narrative: (1)
the gap existing in the earlier gospel stories was filled up; and (2)
it was possible to do this with material which Luke found valuable
and instructive and did not want to omit, and which it was quite
convenient to insert here[2].

---

[1] J. C. Hawkins, Horae synopticae. Contributions to the Study of the
Synoptic Problem, 1899, pp. 84 ff.; id., Three Limitations to St. Luke's
Use of St. Mark's Gospel, in: Studies in the Synoptic Problem by Members
of the University of Oxford, 1911, pp. 29—59, especially 53; B. H. Streeter,
The Four Gospels. A Study of Origins, 1926, p. 204.

[2] Blinzler (cf. above, p. 101, n. 1), p. 34f.

II

What are the characteristics of this material that Luke found worthy of being included in the Travel Narrative? As far as is now discernible, originally it had nothing to do with the journey in question. Only secondarily has Luke used it to illustrate the journey of Jesus from Galilee to Judaea. Accordingly, there must have been other elements in this material that caused him to find it interesting and valuable for his readers.

A survey of the Travel Narrative from this point of view, disregarding its merely secondary function as the report of a journey, shows that the material has in itself an ecclesiastic-didactic character, like the Q traditions in general. Here occur stories about the Lord and sayings of his, which were valuable in answering practical questions discussed by the Church. It is the merit of Form Criticism to have drawn attention to the fact that many Gospel traditions were preserved because the Church discussed what Jesus had done or said in such and such a situation. This insight is easily applicable to the Travel Narrative.

In this context, two main points of view may be considered. The Early Church, in which the traditions adopted by Luke had been developed, was chiefly concerned with two kinds of problems: internal and external, that is, the question of the correct behaviour of Christians in relation to each other, and in relation to outsiders. As for internal problems, those connected with the life of the congregations were specially important to the Early Church, as is proved by the Epistles of the New Testament. As for external problems, some were related to the missionary task of the Church, and others were caused by the attacks of opponents, among which the Jews were at the time the most important. For the education of Christians, especially of such as were to be ministers and missionaries, it was therefore valuable to recollect what Jesus had done and said when instructing his apostles, and when disputing with his opponents. As the ministers and missionaries of the Church were in a quite specific way obliged to fill the role of successors to the apostles, those who were occupied with their education may have been especially interested in what Jesus did and said when instructing the apostles. Furthermore, as these ministers and missionaries at the same time were expected to refute such opponents as Pharisaic Jews, the discussions of the Lord with the Pharisees and others were also of great interest.

Now it is striking to see that the pericopes of the Travel Narrative concern either instruction of the apostles, regarded as leaders of the faithful and as missionaries[1], or discussion with opponents. Instruction and discussion may therefore be regarded as the main themes of the Travel Narrative. More exactly, we have here: (1) instruction of the apostles regarded (a) as leaders and teachers of the Christians, i. e. as ministers, and (b) as missionaries; and (2) discussion with adversaries and opponents. These themes may be supposed to have been especially important with regard to the education of ministers and missionaries. Indirectly, one may infer that such instruction did take place, even if the existence of organized schools is out of the question. Acts 2, 42, where the instruction given by the twelve apostles is mentioned, indicates that the apostles acted as teachers of the Jerusalem congregation. Considering the fact that according to Acts 1, 21—22 every apostle had to be an eye-witness of the life of Jesus, one may postulate that the actions and the sayings of the Lord[2] were an important subject of this teaching. Acts 13, 1 further shows that in a similar way some recognized persons acted as teachers in Antioch, precisely in the centre of the first Christian world mission. They may aptly be regarded as teachers not only of believers in general, but especially of future ministers and missionaries, for according to v. 2 it was they who were responsible for sending out Barnabas and Saul on their first journey. Their teaching activity may be an illustration of the *Sitz im Leben* of the traditions contained in the Travel Narrative. It is only a possibility, but one that must be pondered seriously, that this circle of teachers in Antioch constituted a practical background for the collection of the Travel Narrative traditions, even if these traditions may also be traced back to the apostles in Jerusalem and to the Lord himself. One must not forget that for several reasons Luke may be supposed to have had connections with Antioch, and this not only because one of the teachers mentioned in Acts 13, 1 has a similar name, Lucius of Cyrene.

---

[1] The importance of missionary ideas in the Travel Narrative has been emphasized by E. Lohse, Missionarisches Handeln Jesu nach dem Evangelium des Lukas, Theol. Zeitschr. 10 (1954) 1—13.

[2] This does not mean that there was any radical difference between preaching and teaching, between kerygma and didache. Cf. J. J. Vincent, Didactic Kerygma in the Synoptic Gospels, Scott. Journ. of Theol. 10 (1957) 262—273.

Turning now to the introduction to the Travel Narrative, we find Luke in 9, 51 saying: "As the time for his ascension was due." The Greek word for "ascension", ἀνάλημψις, is certainly to be referred to the ascension of Jesus which is the result of his passion[1]. But it may be asked whether Luke does not also understand this word as a counterpart of the Hebrew word מַעֲלָה, "pilgrimage", which is used in the titles of Ps. 120—134, and which the Septuagint translated with ἀναβαθμός. If this is so, the Travel Narrative is represented as a report of the Lord's pilgrimage to Jerusalem and to the Passover, and at the same time it is connected with his assumption or transition to a higher life.

After this prelude to the Travel Narrative, the attitude of Jesus towards the Samaritans is described in 9, 52—56. This story quite evidently was told because of its specific interest in a situation where the Church discussed its attitude towards people like the Samaritans[2]. This was a question important for the missionaries of the Church who had to do with Samaritans or Gentiles comparable with them; in Acts 8,4—25 there is an illustration of this. The story appears to have been told for their sake, the point being that such as do not receive the messengers of Christ should not be cursed.

The rest of the ninth chapter, 9, 57—62, tells how Jesus answered different claimants to discipleship. This was of great significance for Christian ministers who had to insist that everyone wishing to be a member of the Church should give up all connections with the old order. So this pericope may be understood to be a piece of instruction for ministers.

In the first half of chapter 10 appear some of the most illuminating examples of instruction in the Travel Narrative. It is obvious that the sending out of the seventy — or, according to some manuscripts, seventy-two — disciples as missionaries in 10, 1—12 was retold for the sake of the missionaries of the later Church. Their number corresponded in a symbolic way to the number of the nations of the earth enumerated in Gen. 10, which in the Hebrew text are given as seventy, in the Greek, as seventytwo. This must have had considerable bearing upon the missiona-

---

[1] L. Girard, L'évangile des voyages de Jésus, ou la section 9, 51—18, 14 de Saint Luc, 1951, p. 65; W. Bauer, Griechisch-deutsches Wörterbuch, 5. Aufl., 1957f., col. 113.

[2] K. L. Schmidt, Der Rahmen der Geschichte Jesu, 1919, pp. 267f.

ries who later were sent out by the Church to the Gentiles. It is quite natural to presume that these words of the Lord were preserved by the gospel traditionists for the purpose of instructing missionaries in their environment. And when we compare this speech of Jesus with its parallel in Matt. 10, we are struck by the fact that Luke represents the interests of foreign missions, whereas the speech in Matthew concerns a mission to Israel. This is confirmed by Luke's addition in 10, 13—16 of the judgements pronounced on three Galilean towns, found in Matthew in quite another context. By this addition, Luke has indicated that foreign missions became necessary because of the disobedience of those who were in the immediate environment of Jesus.

The report of the return of the seventy or seventy-two disciples in 10, 17—20 was also meant to be instructive for missionaries of the Church. They are to do wonders like the seventy, but by this word of Jesus they are warned against being proud of their accomplishments.

In 10, 21—24 there is further confirmation of the fact that the sending out of the seventy was regarded by the traditionists as a direct anticipation of the foreign missions of the Church. Quite obviously, Jesus here is represented as the Lord of the missionary Church. His thanksgiving and blessing of the disciples were certainly quoted for the instruction of the later missionaries.

In 10, 25—37 are two sections concerned with the other main theme mentioned above, discussion with outsiders. Being asked by a Jewish lawyer about the meaning of the word "neighbour", Jesus answers with the exemplary story of the Good Samaritan. The point here is that it is not the Priest and the Levite who fulfil the Law, but the Samaritan, who shows love which is the sum of the Law. Thus the story is an illustration of the Lord's discussion with Judaism, and as such it was of value for those in the Church who had to discuss with Jewish lawyers and others the way to eternal life.

In the remaining part of chapter 10 the motif of instruction is again represented by 10, 38—42. The sisters Mary and Martha correspond in a striking way to two functions of Christian ministers which later, according to Acts 6, came into competition with each other: these may be called "liturgy" and "diacony"[1].

---

[1] B. R., Diakonie, Festfreude und Zelos in Verbindung mit der altchristlichen Agapenfeier, 1951, pp. 28—32; Schneider (p. 101, n. 1), pp. 215f.

In that situation, the Twelve chose to be occupied with liturgy
and left diacony to the Seven. Those who recollected what Jesus
had said to Mary and Martha probably had in mind a corresponding debate in the Church as to the value of liturgy in relation to
diacony. It was doubtless a valuable contribution towards the
solution of this problem, to remind people of the attitude of the
Lord in a typical situation like that in the home of Mary and
Martha. So here again we have to do with a piece of instruction.

The following chapter, 11, proceeds with similar problems of
importance for the Church. First comes the question of prayer,
11, 1—4, next that of giving accommodation to a travelling friend
who is evidently the counterpart of a travelling missionary,
11, 5—8; and then that of the answer to prayer, 11, 9—13, with
special regard to such as want accommodation ("it will be opened
to you"). All these sayings of Jesus are directed to the apostles
who have the task of leading the flock of Christ and of going out
into the world as missionaries. They seem to have been quoted
for the instruction of later Christian leaders and missionaries.

In the second half of chapter 11, the motif of discussion appears
again. With a few unimportant exceptions, the whole section 11,
14—54 concerns discussion with the Pharisees who accused Jesus
of being in liaison with Beelzebub.

The rest of the Travel Narrative cannot be studied here in
detail. It appears evident, however, that in 12, 1—18, 14 there
is also striking concentration on such themes as were applicable
to instruction and discussion in the later Church.

Roughly, the distribution of the motifs of instruction and
discussion in the whole Travel Narrative is as follows:

Chapter 10: first half instruction
              second half discussion
        11: first half instruction (including 10, 38—42, about Mary
              and Martha)
              second half discussion
        12: whole chapter instruction
        13: first half instruction, then discussion
              second half instruction, then discussion
        14: first half discussion
              second half instruction
        15: whole chapter discussion
        16: first half instruction
              second half discussion
        17: whole chapter instruction
        18, 1—14: first instruction, then discussion.

There are also exceptions to the above, and the chapter divisions do not always correspond to the material, but on the whole one finds this rhythmical oscillation between the motifs of instruction and discussion.

It may be observed that chapters 12 and 17 are concerned practically entirely with instruction only. Their content corresponds to instructional parts of Matthew that present Q material, Luke 12 corresponding to Matt. 10 and similar specimens of instruction, Luke 17 to Matt. 18 and 24 with their information on discipline and eschatology.

Furthermore, it may be noticed that the first half of Luke 14 contains *Tischreden* of Jesus, which may also be related to conditions in the Church: for according to Acts 20,7 it was a habit of missionaries like Paul to speak about problems of faith at common meals with the brethren.

Another peculiarity to be observed in connection with chapter 14 is that it seems to introduce a new section of the Travel Narrative. For the stories told in chapter 13, and verses 31—33 especially, indicate that Jesus is going to leave Galilee[1]; and in the concluding verses, 13, 34—35, he is presented as if definitely moving towards Jerusalem. Here the Evangelist seems to have forgotten that already in 9, 51 he had described how Jesus left Galilee and began to move towards Jerusalem. It is a discrepancy which may only be explained if Luke is supposed to have used earlier traditions in this context[2]. One has the impression that at an earlier stage of the tradition the so-called Travel Narrative consisted of chapters 10—13, not as a Travel Narrative, but as an illustration of the Lord's last deeds and words in Galilee. Later a new body of similar traditions was added which began with chapter 14, and was attached to the preceding without any connecting link, 14, 1 only saying that Jesus once entered the house of a Pharisee. In this second part of the so-called Travel Narrative there is no topographical indication except for 17, 11 where Jesus is said to be leaving Galilee and Samaria for Jerusalem. So we gain the impression that even in this second part he had not yet definitely begun his journey to Jerusalem, and that at an earlier

---

[1] Schneider (cf. above, p. 101, n. 1), p. 215f.

[2] Schneider, p. 216, with regard to the discrepancy between Luke 9, 51 and 13, 31—33.

stage of the tradition it was only a question of the Lord's last deeds and words in Galilee.

Thus it seems evident that Luke inserted two bodies of tradition into the interval between the Galilean and the Judean activities of Jesus, i. e. 9, 51—13, 35, and 14,1—18, 14 respectively. In themselves, these traditions were to illustrate how Jesus instructed his disciples and discussed with his adversaries, especially during his last days in Galilee. Possibly they were given form in Antioch or at some other similar centre of foreign missions where it was valuable to recollect what the Lord had done and said in situations that corresponded to those in which Christian ministers and missionaries found themselves. Luke, in taking these traditions over, used them to illustrate what Jesus had done and said during the journey from Galilee to Judaea — a journey which it was necessary to presuppose.

III

Here, however, the perspective must also be widened. If we compare the immediate context of the Travel Narrative in Luke, we find that just before its beginning in chapter 9 and immediately after its end in chapter 18 other expressly didactic sections also appear. So the didactic Travel Narrative has been inserted among traditions which already had a didactic character. This is confirmed by a glance at the parallels in Matthew and Mark. For there are parallels in these Gospels both to what precedes and to what follows the Travel Narrative of Luke. These are also expressly didactic, and contain reports of instruction to the apostles and discussion with adversaries that are clearly based upon the needs of the Church. Here are the sections on Church discipline in Matt. 18 with parallels in Mark 9 on the one hand, and the discussions about divorce, children and wealth in Matt. 19 and Mark 10 on the other. In a very pronounced way these sections are intended to be instructive for ministers of the Church. And there is not the least difference between the first and the second part of these traditions. We are told only briefly in Matt. 19, 1 and Mark 10, 1 that Jesus passed from Galilee to Judaea; but what follows is in reality nothing but a direct continuation of the didactic sections of Matt. 18 and Mark 9 respectively. Thus already in the gospel tradition represented by Matthew and Mark there was a series of didactic pericopes that were related in a way to the movement of Jesus from Galilee to Judaea. Accordingly, when Luke inserted here the didactic material of his Travel Narrative, he merely increased a collection of didactic traditions that was already there. This also explains why the Travel Narrative does not end with any remark about the Lord's arrival in Judaea, such as the notices in Matt. 19, 1 and Mark 10, 1. Only at the beginning of the Narrative does Luke draw attention to the fact that from this point on Jesus should be regarded as being on pilgrimage from Galilee to Jerusalem. Toward the end of the Travel Narrative he simply lets the didactic material run along, so that it finally joins again the stream of didactic traditions in Matthew and Mark and proceeds in parallelism with them without interruption.

So the material contained in the Travel Narrative seems to have a setting that throughout is to be referred to the practical needs of the missionary Church. However, it may be emphasized with the greatest force that this ecclesiastic and didactic interpretation of the traditions in question does not at all eliminate the possibility of their essential authenticity. The fact that the traditions are supposed to have been developed in the Church, and with regard to her interests, does not preclude our assuming that the Lord did indeed act or speak in a corresponding way. It is dilettantish to discount the traditions as being not "genuine" only because their formation is ascribed to the later Christian congregation. Instead one should appreciate that the interest in the current problems of the Church led to the preservation of such traditions about Jesus as had especial importance for later generations of Christians.

Finally, the question may again be touched upon as to why Luke, by means of certain allusions, placed all this didactic material in the setting of a journey. We have already observed that he wished to fill up the gap between Galilee and Judaea. But was this his only reason? Considering the fact that the Travel Narrative contains so many traditions intended to be instructive for Christian missionaries, one may ask whether Christ is not described here as being on a pilgrimage toward suffering[1] and glorification, because such pilgrimage is the lot of his messengers on this earth.

---

[1] This point of view is stressed by Conzelmann (cf. above, p. 101, n. 1), pp. 53, 171 f.

The Place of Luke in the Eucharistic Tradition

R. D. RICHARDSON, Boyton Rectory

It is a pleasant thought, generated by words of sufficiently oecumenical authority, that, since the Gospels have their ordained prototypes in the four principal winds, one of these must blow from the South. And if I suggest that this gentle wind is the Gospel according to St. Luke, I do not doubt that I shall have your agreement. To try to assign the points of the metageographical compass to the other Gospels would lead me into difficulties. Enough to say that those who prefer winds that drive more severely — from Matthew, Mark and John — are prone to think less highly of the tender, reconciling and consecutively-minded artist and evangelist whom, without prejudice to questions of authorship, I shall call Luke. Yet, as St. Irenaeus puts it in the passage at which I have already glanced, the Gospel revelation is "quadriform", so that failure to take due account of any part of it must involve us in error or loss. Nowhere is this more true than in the field where we search out the origins of the Christian eucharist; and my testimony today — which in Lucan phrase I trust you will "receive with joy", or at least receive — is that this particular problem will only begin to be solved rightly when the witness of Luke has been assessed rightly. If we can fix the place of Luke in the eucharistic development, as I believe we can, we shall be able to interpret the rest of the evidence with greater security.

The place allotted to St. Luke in the received liturgical tradition has not been great. Although, for example, some Eastern Liturgies include, in their formulae of institution, the word "given", characteristic of the longer Lucan text, they nevertheless subordinate it to their distinctive word "broken"; while it has no place whatsoever in any extant Western Liturgy — except of course the Anglican, which in the sixteenth century showed itself susceptible in other ways to Biblical and Eastern influence. Nevertheless, since the seventeenth century, some of the most distinguished liturgical scholars, irrespective of denomination, forming indeed a succession which soars above the boundaries of churches, have paid a regard to Luke-Acts (and other sources) which inclined them to theories of dual eucharistic origins. With the growth of textual criticism attention was inevitably focused on the two versions of St. Luke's description of the Last Supper, the shorter recounting the sharing of a cup, and then the bread — with only the words "This is my body"; the longer adding the remaining bread-words, "which is given for you. This do in rememorance of me", and a further cup with the words "This cup is the new covenant in my blood, which is shed for you". By the end of the nineteenth century the shorter of these two readings was generally considered inexplicable unless it were genuine, and outstanding conservative scholars treated is as such, while yet regarding it as a curiosity which in no way disturbed the definitive account of the Institution in I Cor. 11. Some, however, took the reading seriously, and found in it support for a variety of views, more or less closely related to the theme that the original Christian rite was a simple memorial-meal, observed in an atmosphere of parousianic excitement, and that St. Paul made a far-reaching innovation by presenting it to the Gentile world as a sacramental act of worship and mystery drama. In our own day there has been a marked swing of textual opinion in favour of the longer Lucan account of the Last Supper, on the ground that it is attested by all Greek Mss. except D. Yet even so, there are differences of opinion concerning Luke's sources: as to whether he made use solely of Mark and Paul; or of these two and a special source; or of but Mark and a special source or sources; and as to whether or not his resultant account may be set alongside those of Mark and Paul as a third and fuller variation of a purely historical record.

From this unsettled basis in the longer text arise a variety of reconstructions of the Last Supper itself. For all of them, this last act of Jesus with his disciples is of basic value and significance, but their variety is bewildering. We learn, for example, that the Last Supper was a *haburah*-supper; and again that it was not; that the first of Luke's two cups was one of the four Passover cups; or again that it was a preliminary relish to a non-Passover meal; or that Luke, more faithfully than the other evangelists, has transmitted an original Semitic tradition which described a first cup of strictly eschatological meaning. On top of this comes also the opinion that Luke's words of actual institution are the liturgical formula preserved by some primitive church other than that of Corinth. Nor is this the sum of variations. Some suggest that the special Aramaic source, or sources, said to have been used by Luke (or by the Lucan editor) in the Third Gospel, provided material also for the beginning of Acts. And as against those who thereon wonder if the Breaking of Bread described in Acts does not best link to a rite according with the shorter Lucan reading, there are those who insist that "Breaking of Bread" is but a cover title, a cryptogram, for a rite based on the full words of institution. If it be asked, Why then was no cryptogram substituted for the formula of institution in the Gospel (and in I Cor.), the answer we receive is that the rule of secrecy belongs to the early second century, and that the shorter Lucan reading was made then, with the deliberate intention of concealment, like the phrase in Acts. Some, notwithstanding, doubt; and think it sounder to accept the shorter reading as, after all, original, and to surmise that the rule of secrecy was already in force when the Third Gospel was written. And then — we begin to fall into the arms of Loisy, who said this long ago. Indeed we workers in this field keep falling in and out of each other's arms all the time — except those of "the straitest sect(s) of our religion". (I am tempted to adopt the rendering, "the straitest party of our rites".)

From the existence of this rich variety of opinions, it is clear that the problem of eucharistic origins is far from solved. I do not propose to examine the opinions in detail, but to comment briefly on four influential books. Sanday's discussion of the Last Supper in his *Outlines of the Life of Christ* is probably still the best representative of conservative English scholarship on the subject. This is his summing up. "If we start from the idea of the Death of Christ as a Sacrifice, then it lies near to hand to conceive of the Supper as the sacred meal which follows the Sacrifice." And "whereas St. Paul emphasizes the redemptive value of the sacrificed Body" ('which is for you'), Mark and Matthew together "do the same for the shedding of the Blood" ('which is shed for many' / 'for the remission of sins'). Paul speaks further of the sacrifice as "spiritual food" and "spiritual drink"; while John, starting from the similar thought that Christ "is given through the sacramental Bread", goes on to express "the larger idea of which the Eucharist is a particular embodiment". The function of Luke's Gospel, according to Sanday, is to confirm the command to repeat the rite; and if the longer text be the result of a later addition "it must" he says, "have been carried out at the head-quarters of the Church", thereby providing still "stronger testimony" to the Church's practice. From these sentences I do not pick out for discussion two underlying assumptions: that we should work backwards to an understanding of the Lord's Last Supper from an Old Testament *Heilsgeschichte* and that a late addition to a peculiar text, if made under authority, is of greater significance than the peculiar text itself "even though the writer was an Evangelist"; I fasten instead on Sanday's opinion that the function of Luke's Supper-narrative is to confirm what is found elsewhere — in other words, that Luke's Gospel has here no independent value of its own. This can hardly be so as regards a matter so outstandingly important as the Eucharist. I submit that there can be no proper solution to the problem of eucharistic origins when one part of the fourfold revelation concerning it is treated as virtually superfluous.

To turn now to a very different book, Lietzmann's *Messe und Herrenmahl*[1], and whilst, in private duty bound, saluting it, I draw attention to the author's verdict that the genuine, i. e. in his opinion the shorter, Lucan account of the Last Supper is simply "the literary result" of reflection on the Marcan source. Lietzmann's view of eucharistic origins, grounded on Luke's evidence as a whole, is that the primitive Christian Supper was centred on a breaking of bread; and since the shorter, no less than the longer, account is derivative and also introduces wine, he traces it ultimately, through Mark, to the tradition of Paul. There is thus a duality in the Lucan evidence; but that part of it which concerns a cup has, in Lietzmann's view, no special significance even for the evangelist himself. This I hold to be impossible, if for no other reason than that every detail of Luke's writing matters to him.

---

[1] The English Tr., with my Introduction and Further Inquiry into Eucharistic Origins, is published by E. J. Brill, Leiden.

Next, concerning the conclusion of J. Jeremias in his *Eucharistic Words of Jesus*, that the Lucan formula of institution has the special characteristics of "liturgical language" and was therefore adopted by the evangelist from the most primitive use of "the sanctuary", I would comment that spiritual fabrics take pattern slowly. The Church, even if militant, is not to be compared with an army in the field, nor liturgical formulae with military order papers. As for the idea that the shorter reading owes its existence to a rule of secrecy, exercised according to Jeremias in the second century, earlier according to others (a theory that I have discussed elsewhere), I must limit myself now to quoting Klauser (the translation of whose paper on *The Western Liturgy* is one of the many things we owe to the promoter of this Congress). I agree with Klauser that in so far as the eucharist was held to embody a *mysterium*, this lay beneath the words of institution. These themselves therefore did not need to be hidden.

With G. Dix's *Shape of the Liturgy*, we encounter another flatly contrary opinion, i. e. that there was probably no liturgical use of words of institution in the primitive eucharist. But this sound judgment is unfortunately set in an elaborate account of eucharistic origins in which all the New Testament versions of the Last Supper, with Luke's two cups in special prominence, are woven together and interpreted by Tractates of the Mishnah without heed to the differing dates of these documents. I am bound to add that all the writers I have cited, in varying degrees, do this. They write history as theologians, not as historians.

And this leads me to my main point, the two parts of which I will apply in turn: i. e., that there can be no escape from all this confusion of opinions, no possibility whatever of reaching a sound settlement of the problem of eucharistic origins, unless attention is paid in the first place to chronology; and in the second place, unless we take account of the situation and intentions of those who wrote the relevant documents.

"The most necessary equipment for the historian" — I quote C. H. Turner's famous Inaugural Lecture of 1920 — "and especially for the historian of a period when the processes of development and growth were so rapid as in the Apostolic Church, is to begin with a firm grasp of the chronological framework." Consider, then, that Luke's Gospel stands chronologically between the Gospels of Mark and John and that, as R. H. Lightfoot stressed, there is palpably in operation here a process of interpretation, advancing from less to more. Lightfoot himself demonstrated, in masterly fashion, how the great doctrinal themes were developed as one evangelist succeeded another. This being so, the possibility that the Gospels likewise reflect a liturgical development cannot be excluded. If Luke advances on Mark in preparing the way for the doctrine of the Incarnation, I suggest that his treatment of Mark's account of the Last Supper may be indicative of an advance of eucharistic worship. Yet when we adopt the fuller Lucan narrative we are faced with the fact that its climax, the formula of institution, is essentially a duplicate, confirming, as Sanday says, what we can read elsewhere. And no Eucharist has ever been heard of in which two cups were drunk. May it not be well, therefore, to look once again, and with greater attention, at Luke's shorter account of the Last Supper? The debate based on the Ms. evidence swings to and fro, and cannot of itself be decisive; and it will be an advantage if we find we can invoke a second criterion of judgment. Does then the shorter Lucan text in any way advance on Mark? a question which is not, I may add, dependent for its answer upon whether Luke used an additional, special, source, or not — although personally I am not convinced that he did.

It is important to weigh the significance of this issue. Three features in particular distinguish Luke's shorter account from that of Mark. Mark sets the blessing and sharing of the bread and wine within the meal, "as they were eating"; Luke removes these words, sets the action markedly at the beginning, and thereby suggests concern that the two sacral moments shall not be confused with the meal itself. Moreover, Luke's inversion of Mark's bread-cup sequence to one of cup-bread links his feeling for shape and order to a well-known Jewish liturgical model, that of the Sabbath supper-rite. Next (and I owe this ultimately to J. M. Creed), there seems to be a peculiar significance in the sentences "With desire have I desired to eat this Passover with you before I suffer, *for* ... I will not eat it until ..."; and again, "Take this and divide it among yourselves, *for* ... I will not drink from henceforth ... until ...". R. H. Lightfoot describes this passage as the commentator's despair, since it begins by seeming to support the idea that the Last Supper was that of a Passover, but then seems concerned to explain why there are no

Passover features in the account of the meal itself. The explanation, I suggest, is that Luke was tied to the Passover setting in
his Marcan source, but also was confronted with the fact that
there was no Passover reference in the eucharistic rite of his
acquaintance. Thereupon he removed the hymn of praise, which
appears to be the Passover-hallel in Mark's account (the only clear
Passover feature of the story), and by his addition of the word
"for", gave his own account a further forward reference to the
time when Christians would drink and eat at the Lord's table in
anticipation of the Messianic feast. In these various ways, then,
we note an advance upon Mark as to the form of the eucharistic
rite. Mark's interpretation of the Last Supper itself is more
advanced than Luke's, but it has no clear liturgical form, nor
any hint that the Supper is to be repeated. Thirdly, there is the
element of sacred discourse which Luke adds to the meal, in
which he lays stress upon self-emptying and taking the rôle of
a servant, and upon such thoughts as that Peter has been kept,
by Christ's intercession, from the power of the Evil One. No
scholar but would agree that these elements of conversation,
parable, prayer and exhortation which Luke introduces —
rearranging and adding to his known sources in the process —
represent a stage of development towards the Farewell Discourses
of the Fourth Gospel. How then can we refuse to see that the
account of the Supper which includes these elements may
represent a development in the form of the rite? The indications
are that Luke here manifests a stage in the life of the Church
when the Supper was taking on the aspect of a definite Table-rite,
in which sacral actions, enshrined in moving memories, were
succeded by a meal whose atmosphere was sustained by elevated
discourse. Doctrine and liturgy, and no doubt locality too, have
all left their mark upon the text.

This conclusion forces itself upon us when, paying attention
to chronology, we set the Third Gospel squarely in the context of
the life and worship of the early church; it is precluded when we
believe, with Wellhausen, that Luke's account of the Last Supper
is "to be understood in a purely historical sense"; or again, when
we insist that the account of the institution in I Cor. 11 is the
standard by which all other evidence of eucharistic practice in
the early church must be interpreted and judged. We are told,
for example, that the breaking of bread, by Paul, at Troas, on

the first day of the week, cannot but signify a eucharist of the
type laid down in I Cor. 11, and that therefore Luke's uses of
the phrase elsewhere inevitably carry the same significance — or
else must be dismissed as having no eucharistic import. And this,
as regards an evangelist whose intention is to tell an intelligible
story, in episodes which he has selected for their relevance and
importance. The opposite approach is to begin with Acts 2,
42—46 and interpret the other passages by these. More cautiously,
the editors of *The Beginnings of Christianity* observe that "the
breaking of a loaf had a special importance for the disciples of
Jesus"; but, they continue, the meaning of the expression "the
breaking of bread" is open to question. And they conclude that
Acts "throws no important light" on the Eucharist. In the whole
five volumes to which we all are indebted, and which treat
learnedly of so wide a range of subjects, there is no proper
discussion of this subject — which is the more surprising in that
Lake, sympathetically, and rightly, shows that Luke's position is
in all essentials Catholic in the best and broadest sense. Moreover
the Preface to the Third Gospel announces an intention "to
trace the course of all things accurately".

Luke's purpose — to which I have now turned — is to set forward the Christianity, both of thought and practice, in which the
convert of his day has been instructed. His philosophy of history,
in part, is that Christianity is foreshadowed, sometimes in the
subtlest ways, in the Septuagintal record of the Old Testament;
but this Biblical theology is lifted on to a Greek plane by the
author's further conviction that the whole universe moves upon
the lines of Jesus. Inevitably, his account of the spread of
Christianity from Jerusalem to Rome is informed by a bold
idealism, which seizes upon the fundamentals of Christianity,
emphasises the underlying unity of the churches and adds its
touch of gold to the record of happenings and of the actions of
the chief *dramatis personae*. That which is taught in the
churches of which Luke himself is representative is the same,
so we are given to understand, as that taught by Paul and
by the Lord's original disciples; it is also essentially the same
as that taught by James and by churches of the Jerusalem
foundation.

If Luke is to be fully understood on the subject of eucharistic
worship, we must now bring together all his references to the

breaking or eating of bread; for the whole purpose, character and genius of the author require us to hold that his statements cannot be haphazard or inconsequent. Now, when Jesus eats bread with the Pharisee at a Sabbath-supper, a fellow-guest exclaims "Blessed is he that shall eat bread in the kingdom of God". Also the multitude for whom food is blessed and broken in the wilderness is taught first of the kingdom of God. Preceding this incident there is a conversation between Jesus and his disciples which is resumed, as Dr. Farrer has pointed out, at the Last Supper, which likewise is associated with the same teaching and whose action, after the drinking of a cup, centres (according to the shorter text) upon the blessing, breaking and distributing of bread. And now we learn that those who are appointed to the kingdom shall eat and drink in it, at my table. Again, just as the miraculous feeding takes place when the day began to wear away, so this same expression, stressing the time of the meal, reappears when the Christ who has entered his glory makes himself known at Emmaus on the first day of the week, in the breaking of bread. Note too that this last phrase is emphasised, for it is repeated when the two return to Jerusalem: he was known of them in the breaking of the bread. That it is the eucharistic rite which is thus signified becomes incontrovertible when we read later, in Acts, that on the first day of the week Christians at Troas were gathered together to break bread.

What of the remaining passages, about which there are such strong and differing opinions? Paul's "eucharistizing" and breaking and taking of bread on a wind-driven ship brought to anchor in the Adriatic sea seems at first sight far from a liturgical occasion. Not even Lietzmann seems to have noted the parallel, in the Vercelli Acts of Peter, where the apostle is said to communicate thy eucharist on a ship which, from the calm of the self-same sea, then runs before a six days' favourable wind. This second-century story, so obviously based on the incident in the Lucan Acts, is the work of a writer whom, says his English editor, we may think of, generously, as orthodox. It may therefore be that Luke, in his reconciling and all-embracing purpose, is giving his blessing to eucharists even of the type of the Acts of Peter when he describes Paul as performing such. Verily "the Lucan account of the institution of the eucharist appears to have

connexions" not only "backwards and forwards", as Sanday
puts it, but sideways too.

There remain the verses in Acts 2, 42. 46: "They continued steadfastly in the apostles' teaching and fellowship, in the breaking
of bread and the prayers"; and: "they continued steadfastly,
day by day, with one accord in the temple and breaking bread
at home". Fortunately I need not venture into the complicated
discussion, from Harnack to Torrey, concerning Luke's sources
for his account of these first days of the Church. Nor is there
much point in contrasting the two verses just quoted. I am however bound to note that both occur in one of what are called by
textual critics Luke's "summaries", i. e. the generalizing links
between his "panels" of material. These summaries are usually
thought to be the author's own work as editor; although Kirsopp
Lake's final, reconsidered, verdict on the summary which contains our two relevant verses is that it may represent the more
original of two forms of the same document, Jerusalem Source B.
The point to note however is that, whether or not we are here in
touch with a virtually first-hand record of Aramaic origin, Luke
himself includes the verses as significant and related to the rest of
his picture. They show the Jerusalem church, numbering "about
3000 souls", gathered for the Breaking of Bread in convenient
homes such as provided an "upper-chamber", presumably when
the evening sacrifice in the Temple had been offered, i. e. as the
day was drawing on; and as doing so daily. Luke thus, I suppose,
embraces, in his references to the eucharistic rite, members also
of the Jewish Christian church who, in his own day, were zealous
for the keeping of the Law in all its aspects, resented all developments, observed the Breaking of Bread at the beginning of every
meal and were, no doubt, well on the road to Ebionism. At the
same time, with his dramatic and historic sense, the evangelist is
also picturing vividly what to him was the earliest practice of the
Table-rite. A written source may have aided him; undoubtedly
there was tradition; it is unlikely that the story proceeded from
an exuberant imagination. Moreover the rite of Luke's own
practice, since it can still be called the Breaking of Bread, as in
Didache even later, reveals by this same title what its beginnings
are likely to have been and the line of its development: a primitive
Supper has become conformed to a weekly Sabbath-pattern, at
which a cup of wine was drunk solemnly before the bread was

broken, the meal then proceeding as a holy "convocation". The
only obstacle to believing that so natural a development actually
took place would be evidence that during the first century A. D.
the *kiddûsh*-cup interrupted a meal begun before the inception
of the Sabbath. Elbogen argued that this was the Jewish custom
until the end of the second century A. D. Louis Ginsberg however
maintained otherwise, and I have the assurance of the Jewish
scholars who are working on the publication of his papers that "his
views are regarded as authentic and authoritative on this, as on
other subjects". The probable solution, in which after much
inquiry I have some confidence, is that Jewish custom as to
the hour of beginning the Sabbath-meal was still fluid during the
first century.

But Luke's rite, as patterned in the shorter account of the Last
Supper, does not represent development under Jewish influence
only. It goes far beyond this, except as to its cup-bread form, for
it interprets the breaking and distributing of the bread in the
light of the words "This is my body", and thus approximates also
to the eucharistic teaching of I Corinthians. When Luke presents
his Breaking of Bread as the Pauline, no less than the Palestinian,
rite, he says no more than what is broadly true — although the
rite of which he is thinking is surely not that of I Cor. 11, but that
of I Cor. 10. And only if he were accustomed to a rite of this type,
in which the meaning of the cup was subsumed under that of the
bread as "a communion of the body of Christ", could he possibly
have made his particular selection of words from the Gospel of
Mark which lay before him. The fact that he omits Mark's
reference to the blood of the covenant, while retaining the
sharing of the cup, shows that Mark's account of the Last Supper
could not possibly have represented a universally-accepted
tradition. But in Luke's reconstruction, there is nothing to show
that he knew better than Mark what actually happened at the
Lord's Last Supper, while there is a great deal to show that he was
writing under pressure of his knowledge of the Table-rite as this
was being practised in churches of his acquaintance. Thus Luke's
purpose as an evangelist, his treatment of his Marcan source and
the Ms. evidence for the shorter text combine to make a threefold
cord, not easily to be broken.

It is of course open, as I fully recognize, to give pride of place to
the longer Lucan reading and to try to work out from this, instead

of from the shorter, account of the Last Supper connections with
the meals which took place before and after it as described in
the various passages I have cited. But no one has yet done this
without reducing Luke's record to secondary importance and
without tarnishing the repute which he otherwise merits for intelligibility. As against writers like Dix and Jeremias, and even
the magisterial Lietzmann, I see another interpretation of Luke's
place in the eucharistic tradition: one which requires no hypothesis to help it out, but simply a straightforward reading of the
evidence as it stands in the chronological framework of the New
Testament and in the light of Luke's known purposes. We see in
Luke the moment when the earlier continuance of the Jewish
daily meal — always begun with the blessing and breaking of
bread — is being transformed into a conscious and deliberate
weekly commemoration of Jesus' Last Supper before his sacrifice.
Luke's is not yet the fully-developed doctrine of the Covenant
Lamb; but neither is his eucharist simply the remembrance of a
tragic parting. It is St. John, the first formulator of the doctrine
of the Incarnation, who likewise sets the Church's eucharistic
faith and practice on their tremendous course; but he does so by
fusing elements in Paul and Mark and Luke. His link with Luke
is evident in that he lays primary stress upon the bread: "This is
the bread which came down out of heaven", "I am that bread of
life".

Does it follow from what I have said that we must think of a
multiple origin for Christian eucharistic worship? or at least of
an original duality of rite, centred in the one case from the beginning on the words of institution, in the other on the breaking
of bread?

These questions cannot be answered without reference to the
place, not only of Luke, but also of Mark, John, Matthew, and
all the second-century witnesses in the developing eucharistic
tradition. It is however my conviction that every development of
value can be related to what took place in the Upper Room on the
night that Jesus was betrayed. From then on, it would seem that
the rite developed differently in different localities. With the
second century we reach a veritable reservoir of rites, as likewise
of New Testament texts. And just as the second-century popular
text had inexaustible variety but basic identity, so it is with the
second-century rites. Out of them flowed two main streams, one

East, one West, and from thence onwards the story is sufficiently plain. Our concern should be to know the basic identity; and a true estimate of what was done in the local churches of St. Luke's acquaintance must be helpful in seeking to unveil that primal scene, in one locality, where what was said and done by Jesus gave birth to all the texts and all the rites which have arisen to unfold and to proclaim its meaning.

The Gospel Tradition and its Beginnings

H. Riesenfeld, Uppsala

The inexhaustible significance of the Gospels lies pre-eminently in the fact that they are our principal source for any account of the life of Jesus. The sparse biographical *data* in the rest of the New Testament writings and in the other early Christian and non-Christian literature, though they may have a certain interest of their own, contribute nothing to our conception of the figure of Christ. The question is often raised whether there is not something unfitting in the fact that our account of the life of Christ should have come down to us not in a single Gospel, but in four, and, what is more, in accounts which differ in some of their details. Should we not have been better served by a single Gospel? To such questions we must reply emphatically "No!". Had this been the case, we should have been seriously perplexed whether we were not in the presence of a literary fiction, or in any case, of a very subjective interpretation of the figure the Gospels depict. It is by reason of the fact that we have several, to be precise four, accounts, that we have been granted a more sharply defined and a more realistic presentation of the person of Jesus, just as in a stereoscope we obtain a far superior three-dimensional impression from pictures which, when examined side by side without the lens, differ among themselves. These differences between the Gospels naturally create for the student a never-ending problem; but for our assurance of the historicity of Jesus and for our general knowledge of who and what he was, the fact that we have a plurality of four Gospels is a fundamental advantage.

Now what precisely is a Gospel? In the history of religion and of literature alike a Gospel is something wholly unique. It is true that there are distant parallels in the biographies of philosophers or rulers in the Greek literature of the Hellenistic age. This is

more particularly so in the case of St. Luke's Gospel, the only
one of the four which has been in any degree moulded by literary
considerations. On the other hand, there exist certain parallels
on Palestinian soil, notably in the Prophetic Books of the Old
Testament. Here we have parallels, in matters of outward form,
to the preaching of Jesus and to his appearances before his
hearers as these are portrayed in the Gospels. But none of these
parallels takes us beyond individual items. To the Gospels as a
whole there is no known parallel or analogy. The same negative
verdict is given by the much discussed and much debated manuscripts from the Dead Sea. It is true that in these new texts we
have *data* which assist our understanding of primitive Christianity,
its mode of thought and its method of organization, its writings
and its vocabulary, for we owe them to a religious movement
in Judaism roughly contemporary with Jesus of which we have
been hitherto almost wholly unaware. There is also much in the
New Testament whose origin was previously sought in distant
countries, such as the Johannine symbolism of light and darkness or the ministerial offices in the early Christian communities,
which has now been proved to be the native product of Palestine.
We also have in the writings of the so-called Sect countless instructive parallels to the very free way in which primitive
Christianity often used and interpreted its quotations from the
Old Testament. But how gratified we should have been to have
discovered among these texts and fragments a Gospel concerned
with the leading figure in this Jewish movement, the so-called
"Teacher of Righteousness". Yet of such a Gospel we have found
no trace. And it is certain that we shall find none.

Now where did our Gospels come from? Obviously it is no
sufficient answer to say that they came from their evangelists'
pens. It is true that the Gospels in their several forms are the
products of writers and theologians who were consciously creative.
And to this extent we can reckon either with individual authors
or with circles or schools from which one or more of the Gospels
came. In the former class we must certainly put Luke, and probably also Mark, both of them Gospels which reflect certain individual characteristics either of their actual authors or of the
early tradition from which they came; in the other class perhaps
the Gospels of Matthew and John which issued from the form-
ative influence of a school. But what each of the four evangelists

has done is to create this or that Gospel, with its characteristic marks, with its individual style, its structure, its theology and its peculiar features in its picture of Jesus. Nevertheless, it is no chance that the titles given to the Gospels in the early Church were: "The Gospel according to Matthew", "The Gospel according to Mark", and so on. The evangelists took over their material from the tradition as it lay before them. And though it may be possible to establish points of interdependence in the existing Gospels, none of the four is the religious or literary prototype of the Gospel proper; this must be sought in their pre-history which is not directly accessible to us. It is important to recognize, as is clear from a study of the extant Gospels, that the tradition which lay before our evangelists already had the characteristic *traits* of the class of literature which we describe as Gospels, and that even if it had not yet reached full definition, it could none the less be already identified as such.

We shall not endeavour to deal here with the origin of the several Gospels in their present form, each with its own characteristics. To do so would be to enter upon four far-reaching and separate fields of study. What we shall attempt to do is, with th aid of the material embodied in our four Gospels, to make clear the pre-history and, as far as we can, the very beginnings of the tradition which finds its written embodiment in the Gospels as they have come down to us. How then did the tradition arise, the tradition of the words and deeds of Jesus? Where shall we find its "situation in life" (*Sitz im Leben*)?

Nearly forty years ago an important hypothesis was propounded to answer this question. Though at the time it opened up new and fruitful paths of study, and in many respects was of abiding importance, yet in its one-sidedness it became one of those scientific dogmas or myths which have their day and then must gradually be set aside if they are not to impede the further development of investigation. I am here referring, of course, to the solution put forward by the so-called Form-criticism. The names of the distinguished scholars associated with this school are well known to all professional students of the Gospels. What concerns us here is the subject more than personalities[1]. The

---

[1] See e. g. M. Dibelius, Die Formgeschichte des Evangeliums, 1919, 2nd ed. 1933; K. L. Schmidt, Der Rahmen der Geschichte Jesu, 1919; R. Bultmann, Die Geschichte der synoptischen Tradition, 1921, 3rd ed.

permanent achievement of form-critical investigation is the
formal analysis of the individual elements in the Gospel material,
of the parables and other words of Jesus, of the accounts of the
deeds of Jesus or of happenings in the life of Jesus. These elements were assembled from the tradition which was originally
oral, but gradually as time went on, also written down, and
then transmitted, as individual fragments or in small groups,
until they found their final embodiment in the compilations
known to us as our Gospels. From these studies we now know,
for instance, that a parable or an account of a miracle took shape
in accordance with definite stylistic laws which can be seen at
work in transformations of all items of the same kind. And from
our knowledge of these laws we can the better appreciate and
judge the peculiarities of the several evangelists. One fact of the
first importance which we have learnt is that these elements of
tradition have been subjected to certain influences through the
Church life of the particular place or *milieu* where they were
handed down or received their final written form. Thus by studying details of expression in the pericope on Martha and Mary in
Luke 10, it is possible to recognize questions which arose about
the position of women in the communities and on the importance
of *diakonia*.

But often the exponents of Form-criticism went farther than
this. They held that their method enabled them to explain the
very beginnings of the Gospel tradition. To the question: "What
was the situation in life of the earliest Gospel tradition?" their
answer was "Preaching" or "Catechetical Instruction" or "Controversy". This was because the first missionaries of the new
movement that suddenly arose from belief in the Resurrection,
were at once forced to base their preaching on the words of Jesus
or on accounts of events in the life of the great Master of Nazareth. This solution presupposes an extraordinary creative capacity in the first Christian generations. A considerable part of the
material which is contained in the Gospel was freely invented
and then given definite shape. We may take an instance of the
way in which the origin of the miracle stories was conceived.
When Christianity made its way outside Palestine, into the wide

1957; E. Fascher, Die formgeschichtliche Methode, 1924; P. Benoît,
Réflexions sur la "formgeschichtliche Methode", Rev. Bibl. 53 (1946)
481—542.

area of the Mediterranean world with its Hellenistic culture, the Christian missionaries found themselves competing with wandering preachers of salvation and miracle-workers of a Graeco-Oriental type. They therefore felt it incumbent on them to present the greatness and importance of the Christ whom they proclaimed by the same means as those which their competing miracle-men employed. To this end they invented stories of miraculous acts done by Jesus and thus conveyed to their hearers a striking impression of the power of their Saviour.

I cannot enter here into a detailed critique of these theories. The very existence of such an anonymous creative generation in primitive Christianity presupposes, in view of what we know from the New Testament about the apostles and the other members of the early Christian community, a truly miraculous and incredible factor in the history of the Gospel tradition. And the hypothesis that the miracle narratives arose on Hellenistic soil can be directly refuted. If we analyse the motives which form the content of the miracle narratives—and we must interpret the miracles as actions with a symbolic purpose which have their clear counterparts in the analogous symbolic acts of the Old Testament prophets—we find that the symbolism of all the miracles which occur and are described in the Gospels rests on a genuine Old Testament and Jewish basis. It certainly did not arise somewhere in the Hellenistic world. It is in just such points that the improved methods of observation of the last few years have succeeded in correcting the false conclusions of earlier students. Indeed, the analysis of the language of symbolism as we find it in the New Testament, offers us far more reliable guidance in determining the modes of thought of the primitive tradition.

Another point to be noted is that modern judgements essentially inapplicable to the material under consideration are introduced into these analyses. Scholars have set out from a conception of Jesus which has been constructed *a priori* and have then asked what portions of the Gospel material accord with this conception. They have more or less unconsciously used as the measure of their inquiry what Jesus can or cannot have done, without taking account of the fact that from the very first the tradition understood the deeds no less than the words of Jesus as something wholly unique which can be understood only in an eschatological setting. But an imperative requirement in the matter of method is that the nature of the investigation, and the criteria by which the material is judged, should be appropriate to the subject of inquiry. And this is something that we can now see more clearly than was possible a few decades ago[1].

But—to come at last to the main point—Was mission preaching in the earliest years of Christianity one of the principal sources from which the Gospel tradition derived? We must ask the scholars who have reached this conclusion whether they have not allowed themselves to be influenced unawares by picturing in their minds a preacher of our own times. They have in view a conscientious pastor who, unrestrained by any prescribed lectionary, searches out a suitable text for his Sunday sermon. So, they suppose, it must have happened nineteen hundred years ago—except that on many occasions the text could not be found ready-made at all, but had first to be invented. But this picture, surely, is scarcely credible.

Nor, indeed, need we rest content with such general considerations. Scientific study of the material puts in our hands the means of demonstrable proof based on empirical facts. It is now many years since C. H. Dodd showed that we can, as it were, distil from the speeches of the apostles in the first chapters of Acts, characteristic elements of the earliest Christian preaching[2]. The content and final challenge of this preaching, whose object was to win its hearers to faith in Jesus Christ and which is hence commonly known as mission preaching, constitutes the so-called *Kerygma*, a compressed summary of the saving work of Christ. Its content was as follows: "Jesus of Nazareth, the man divinely accredited to you by works of power, prodigies, and signs which God did through him in your midst, was, as you yourselves know, delivered up by the determinate counsel and foreknowledge of God; him you have slain by the hands of the Gentiles on the cross. But God raised him up, having loosed the pangs of death, because it was not possible for him to be held by death. This Jesus God raised from the dead, whereof we are witnesses. Being exalted at the right hand of God, and having received the promise of the Holy Spirit from the Father, he poured out this which you see and hear. Assuredly shall the whole House of Israel

---

[1] Cp. e. g. F. V. Filson, The New Testament against its Environment, 1950, pp. 43—50.

[2] C. H. Dodd, The Apostolic Preaching and its Developments, 1936.

be made aware that God hath made Lord and Christ the very Jesus whom you have crucified.—And when they heard this they were pricked to the heart." We have here typical elements in the primitive Christian preaching: A summary of the Redemptive Act, developed in close relationship to the religious situation of the hearers, and the whole culminating in a missionary reference, and insistence on the imperative need for conversion and faith. As far as the mission preaching to the Jews is concerned, the point of contact was on the one hand demonstration from Old Testament citations that Jesus is in very truth the promised Messiah who now exercises his dominion as the Risen One, and on the other the threat of the final judgement, which all Jews awaited with fear, as directly imminent and the proclamation of salvation in this judgement through faith in the Messiah Jesus. Such was the mission preaching as it was directed to Jews. But in the same Book of Acts we have also pointers, at any rate, to the preaching to the Gentiles, as it was set forth, among others, by Paul, the great Gentile missionary. It is probable that Paul's so-called Areopagus speech at Athens represents, to some extent, an abbreviated and schematized, yet none the less typical, example of such a sermon to the Gentiles in Pauline modes of thought[1]. And here again we find direct contact made with the religious presuppositions of the hearers, though in this case they were different: "For as I passed along and observed the objects of your worship I found also an altar with this inscription: 'To an Unknown God'. What therefore ye worship in ignorance, this set I forth unto you. The God that made the world and all things therein, he, being Lord of Heaven and earth, dwelleth not in temples made with hands" (Acts 17, 22—24). And then at the end, with the demand for conversion, we have a reference to precisely the preaching of Jesus Christ: "But now he commandeth men that they should everywhere repent, inasmuch as he hath appointed a day in the which he will judge the world in righteousness by the man whom he hath ordained, whereof he hath given assurance unto all men in that he hath raised him from the dead" (17, 30f.). Mgr. L. Cerfaux has accurately observed how Paul in his earlier letters, where he sets out from the Jewish situation, makes the fear of the approaching judgement the principal point

---

[1] See B. Gärtner, The Areopagus Speech and Natural Revelation, 1955.

of contact with his hearers in his mission preaching, whereas in his later letters he has chiefly in the foreground the fear of death which was the question of existential import in the Hellenistic world that knew little of the threat of judgement[1].

Thus, with the help of Acts and of certain echoes in the New Testament epistles, we can construct notions of the early Christian missionary preaching to Jews and Gentiles alike. And, as we have already said, we have fragments of kerygmatic formulae about the saving work of Christ. But of anything which recalls the materials from which our Gospels were constructed we have, alas! not the least trace. It is true that claims have sometimes been made to have recovered them. For instance, there is a passage about Jesus put into the mouth of Peter in Acts 10 where we read: "Jesus Christ is Lord of all. You yourselves know what took place throughout Judaea, beginning from Galilee after the baptism which John preached. You know of Jesus of Nazareth, whom God anointed with the Holy Ghost and power, who went about doing good and healing all that were oppressed by the devil, for God was with him. And we are witnesses of all that he did both in the country of the Jews and in Jerusalem. Him they brought to the gallows and slew" (Acts 10, 36—39). May not this summary of the life and death of Jesus be conceived as an epitome, so to speak, of the Gospel tradition? And could not the latter have been expanded from such rudiments into its later fullness? Along these lines the course of development is often still conceived. But is not such a solution another hypothetical dogma or myth? Facts are wholly wanting to support such a process of expansion and there is certainly nothing in our Gospels, especially if we compare the three Synoptics with the Fourth Gospel, which gives the slightest basis for such an hypothesis. Here we must refrain from adducing further considerations, and summarize our conclusion: "Mission preaching was not the *Sitz im Leben* of the Gospel tradition."

Side by side with mission preaching the announcement of the Gospel went on within the Christian communities. On the one hand there was the instruction of catechumens, on the other edification of the community's members. This preaching in the framework of the communities took place not so much through appeal

---

[1] L. Cerfaux, Le Christ dans la théologie de saint Paul, 1951, pp. 45, 90 ff., 121 f., 125.

to the emotions as by instruction in matters of fact and in the
Christian way of living. This teaching would have included both
Christological and other theological matters as well as ethical
admonitions, this last in the form of the so-called "parainesis".
In this connexion we may recall, for instance, the catalogues of
virtues and vices, and also the "household instructions" (*Haus-
tafeln*). Nor are we here wholly dependent on speculation. From
certain of the New Testament Epistles—especially the non-
Pauline ones—we can see to some extent what the subject-
matter of such preaching was. For there can be no doubt that
these epistles were composed and despatched to be read in the
communities as formal utterances, that is, as sermons. And
while it is certain that few unwritten sermons, in the matter
either of content or form, could be compared with the letters of
St. Paul, yet in respect of the species and kind of utterance,
we can assuredly here build on analogies.

We have now to ask: "Can we find in this preaching within the
framework of the communities the primitive Gospel tradition?"
Here, too, scholars have sought to draw positive conclusions.
Thus in 1 Cor. 7, 10f. Paul expressly appeals to Jesus' teaching
on marriage: "But to the married I give charge—yea not I, but
the Lord—That the wife depart not from her husband. But and if
she depart let her remain unmarried or else be reconciled to her
husband: and that the husband leave not his wife." Doubtless
the apostle is appealing here to the words of Jesus on marriage
transmitted, e. g. in Mark 10. The situation is still clearer in the
Epistle of James, where at almost every step we meet with allusions to parainetic sayings of Jesus. Have we not a proof here
that in any case the sayings of Jesus with an ethical import were
transmitted, if indeed they were not created, in connexion with
the early Christian parainesis? Yet this is another conclusion
which I find it hard to accept for the following reasons, mainly
based on considerations issuing from recent studies carried out
in Uppsala[1].

For if we suppose the existence of such an interrelation between early Christian community preaching and Gospel tradition,
then it remains inexplicable that while in the Christological and
parainetic parts of the New Testament Epistles we have countless

---

[1] To be published in a thesis by B. Gerhardsson.

allusions to the sayings of Jesus (though not to the narrative
material of the Gospels), we have no express citations of his
words. There can be only one explanation of this strange fact,
namely, that the primitive Christian letter-writers, and among
them Paul, took express pains to avoid citing the sayings of
Jesus in the context of their original utterance. Their method, that
is, was directly the opposite of that of preachers of our own day.
The sayings of Jesus, and hence the tradition about Jesus, were
presumed to be already known, but this tradition was not cited
in its verbal form.

Two examples will illustrate this point. Let us compare the
Epistle of James 2, 5: "Hearken, my beloved brethren. Did not
God choose them that are poor in the world to be rich in faith
and heirs of the Kingdom?" with Matt. 5, 3 and 5, 5: "Blessed
are the poor in spirit; for theirs is the Kingdom of Heaven. . . .
Blessed are the meek for they shall inherit the earth." And again
the saying in Jas. 1, 25: "But he that looketh into the perfect
law of liberty and so continueth therein, being not a hearer that
forgetteth, but a doer that worketh, this man shall be blessed in
his doing", has its counterpart in John 13, 17: "If ye know these
things, blessed are ye if ye do them." Of the eight Matthaean
beatitudes, four are to be found in the Epistle of James and in
the same order, a fact, by the way, which cannot be accidental.
In any case the author of this epistle presupposes parts of the
Sermon on the Mount as clearly well known to his readers.
Indeed, we can establish that the verbal form of the sayings of
Jesus which James presupposes is that of Matthew and not of
Luke.

From the analysis of Paul's epistles there is much that might
be adduced on this subject, though here we must confine ourselves to a few brief remarks. It is clear that Paul was acquainted
with the tradition of the sayings of Jesus, and at many points
in his epistles makes express allusion to sayings of his. This means
in turn that Paul could presuppose these sayings as known to his
readers. The words in Romans 12, 14: "Bless them that persecute
you, bless and curse not" are simply a paraphrase of the saying
of Jesus: "Love your enemies and pray for your persecutors"
(Matt. 5, 44). Hence scholars have concluded—and certainly
correctly—that such a section as Rom. 14, 13ff. records parainetic words of Jesus and that the Epistles to the Thessalonians

have their basis in apocalyptic teaching in the Synoptic tradition[1].

Once we have perceived this, very wide vistas open up. It is
one of the characteristic features of the New Testament that
the Messianic title, "Son of Man", is virtually confined to the
Gospels. Though it must certainly have been known to the authors
of the New Testament Epistles, they could not bring themselves
to use it. And this, too, cannot be an accident. On the other hand,
there are essential elements of the Pauline Christology which can
be explained as the interpretation or "theologization" of the
Son-of-Man-sayings of Jesus.

We will again epitomize the negative result of our investigations
up to this point: The *Sitz im Leben* and the original source of the
Gospel tradition was neither mission preaching nor the communal
instruction of the primitive Church.

It is now high time to enter upon the positive aspects of our
problem. And only one possible answer remains, even if it
demands an extended analysis, namely: The Gospel tradition
belongs to a category which is *sui generis* and, to put the matter
concisely, it has its own setting. It is a conclusion which has been
forcing itself upon us with ever growing insistence. It is true that
even when we have recognized this, we are still at the outset of
our task. Yet to have seen this much enables us to break through
the fetters which arise from a one-sided application of the form-
critical method.

It is not incompatible with insistence on the unique character
of the primitive Christian message, and hence of the Gospel
tradition, to draw attention to analogies from the *milieu* in
which this Gospel tradition arose. Strangely, these have been
insufficiently heeded hitherto. Preaching and instruction were
commonplaces alike in Palestinian Judaism and in the Jewish
Diaspora of the Mediterranean world, even though their character
was far less intense than in the early Church. But no real student
of Judaism in the Hellenistic age would for one moment imagine that their authoritative or "holy" words originated from

---

[1] See e. g. W. D. Davies, Paul and Rabbinic Judaism, 1948, 2nd ed.
1956, pp. 136ff.; E. E. Ellis, Paul's Use of the Old Testament, 1957, pp. 86
—92; G. R. Beasley-Murray, Jesus and the Future, 1954, pp. 232—234.
— Cp. E. G. Selwyn, The First Epistle of St. Peter, 1946, pp. 23f., 158f.,
268ff., 376ff., 442—449.

preaching or from instruction of the community or from controversy with the surrounding world.

As regards the writings of the Old Testament, their literary content was already fixed at this period. Hence in this case there could be no question of any oral tradition. But side by side with the text of the Old Testament there existed an extensive and important complex of tradition. This was the so-called "Sayings of the Fathers", that comprehensive exposition and elaboration of the Law which was carefully handed on from generation to generation and finally found its literary embodiment in the Mishnah c. A. D. 200. In this case we have indeed an authoritative "holy" tradition which it was sought ultimately to derive from the revelation of Jahweh to Moses on Mount Sinai.

As regards the nature of this Jewish tradition and its transmission, we are, as it happens, relatively well informed[1]. But what justifies us in drawing from it a number of conclusions relating to primitive Christianity is the fact that the terminology used of the Jewish process of tradition reappears in the New Testament. It appears here, indeed, in Greek translation, but it is easily recognizable. But we must add at the outset—to guard ourselves from conveying the misleading impression of putting the Gospel tradition on the same level as the Jewish interpretation of the Law—that we are here concerned only with the formal side of the process of tradition and not directly with its content as such.

Παραλαμβάνειν, "take over", Heb. qibbēl, denotes the imprinting of a tradition of doctrine with which one had been entrusted, while παραδιδόναι, "hand over", Heb. māsar, is used of its commitment to a particular pupil. The situation as here conceived is not the vague diffusion of narratives, sagas, or anecdotes, as we find it in folk-lore, but the rigidly controlled transmission of matter from one who has the mastery of it to another who has been specially chosen to learn it. The bearer of the tradition and the teacher (rabbi) watched over its memorizing by his approved pupils (talmīd) and what was passed on in this way was, in the matter both of content and form, a fixed body of

---

[1] E.g. W. Bacher, Tradition und Tradenten in den Schulen Palästinas und Babyloniens, 1914; G. Kittel, Die Probleme des palästinischen Spätjudentums und das Urchristentum, 1926, pp. 7ff., 63—70; O. Cullmann, Die Tradition, 1954, pp. 12ff.

material. Especially was this so as regards the Halachic material
of the Mishnah tradition, that is, as regards its specially important, "holy", constituent. The ideal pupil was one who never lost
one iota of the tradition. That variations in the material took
place in the process of tradition for psychological reasons is
obvious, and this circumstance enables us to investigate the
development of the tradition from another angle. For, however
great its receptive capacities, even an Oriental mind is not a
tape-recorder.

From the circumstance that the Rabbinic tradition was strictly
controlled and its transmission regulated by firmly established
laws—a fact bound up with the conception of the transmitted
material as holy Word—it follows that the oral tradition was
esoteric, and this not in the sense that it was treasured as a dark
secret, but that it was not entrusted to everyone nor was it at
everyone's disposal to use as he wished.

All this means, therefore, that in New Testament times the
specifically Jewish tradition, at any rate, was not possessed and
shaped by an unlimited and undefined anonymous multitude. The
people or the synagogue community were, of course, instructed
in the Scriptures and in the tradition of the Law, but such instruction never made a community as such bearers of the tradition. On the contrary, those who performed this task were an
exactly defined group within the community.

From this point we can now explain, or at least throw light
on, the New Testament conception of παράδοσις, "tradition".
For it has been one of the defects of Form-criticism, as it has
been employed hitherto, that all too little notice has been taken
of the relevant analogies in the Palestinian conception of
tradition.

Let us, then, return to the New Testament. There is a characteristic passage in Paul which is relevant in this connexion. He
writes: "Finally, brethren, we beseech and exhort you in the
Lord Jesus that as ye received of us [i. e. the tradition] how ye
ought to walk and to please God, even as ye do walk, that ye
abound more and more" (1 Thess. 4, 1). Here the apostle is
using the terminology to which we have already referred: the
community has received a tradition through his mediation. But
what sort of a tradition? Examination of the use of similar expressions elsewhere in Paul justifies us in assuming that they

were words of Jesus about the nature of discipleship and the
mode of life to be followed by the brethren.

To be brief, I will merely state one of the conclusions which
follow from a large body of evidence. Paul was himself the bearer
of the Gospel tradition, that is, he carefully took it over and
gave it shape. In the long autobiographical passage at the beginning of the Epistle to the Galatians he says that he spent three
years in Arabia after his conversion and then went to Jerusalem
and visited Peter with whom he stayed fifteen days. It is reasonable to conclude that his chief concern in these weeks was not
theological discussions or ecclesiastical projects but something
which was a precondition of the fulfilment of his apostolic work,
namely that Peter should test whether he, Paul, during his term
of preparation, had really made the tradition of the words and
deeds of Jesus his own, in the form, that is, which these words
and deeds had assumed by that date. For in the Pauline Epistles
we see that the apostle is dependent on an overmastering tradition, and this must have been mainly the Gospel tradition in
its own individuality. If Paul, like the other writers of the New
Testament Epistles, usually refrains from expressly quoting this
tradition—and this reticence, of which we still have to speak, is
certainly intentional—yet in certain specially important places
he makes it clear that he has access to the verbal tradition, e. g.
in the passage where he solemnly introduces as a quotation the
Words of Institution at the Last Supper (1 Cor. 11, 23—25).
The way in which Paul handles such a quotation shows that the
words of the tradition did not, in fact, normally find a place in a
letter.

Now just because Paul was in a special way the bearer of the
tradition of the words and deeds of Jesus, he could consider himself as on a level with the other apostles, and especially with the
Twelve. For the chief obligations of the apostles included not
only preaching and the oversight of the communities, but also
the safe-keeping and committal to trustworthy persons of the
words and deeds of Jesus, that is of the Gospel tradition. We can
see this especially clearly from certain passages in the Lucan
writings. In Acts 6 the activity of the apostles is described with
some exactness: "It is not meet that we should forsake the Word
of God and serve tables" (6, 2). Hence seven collaborators were
selected for the latter task, while the apostles devoted themselves

to prayer and the "service" (διακονία) of the "Word". Wherein
this service consisted, and that it was not regarded as being primarily preaching, follows from the phrase here employed: λόγος
τοῦ θεοῦ, the "Word of God". We may also recall the prologue
to St. Luke's Gospel, which comes from the same writer as Acts.
Here we read of the events of the life of Jesus, "how they have
been transmitted to us [we may note the *terminus technicus*] by
the original eye-witnesses and ministers (ὑπηρέται) of the Word"
(Lk. 1, 2). The words and deeds of Jesus are a holy Word, comparable with that of the Old Testament, and the handing down
of this precious material is entrusted to special persons. And just
for this reason it was so important, when the twelfth place in the
circle of the disciples had become vacant through the fall and
death of Judas Iscariot and had to be filled again, to find someone
who—as we read—"belongs to the people who have companied
with us [i. e. with the Twelve] all the time that the Lord Jesus
went in and went out among us, beginning from the baptism of
John until the day that he was received up from among us. He
must with us be a witness of the Resurrection" (Acts 1, 21 f.).
Hence to be an apostle or witness of the Resurrection it was not
sufficient to have met the Risen Christ, but that person had to
possess such a living impression of the life and work of Jesus as to
make him qualified to transmit the holy tradition of the words
and deeds of Jesus.

Now can we find in the most primitive Christianity any *Sitz im
Leben* of such a special "holy" tradition about Jesus? We are
helped in answering this question if we consider the literary genus
of this tradition which precedes the Gospels in their definitive
written form. Comparison with the style of the Prophetic discourses of the Old Testament on the one hand and with the
Rabbinic material on the other, suggests that the tradition was
recited; and, since the tradition was not esoteric in the narrower
sense, that it was recited not exclusively to hearers who were
destined to become future transmitters of the tradition. But as
soon as ever one reflects on the character of this Christian tradition as holy word, as the Word of God and as something parallel
to the holy writings of the Old Testament, the very smallest
knowledge of religious life in Palestine forces the conclusion
that the words and deeds of Jesus were not just improvised, that
there was no question of freely narrating or of inventing, even

when the speaker was possessed by the Spirit. On the contrary, the strict laws relating to holy tradition will have prevailed from the outset and determined both what was uttered and what was transmitted, in spite of the fact that in points of detail variations could not but appear and, indeed, did appear.

But where, we may ask, was this traditional material uttered or recited? Here too we can give the answer. It would evidently have been in the assemblies of the community. We must again picture in our minds analogies drawn from the use of the sacred books of the Old Testament in Judaism. It is significant that the original New Testament designation for the Gospel tradition was not εὐαγγέλιον—this word stands for its missionary appeal— but λόγος and λόγος θεοῦ—terms which correspond with the names current in Judaism for Holy Scripture[1]. The words of Jesus and the reports of his deeds and his life, although originally transmitted by word of mouth, were conceived from a very early date to be the New Torah, and hence as the Word of God of the new, eschatological covenant.

Now we know from the accounts in Acts that the original Jerusalem community took part in the services in the Temple and in the synagogues, and they did so, we may conclude, for the sake of the prayers and Bible readings. But besides this public worship the community which believed in the Risen Lord gathered in a closer circle—first in the Upper Room and soon also in private houses—for the breaking of bread, for prayer and for instruction by the apostles, διδαχὴ τῶν ἀποστόλων, which took place in the presence of the whole community (Acts 2, 42). In view of such participation in the Jewish worship, it is natural to regard the apostles' instruction as being in the first place the recounting of the words and deeds of Jesus, as the complement to the sacred Word of the Old Testament which the community had already heard. Indeed, it would have been not only its complement but also its fulfilment. As in the synagogue, exposition followed the recitation, and of this exposition we have some indications in the New Testament Epistles.

Here we have the reason why the words and deeds of Jesus were probably never quoted verbally in the missionary preaching and only on rare occasions in the community instruction. The

---

[1] Cp. G. Kittel, λέγω, λόγος: Theol. Wörterb. zum N. T. 4 (1942), pp. 114—124.

tradition which was recited was holy and hence, in contrast to present-day practice, was not readily mentioned by word of mouth. Mission preaching, indeed, pointed and led to it. The instruction in the community presupposed it and linked itself up with it. But in its verbal form and in its function in the community it was *sui generis*.

From this point we can gain light on the transmission of the tradition in the early Church and on the process of its literary fixation. In view of the fact that the recitation of the tradition about Jesus as the sacred Word of the New Covenant was an essential constituent in Christian public worship, it is certain that the need for authorized transmitters of this tradition became greater as the Christian Church itself grew and its communities increased in number. This need must have contributed fundamentally to the growth of the Christian ministry. It was the same set of circumstances which, again in analogy with the Old Testament, led to the written fixation of the text at a comparatively early date. In this process it was the words of Jesus which were brought together first, just as in Judaism special importance was attached to the Sayings of the Fathers. The earliest step away from the original exclusiveness of the holy tradition is the Gospel of Luke which already places the words and deeds of Jesus in a literary and apologetic framework.

But fully to understand the origin of the Gospel tradition we must go back further still. How can we explain the fact that in the first age of the Church the tradition about Jesus already possessed its special character as holy Word? The answer must be: That this tradition, *qua* tradition, was derived from none other than Jesus. Hence our thesis is that the beginning of the Gospel tradition lies with Jesus himself.

In the Gospels we are shown very clearly that Jesus was a teacher, and especially in his relation to his disciples[1]. This means more than his mere preaching in their presence. He gave them instruction and in this we are reminded, *mutatis mutandis*, of the method of the Jewish rabbi. And this implies that Jesus made his disciples, and above all the Twelve, learn, and furthermore that he made them learn by heart.

---

[1] K. H. Rengstorf, διδάσκαλος: Theol. Wörterb. zum N. T. 2 (1935), pp. 155—159; W. Manson, Jesus the Messiah, 1943, pp. 51ff.

And, if we view the matter from the other side, it is also evident that some of the main portions of Jesus' sayings in the Gospels are formulated so as to be suited to transmission and memorization. Here too we can make comparisons with the stylistic laws of the sacred tradition of the Jews, though we must not overlook the differences. Of the Lord's Prayer it was expressly said that Jesus taught his disciples this (Lk. 11, 1f.; cf. Matt. 6, 9). But, apart from this, many of the words of Jesus are in such a form that not only is it possible to hear the echoes of the Aramaic original, but also to deduce that they were carefully formulated so as to be apt for transmission[1]. We may take the case of the Parable of the Building of the House with which the Sermon on the Mount in the First Gospel concludes:

"Everyone who heareth my words and doeth them
    is like a wise man
    who built his house upon the rock

"And the rain came down and the floods came and the storms
    and they fell against that house   [blew
    and it fell not
    for it was built upon the rock.

"And everyone that heareth these my words and doeth them not
    is like a foolish man
    who built his house upon the sand

"And the rain came down and the floods came and the storms
    and they beat against that house   [blew
    and it fell
    and its fall was great" (Matt. 7, 24—27).

In accord with this is the fact that even after the translation of the tradition into Greek, certain words of Jesus were preserved in their original Aramaic form, as for instance *Talitha qūm*, "Young maid, Arise", in the narrative of the awakening of Jairus' daughter (Mk. 5, 41). It is not here a case of the use of magical words in acts of healing in the primitive community. What we have are formulae which were treasured in the memory for the sake of Jesus, and this because they came from him and not for any miraculous power they might possess.

---

[1] C. F. Burney, The Poetry of our Lord, 1925; M. Black, An Aramaic Approach to the Gospels and Acts, 1946, pp. 105 ff.

The preaching of Jesus before the Palestinian crowds was revelation, the announcement of a Divine secret, μυστήριον. We
must think of the disciples, in their relation to this message, as
sitting at Jesus' feet, partly in order to hear once again the words
and to get to know them by heart, partly that they might be
instructed in their meaning as, e. g. (in the matter of method),
in Mark 4, 11: "When they were alone those that were around
him with the Twelve asked him about the Parables." In this way
they were taught the destiny of the Son of Man and the conditions
of following after him, matters which in Jesus' lifetime were
intended for a more esoteric and narrower circle of disciples[1].

In modern times such a picture of the origins of the Gospel
tradition as the following is often met with: The preaching of
Jesus, who was possessed by the prophetic Spirit, was free and
without restraint. Some of this preaching survived with more
or less verbal accuracy in the memories of his hearers. Besides, it
was the custom in the primitive Church to preach freely and
without restraint, and in this process sayings and narratives were
created and invented. And then from this extensive body of
material the evangelists or their predecessors made a well-con-
sidered selection. But this romantic picture has no relation to
reality. On the contrary, it is probable both that from Jesus'
own days the material was far more strictly limited and also that
it was handed down in a far more rigid and fixed form. One indication of this is the very limited extent of the extra-canonical
tradition of Jesus. It is evident that Jesus did not preach indiscri-
minately nor continually, but that he imposed certain limitations
on his preaching as he did in the case of his miracles. And what
was essential to his message he taught his disciples, that is, he
made them learn it by heart. Doubtless there are small parts of it
which have fallen by the way, but we may well ask whether the
bulk of it is not preserved in our Gospels. Such a statement as
John 21, 25 is clearly an exaggeration.

Along this road we can advance still farther. We can inquire
whether the tradition of Jesus' deeds cannot also be traced back
in its beginnings to Jesus himself. Naturally this cannot apply to
the Passion narratives, which form a unit apart, with their own
problems. But there are indications in connexion, e. g., with the

---

[1] Cp. Jn. 16, 1 ff.

Miracles of the Feeding (Mk. 8, 19—21) which lead to the conclusion that Jesus also spoke with his disciples about deeds and
their significance. We may also compare the reply to the Baptist
on the subject of miracles (Mk. 11, 4f.). And it is probable that
the kernel of the narratives on the Baptism and the Temptation
are to be derived from Jesus' teaching in the circle of his disciples.

The account of the anointing at Bethany (Mk. 14, 3—9) concludes with a saying of Jesus about the woman with the alabaster
vessel and her gracious act: "Verily I say unto you, Wheresoever
the gospel shall be preached throughout the whole world, that
also which this woman hath done shall be spoken of for a memorial
of her." This remark at the end of the narrative is generally
regarded as a secondary addition from the days of the primitive
Church. But the question arises whether the thought expressed
in the passage is necessarily incompatible with the situation and
the intention of Jesus, either in the actual setting here given to
it or in some other of a similar kind. That Jesus reckoned with
an intervening epoch between his death and the parousia, that
is, with the epoch of the Church, appears to me a necessary
consequence of the institution of the Lord's Supper. The sacra-
ment is intended as a symbolic action which derives its meaning
from its relation to the Church. But is it possible to conceive of
any such action in the intention of Jesus without the complement
of the Word? Hence we must seriously ask whether Jesus did not
reckon with the announcement of the Good News in the epoch
of the Church, and whether he did not, in view of this preaching,
transmit to his disciples a λόγος whose outlines were already
defined. There is the duality of word and action both with Jesus
and in the Church. Between the deeds of Jesus and the sacramental symbolic action of the Church there exists an ascertainable
connexion. Should not a like connexion also exist between the
preaching of Jesus and the tradition of the words and deeds of
Jesus in the Church? I therefore make bold to conjecture that
Jesus reckoned with what we may call the recital of the Gospel
tradition in the epoch between his death and the parousia.

In asserting this we are naturally not saying either that the
Gospel tradition existed from the very first in its settled form as
we find it in the Synoptic tradition, or that it can be traced back
to Jesus in its definitive shape. It is self-evident that the moulding

of the tradition—e. g. by the collecting and grouping of individual pericopes, through its transformations and also through its additions—came about gradually in the life of the primitive Church. The essential point is that the outlines, that is, the beginnings of the proper genus of the tradition of the words and deeds of Jesus, were memorized and recited as holy Word. We should be inclined to trace these outlines back to Jesus' activity as a teacher in the circle of his disciples. Another consequence of such considerations is that we reach a more positive attitude to the question whether the essential constituents of the Christology and ethics, as we now have them in the bulk of the tradition, may not go back to Jesus himself.

Along these lines we also reach vantage points from which to judge of the Johannine tradition. It is clear that the development of the material in this Gospel took place in accordance with rules which in some ways differed from those which controlled the Synoptic material. It is a characteristic of the Johannine mode of presentation that the words and deeds of Jesus are, so to speak, commented on, that they became the object of "meditations". Here too I should incline to the view that the Gospel of John rests on an independent line of tradition, which had its original starting-point in the activity of Jesus, and which then ran parallel with the Synoptic line of tradition. And here the starting-point is to be found in the discourses and "meditations" of Jesus in the circle of his disciples, such as certainly took place side by side with the instruction of the disciples proper, with its more rigid forms. Such a view is not incompatible with this line of tradition having also undergone a long and complex development.

But in the last resort the solution given to the whole problem of the Gospel tradition depends on the inquirer's attitude to the problem of the Messianic self-consciousness. Here again we find that this is the central question for the interpretation of the New Testament and the point at which the ways divide.

If we take in all seriousness the position that Jesus regarded himself in some way as the Messiah and that as a result of this he also drew the consequences of a fully developed Messianic system of ideas[1], then we need not be surprised if Jesus was

---

[1] Cp. W. Manson, op. cit., pp. 97f.

conscious of himself as the bearer of revelation, as the bringer of
the new law and as a teacher[1]. Granted the Messianic consciousness, then the circle of the disciples formed the kernel of the
corresponding eschatological community. In view of the Old
Testament background and the Messianic hopes of the Jews, we
can legitimately assume that Jesus entrusted to his disciples, and
hence to the eschatological People of God, an already formulated
holy Word for it to transmit, and that this was the starting-point
of a tradition. For if we assume the Messianic consciousness, then
Jesus must also have spoken about the significance of his person
and the rules for the conduct of life in the Messianic community.
In this particular matter the writings from the Dead Sea at least
point the way.

In modern handbooks on the theology of the New Testament
the appearance and proclamation of Jesus are sometimes treated
as prolegomena[2]. So regarded, Jesus of Nazareth belongs to the
history of later Judaism. Christianity—that is, faith in Jesus
as Messiah and Redeemer—first arose in the primitive community
after the Resurrection and hence is to be treated as a subject
separate from the preaching of Jesus. Over against this view, the
considerations which have just been urged lead us back to the
"classical" method of interpretation. The belief in Christ is to be
found already in the words and deeds of Jesus just because Jesus
regarded himself as the Messiah. The faith of the primitive
Church had its origin in what Jesus proclaimed and set forth in
symbolic form. One of the preconditions of this has already
been established: It was owing to the tradition of the deeds
and words of Jesus which began from Jesus himself that the
primitive Church had the basis for its faith. This gives us a
profitable starting-point from which to compare our four Gospels,
both among themselves and also with the rest of the New
Testament writings, as the expression of the faith of the first
Christian generations.

When we reckon with the fact that Jesus is the founder of
the Gospel tradition, both as to its essence and its original starting-point, we arrive naturally at a synthesis which is again
classical and see in the "Gospel of Jesus Christ" ($εὐαγγέλιον$

---

[1] W. D. Davies, Torah in the Messianic Age and / or the Age to come,
1952, pp. 90 ff.

[2] R. Bultmann, Theologie des Neuen Testaments, 1948—53, pp. 1 ff.

Ἰησοῦ Χριστοῦ, cf. Mk. 1, 1) both the Good News brought by Jesus Christ (subjective genitive) and the Good News about Jesus Christ (objective genitive). By simply tracing their descent we find the two lines here united in the person and work of Jesus.

We have here attempted to give an answer to the question as to the origin of the Gospel tradition. We must seek its origin ultimately in Jesus and his Messianic self-consciousness. Jesus is not only the object of a later faith, which on its side gave rise to the growth of oral and also written tradition, but, as Messiah and teacher, Jesus is the object and subject of a tradition of authoritative and holy words which he himself created and entrusted to his disciples for its later transmission in the epoch between his death and the parousia.

The New Look on the Fourth Gospel

J. A. T. ROBINSON, Cambridge

I should like to say, before anything else, in the company of so many more learned than myself, who have spent many more years in the study of the fourth Gospel than I, that I put forward these observations with the very greatest diffidence. This is not simply due to modesty, false or genuine, but to the fact that I am not finally convinced whether there is a "new look" on the fourth Gospel or not; but I think there is. The reason for my diffidence is that I am really doing no more than trying to assess straws in the wind: the ground of my conviction, such as it is, is that all the straws seem to be blowing in much the same direction. But I am only too well aware that this may be an optical illusion and that it is I who am being carried along by the wind, and that the new look may represent no more than my look. But with this quali- fication — and I mean it to be taken seriously — let me come at once to explaining what I mean by this "new look".

Obviously it can be understood only with reference to the "old look"; and by the "old look" I do not here mean the pre- critical assessment of the Gospel which served the Church for seventeen centuries and which indeed still serves most of its members to-day. I mean what might be called the "critical orthodoxy" which has taken shape over the last fifty years and which is still represented in the most recent commentaries and text-books. Now this is clearly a vast and inclusive term. In fact, one has only to glance at the swings and roundabouts of Johan- nine criticism in this period[1] to question whether it means any- thing at all; and indeed for positive definition it is far too wide a classification to be useful. But negatively, I think, it may serve

---

[1] Vide W. F. Howard, The Fourth Gospel in Recent Criticism and Interpretation, 1931; revised by C. K. Barrett, 1955; P.-H. Menoud, L'évangile de Jean d'après les recherches récentes, 2nd ed. 1947.

some purpose. For the "new look", if I discern it aright, may best
be understood as a questioning of certain presuppositions that
have underlain this approach in all its multifarious manifestations. These presuppositions do not, of course, apply equally to
all its representatives, and anyone will be able to single out
exceptions to whom perhaps they do not apply at all. But for our
purposes we may say broadly that current critical orthodoxy on
the fourth Gospel rests on five generally agreed presuppositions.

In passing, it is worth noting that the very title "the fourth Gospel"
itself reflects these presuppositions, and I cannot refrain from quoting
some rather naughty words from James Montgomery's little book, *The
Origin of the Gospel According to St. John*, published in Philadelphia as
long ago as 1923. "I may", he wrote (p. 3), "have academically 'declassed'
myself by using the name 'Gospel of St. John' in the title ... I frankly
think that 'Fourth Gospel' is a scholastic affectation. Why not the First,
Second, and Third Gospels? Are we any surer of their authors? Any tyro
knows that Deuteronomy is not 'the Second Giving of the Law', but are
we obliged to make constant profession of our critical attainments by
calling that document the Fifth Book of Pseudo-Moses?"

But let us return to the five presuppositions I mentioned.
These are:

(1) That the fourth Evangelist is dependent on sources,
including (normally) one or more of the Synoptic Gospels.

(2) That his own background is other than that of the events and
teaching he is purporting to record.

(3) That he is not to be regarded, seriously, as a witness to the
Jesus of history, but simply to the Christ of faith.

(4) That he represents the end-term of theological development in first-century Christianity.

(5) That he is not himself the Apostle John nor a direct eye-
witness.

Now the effect of each of these presuppositions is to place the
Evangelist at one remove or more from the events he is narrating.
This may be no loss — it may even provide a gain in perspective —
but it does determine the sort of questions which it is worth
asking of the Gospel. The "new look", if I may use the term, is
characterized by a certain impertinence, an insistence that it may
be worth asking other, often apparently naïve, questions, which
these presuppositions would rule out as ones that the Gospel was
never meant to answer. This is partly because if one does ask
them one frequently seems to get what look like astonishingly

sensible answers, and partly because the foundations of these
presuppositions themselves are beginning to appear a good deal
less certain than they did.

Let us consider them each in turn.

(1) The first is that the fourth Evangelist is dependent on
sources, including (normally) one or more of the Synoptic
Gospels.

That John is dependent on the Synoptists, or at any rate on
Mark, is perhaps the presupposition into which the acids of
criticism have themselves eaten most deeply. It is indeed a
presupposition shared, like all the rest, by the most recent
critical edition of the Gospel, that of Dr. C. K. Barrett[1], as well
as by the late Professor R. H. Lightfoot's posthumous commentary[2]. But the work of Mr. P. Gardner-Smith[3] and others has had
its effect, and I notice a widespread tendency to-day, which I
fully endorse, to regard the case for literary dependence as quite
unproven.

The effect of this has been to emphasize the independence of
the Johannine tradition, which in the nineteenth century was the
main count against its authenticity, while in the twentieth,
paradoxically, it has been its dependence which has discredited it
as an original witness. But if the Johannine stream is independent
of the Synoptists (whether John actually knew of them or not),
then potentially it is as near the source as any of the other
independent streams of tradition — Mark, "Q", special Luke, or
special Matthew. I do not say that it is as near; and in each case
one has to test the waters as critically as one can to assess how
far they have flowed before they have reached one and how much
they have picked up on the way. But potentially one can put the
same questions, with the expectation of comparable results, to
the Johannine tradition as one can to the Synoptic. This places it
on all fours with the Synoptic tradition from the point of view of
its relation to source — or, in plain language, its historicity. That,
again, is not to say that it is equally historical, but simply that
one can approach it with the supposition that it equally might be.
We should according to this "new look", be prepared to approach
both the traditions — or rather all the traditions, since the

---

[1] The Gospel according to St. John, 1955.

[2] St. John's Gospel, 1956.

[3] St. John and the Synoptic Gospels, 1938.

Synoptic tradition is not homogeneous — impartially, with an open mind as to which, at any given point, may be the most primitive. We shall still give priority to material that is confirmed by two independent traditions, for instance, by "Q" and Mark, or by Mark and John. And when it comes to material peculiar to one source, be it special Matthew or John, we must be prepared to scrutinize it very carefully. But we should not adopt different criteria just because it is Johannine.

Then there is the further question of the non-Gospel sources upon which the fourth Evangelist has been said to draw — for instance, the *Offenbarungsrede* (revelatory discourses) and the *σημεῖα-Quelle* (signs source) of Professor R. Bultmann[1]. Again, I notice an increasing reluctance to admit the evidence for such sources. As a recent writer has put it, "It looks as though, if the author of the Fourth Gospel used documentary sources, he wrote them all himself"[2]. The detailed examination of the Johannine characteristics undertaken by Professor E. Schweizer[3] and others[4] has told heavily in favour of a unity of style throughout the Gospel, including the last, additional chapter. Professors P.-H. Menoud[5], E. Ruckstuhl[6] and B. Noack[7] have examined Bultmann's source criticism most carefully and conclude that it cannot stand. In John we are dealing with a man who is not piecing together written sources but placing his stamp upon an oral tradition with a sovereign freedom. As Menoud[8] puts it, it is as if he is saying to us from beginning to end: *"La tradition, c'est moi!"*

(2) The second presupposition which is being re-examined is that the background of the Evangelist himself is other than that of the events and teaching he is purporting to record.

---

[1] Das Evangelium des Johannes, 11th ed. 1950.

[2] P. Parker, Two Editions of John, Journal of Biblical Literature 75 (1956) 304.

[3] Ego Eimi, 1939.

[4] E. g. J. Jeremias, Johanneische Literarkritik, Theologische Blätter, 1941, 33—46; E. Ruckstuhl, Die literarische Einheit des Johannesevangeliums, 1951.

[5] Op. cit., pp. 17—21.

[6] Op. cit., pp. 20—179.

[7] Zur johanneischen Tradition, 1954, pp. 9—42.

[8] Op. cit., p. 77.

I have deliberately put this as generally as I can since the proposed "backgrounds" for the fourth Evangelist are legion[1]. But they all have this in common that they locate him, whether in time or place or mental environment, at a distance from the milieu and thought-forms of Palestine prior to the Jewish war of A. D. 66—70. Now the kind of reaction that I am describing would not deny that in a real sense this was true. It is perfectly clear that the Evangelist is writing for a non-Palestinian situation where common Jewish customs, of purification (2, 6) and burial (19, 40), have to be explained and even the simplest Semitic words, like *Rabbi* (1, 38) and *Rabboni* (20, 16) (which Mark [9, 5; 10, 51] does not bother to translate for his Roman public), need to be made plain. Nor, I imagine, could any responsible person deny that his language has echoes and overtones which would evoke a response, and were intended to evoke a response, in circles far wider than those within which the words and works of Jesus himself were circumscribed. It is essentially the Gospel for those who have not seen, because they were not there to see.

And yet, though this may be true of the environment in and for which the Gospel was published, that is not to say that the Evangelist or the tradition he represents was native to that environment. When we look to the background, strictly speaking, rather than to the eventual environment, of the Evangelist and his tradition, I detect a growing readiness to recognize that this is not to be sought at the end of the first century or the beginning of the second, in Ephesus or Alexandria, among the Gnostics or the Greeks. Rather, there is no compelling need to let our gaze wander very far, either in space or in time, beyond a fairly limited area of southern Palestine in the fairly limited interval between the Crucifixion and the fall of Jerusalem. This area and this interval will not tell the whole story: but I suspect they will be found to tell us a great deal more than we had previously imagined.

This judgment has, of course, received considerable stimulus and support from the evidence of the Dead Sea Scrolls. Their connections with the thought-forms of the fourth Evangelist have

---

[1] For a survey of the most important, vide C. H. Dodd, The Interpretation of the Fourth Gospel, 1953, pp. 1—130; also Menoud, op. cit., pp. 30—50.

been widely noticed[1] and need not be repeated here. Let me simply say why I think they are significant in this respect. They are important for Johannine study not because they offer closer or more numerous parallels with the language of the fourth Gospel than any other literature. I doubt really if they do. They are decisive, in my judgment, because for the first time they present us with a body of thought which in date and place (southern Palestine in the first century B. C.—A. D.), as well as in fundamental, and not merely verbal, theological affinity, may really represent an actual background, and not merely a possible environment, for the distinctive categories of the Gospel. And when this is combined with the evidence connecting the Johannine tradition with circles that entered Christianity through the Baptist movement, and with the hypothesis, which I believe to be strong, that the Baptist himself had had associations with Qumran[2], then the sort of thinking represented in that Community becomes a very probable and not merely a very possible background for the Gospel. This does not mean that other suggested backgrounds are ruled out. Indeed, I believe that what Professor B. Reicke[3] has aptly called these "pre-Gnostic" thought-forms will help us to fill in other connections[4], and in particular to understand more clearly why later this Gospel was to have such an appeal for the Gnostics. The new evidence has not changed the whole picture; but it has changed the perspective.

---

[1] E. g. W. Grossouw, The Dead Sea Scrolls and the New Testament, Studia Catholica 26 (1951) 295—299; F. M. Braun, L'arrière-fond judaïque du quatrième évangile et la Communauté de l'Alliance, Revue Biblique 62 (1955) 5—44; R. E. Brown, The Qumran Scrolls and the Johannine Gospel and Epistles, Catholic Biblical Quarterly 17 (1955) 403—419; 559—674 (reprinted in The Scrolls and the New Testament, 1957, ed. K. Stendahl). For a fuller bibliography, cf. my article in the Harvard Theological Review cited below.

[2] Cf. my article, The Baptism of John and the Qumran Community, Harvard Theological Review 50 (1957) 175—191. To the bibliography there given should now be added: J. Steinmann, Saint Jean-Baptiste, 1956, pp. 58 ff.; E. Stauffer, Jerusalem und Rom, 1957, pp. 88—93.

[3] Traces of Gnosticism in the Dead Sea Scrolls?, New Testament Studies 1 (1955) 137—141.

[4] Cf. R. McL. Wilson, Gnostic Origins, Vigiliae Christianae 9 (1955) 193 ff.; Gnostic Origins Again, ib., 11 (1957) 93 ff.; Simon, Dositheus and the Dead Sea Scrolls, Zeitschrift für Religions- und Geistesgeschichte 9 (1957) 21 ff.

The other influences fall into a different place, and many of them will, I believe, be seen to be more important for understanding the reception of the Gospel than for interpreting its background or assessing its purpose.

(3) Now both these first two considerations, that the Evangelist represents an independent tradition and has his background, as it were, on the spot, have naturally affected the third presupposition, namely, that he is not to be regarded seriously as a witness to the Jesus of history, but only to the Christ of faith.

That he is primarily, and indeed all the time, a witness to the Christ of faith is, of course, not to be questioned. "These things are written that you may believe that Jesus is the Christ, the Son of God" (20, 31). That is his purpose — as it is also Mark's purpose — and his sole theological concern. But for him the Christ of faith includes the Jesus of history; and the notion that the former can be had apart from, or at the expense of, the latter was exactly the error which, to judge from the Prologue and the Epistles, he was most concerned to combat.

However, concern for the "flesh" of Christ as a theological truth and reliability as a historical witness are not the same thing — though it is astonishing how readily critics have assumed that our Evangelist attached the greatest importance to historicity in general and had but the lightest regard for it in particular.

But what marks the newer approach is, as I said, an openness to recognize that in the Johannine tradition we may at points be as near to the Jesus of history as in the Synoptic Gospels. This is not to deny that a good deal of peeling and paring away may be necessary in both, as Professor J. Jeremias has shown in his book on the Parables[1]. But recent studies indicate that when sayings and incidents in the fourth Gospel are subjected to this process the results are often such as to uncover tradition at least as primitive as in comparable Synoptic material, and sometimes more so[2].

From another side, it is becoming clear that the Dead Sea Scrolls may force us to think again about the Johannine picture

---

[1] The Parables of Jesus, English translation by S. H. Hooke, 1954.

[2] Cf. my article, The Parable of John 10, 1—5, Zeitschrift für die neutestamentliche Wissenschaft 46 (1955) 233—240; and Dodd, Some Johannine "Herrnworte" with Parallels in the Synoptic Gospels, New Testament Studies 2 (1955) 75—86.

of John the Baptist. Professor W. H. Brownlee[1] and others[2] have claimed, and I would agree with them, that one of the most remarkable effects of the Scrolls has been the surprising vindication they appear to offer of ideas and categories attributed to John by the fourth Evangelist which recent criticism would never have allowed as remotely historical. Indeed, nothing, I prophesy, is likely to undergo so complete a reversal in the criticism of the Gospel as our estimate of its treatment of the Baptist, and therefore of the whole Judean ministry of Jesus with which it opens. This treatment has almost universally been assumed to spring from purely theological motives of a polemical nature and thus to provide evidence for a very minimum of historical foundation — about as much in fact as I should be prepared to allow to the Baptist group claiming John as Messiah against which the whole construction is supposed to be directed[3]. On the contrary, I believe that the fourth Evangelist is remarkably well informed on the Baptist, because he, or the witness behind that part of his tradition, once belonged to John's movement and, like the nameless disciple of 1, 37, "heard him say this, and followed Jesus".

It is for this same reason that he appears also to be being vindicated in his knowledge of the topography and institutions of Palestine prior to the Jewish war. This is not to imply that he is flawless; but it is equally ridiculous to believe that he is as clueless as some recent criticism has made him. The one thing he is not is vague — as Luke, the historian, is frequently vague about Palestine (compare the "certain village" of Luke 10, 38 where Mary and Martha lived, which in its Lucan setting might be anywhere from Galilee to Judaea, with John's "Bethany", "fifteen furlongs from Jerusalem", John 11, 18). And his details of name and place certainly seem to be being borne out, as far as I can judge, by such findings as those of Professor W. F. Albright in his *Archaeology of Palestine*[4] and in his article for the Dodd

---

[1] John the Baptist in the New Light of Ancient Scrolls, Interpretation 9 (1955) 71—90.

[2] E. g. B. Reicke, Nytt ljus över Johannes döparens förkunnelse, Religion och Bibel 11 (1952) 5—18. For a fuller bibliography cf. my article in the Harvard Theological Review cited above.

[3] Cf. my article, Elijah, John and Jesus, New Testament Studies 4 (1958) 263—281.

[4] 1956, pp. 243—249.

Festschrift[1] and of Professor Jeremias in his monograph on the rediscovery of Bethesda[2].

I would repeat that the fourth Evangelist is not interested in historical accuracy for its own sake. Indeed, it is precisely because his detail is often so incidental and irrelevant to his overriding theological purpose that it is the more impressive. But, however impossible it may be to draw the line, he would, I think, subscribe to the dictum of C. P. Scott of *The Manchester Guardian* that "fact is sacred, comment is free". If only because he is the New Testament writer who, theologically speaking, takes history more seriously than any other, he has at least the right to be heard — on the history as well as on the theology.

(4) And so we come to the fourth presupposition, that the fourth Evangelist represents the end-term of theological development in first-century Christianity.

Again, this is not to be disputed — in so far as he bestrides the whole development of New Testament thinking like a colossus. But so also does Paul; and, like Paul, he will be seen, I believe, to represent its *Alpha* as much as its *Omega*.

At points where his tradition has been tested he is, as I said, often remarkably primitive in his witness. And this is coming to be recognized also of his theology. Again, no one is saying that it is not an extraordinarily mature theology, the more extraordinary if, as I believe (in substantial agreement with Professor E. R. Goodenough[3]), it had reached its essential, if not its formal, maturity by about the same time as St. Paul's, at a date, that is, before any of the Synoptic Gospels were written. But while it is mature, it also stands very near to the primitive apostolic witness.

I will illustrate this from the point above all at which the fourth Evangelist is normally regarded as standing at the end of a line of doctrinal development and administering a "supreme and final corrective"[4] — namely, in his eschatology. The primitive

[1] Recent Discoveries in Palestine and the Gospel of St. John, in: The Background of the New Testament and its Eschatology (ed. W. D. Davies and D. Daube), 1956, pp. 153—171.

[2] Die Wiederentdeckung von Bethesda, 1949; cf., from an earlier period, K. Kündsin, Topologische Überlieferungsstoffe im Johannes-Evangelium, 1925.

[3] John a Primitive Gospel, Journal of Biblical Literature 64 (1945) 145—182.

[4] J. E. Fison, The Christian Hope, 1954, p. 145.

eschatology is taken to be what John came to see as "the apocalyptic *faux pas*", and in his writings this crude adventism is held to be quite — or almost quite — refined away in favour of a more "mystical" or "timeless" or "realized" understanding of the gospel of the Kingdom or "eternal life". This reconstruction I believe to be correct at one point, namely, that the path into apocalyptic was a *faux pas*. It was not, I am persuaded[1], the original eschatology of Jesus, which was much more in the line of the Prophets than of the Apocalyptists, nor was it that of the most primitive Church. The Synoptists witness to a progressive apocalypticization of the message of Jesus, as recent study has shown, and as the Gospel of Matthew most forcibly illustrates. The fourth Gospel does not, I believe, stand at the end of this progress, as a reaction against it, for which I think there is no internal evidence. Rather, as Dr. Dodd in his later work has hinted[2], it represents a form of the tradition which has never seriously undergone this process at all. While, in the Synoptists, elements in the eschatological teaching of Jesus were gradually detached from the supreme crisis in which he stood to his own generation and referred to a second separate moment, in the fourth Gospel the original unity is not broken: its picture of the vindication and the visitation of the Son of man is still essentially that, I believe, of Jesus himself and of the most primitive tradition, however immeasurably it may have been deepened by the recognition that it was in the Cross and not merely in the Resurrection that, in the terminology of the earliest preaching, God "glorified" and "lifted up" his Son.

What I think we detect in the history of the Johannine tradition is an increasing rather than a decreasing contact with the more apocalyptic stream of interpretation. The so-called traditional concept of the *Parousia* which makes its appearance in the epilogue to the Gospel and in the Epistles is not the trace of an earlier eschatology not wholly refined away. It points rather to the contact of the Johannine tradition with this stream of thought after it had been thrown by events from the relative isolation of its Palestinian milieu into the more cosmopolitan world of Asia Minor. By then, I believe, the material of the Gospel, whether in

---

[1] Cf. my book, Jesus and His Coming, 1957, particularly the final chapter.

[2] The Interpretation of the Fourth Gospel, p. 447.

oral or written shape, had essentially come to formulation, though it may have been edited and published for its present public, and the Epistles written, perhaps considerably later. The last term of this process is represented by the complete merger of the Johannine tradition with the world-view of apocalyptic in the book of the Revelation.

(5) This reconstruction, which is inevitably very tentative, brings us inescapably to the fifth and final question, that of authorship.

That the Evangelist is not himself the Apostle John nor a direct eye-witness is, Dr. Barrett says[1], a "moral certainty". It is naturally impossible here to go into the evidence, which has been so worked over that there would seem perhaps to be nothing more to be said. Again, I think that any change we see — and so far the question has not really been reopened — is likely to be reflected not so much in a flat denial of the answer just given as in a shift in the questions asked.

It is clear to anyone observing the protagonists on each side of the debate — and the conservative position, still presented so monumentally in J. B. Lightfoot's *Biblical Essays*[2], continues to have protagonists who are no fools[3] — that it is the presuppositions they bring to the evidence which are decisive. Indeed, the combination of the four preceding theses, all of which have the effect of setting the Evangelist at a distance from the events, makes the fifth conclusion of the reigning critics well-nigh inevitable. Long before they train their guns on the hapless Papias and Irenaeus and the ignorant Galilean fisherman we know what the result will be.

Incidentally the particular argument that runs, "This couldn't have been written by a Galilean fisherman", always seems to me singularly inept. You might have said of Ernest Bevin's speeches as Foreign Secretary, "These couldn't have been written by a barrow-boy in east Bristol" — to which, of course, the answer is that they weren't: they were written by a man who had been a barrow-boy in east Bristol.

---

[1] Op. cit., p. 112.

[2] 1893, pp. 1—198.

[3] E. g. recently in England: A. C. Headlam, The Fourth Gospel as History, 1948; A. H. N. Green-Armytage, John who Saw, 1952; H. E. Edwards, The Disciple who wrote these Things, 1953; R. A. Edwards, The Gospel according to St. John, 1954.

But my object here is not to argue the case for Apostolic authorship. What I want to do is to indicate, in conclusion, how the form of the question is now being changed.

Let me make a further comparison with Synoptic criticism. Until lately the question that dominated the study of the first three Gospels was, to cite Professor Bultmann's title, "the history of the Synoptic tradition"[1]. That is to say, the centre of interest was not the Evangelist, who was little more than an editor, but the tradition and the community behind the tradition. In the fourth Gospel, however, the Evangelist filled the eye. He may indeed have used sources, but for the most part the discussion ranged round what he made of them, what was the Johannine purpose, the Johannine theology. The difference corresponds, of course, to a real difference in the material; but it is now recognized as exaggerated. There is a great deal more interest in the purpose and theology of the Synoptic Evangelists themselves. And there are now signs of a corresponding interest in the Johannine tradition as such and in the community behind it — as witness, for example, the title of Bent Noack's recent book, *Zur johanneischen Tradition,* or of the article by the Finnish professor, Rafael Gyllenberg, in the latest Bultmann *Festschrift*[2], *Die Anfänge der johanneischen Tradition.*

Until now the discussion of the fourth Gospel has been dominated by the person of the Evangelist, and therefore by the question of individual authorship. The conservatives maintained the author was John son of Zebedee and they thus preserved the link with the Jesus of history — through one man. Their opponents found this link too weak to sustain. But having, as they felt, broken it, they tended to assume that there was no link: any statement in the Gospel belonged to the last decade of the first century or to the first of the second, and could therefore show no serious claim to be considered as history.

The question of authorship is still important, if only because the narrative is patently presented as that of an eye-witness and if that claim is groundless it affects our total assessment of it, and also because in this case the dominance of a single mind is so powerful that we have the impression, as we said earlier, that

---

[1] Die Geschichte der synoptischen Tradition, 1921.

[2] Neutestamentliche Studien für Rudolf Bultmann (ed. W. Eltester), 1954, pp. 144—147.

"*la tradition — c'est moi*[1]". But the question of authorship is not, I believe, the decisive one for the valuation of the Gospel as history. The decisive question is the status and origin of the Johannine tradition. Did this come out of the blue round about the year A. D. 100? Or is there a real continuity, not merely in the memory of one old man, but in the life of an on-going community, with the earliest days of Christianity? What, I think, fundamentally distinguishes the "new look" on the fourth Gospel is that it answers that question in the affirmative.

---

[1] Menoud continues: "Au terme de l'âge apostolique il ne restait qu'un homme qui ait pu parler ainsi" (op. cit., p. 77).

The Purpose of St. John's Gospel

W. C. VAN UNNIK, Utrecht

The subject of this evening's lecture will be familiar to everyone of you. One of the first questions asked in reading and explaining the Bible is always: what was the author aiming at? And the particular features of the Fourth Gospel as distinct from the Synoptics are so marked that the question cannot be suppressed: what led this writer—whoever he was—to draw this picture of our Lord so different from the others?

Perhaps everyone in this illustrious audience knows the answer, because no commentary on St. John and no Introduction to the New Testament is published without paying due attention to this point. I could enter into your feelings, if you said after reading the title in the programme: "This theme has been discussed for so many generations that we are at a dead-lock." You are right; this subject is well-worn. Of course there are still some greater or smaller differences left, but that is mainly due to differences in the background of the gospel as seen by various scholars.

It is therefore not without some hesitation — to put it mildly — that I have chosen the subject. While I was preparing this lecture I seemed to hear the voice of a British subject: "If somebody is going to speak, it is undoubtedly to shed new light on the subject; why else does he speak?" This heart-searching question could not easily be silenced by observing that the man who said it, Thomas Carlyle[1], is long dead. In coming to this place of learning and this congress people have not gathered to hear a number of truisms, the repetition of text-book sentences, even if with the new look, or "old favourites". Does the characteristic of a university-town in New Testament times not hold good in

---

[1] This saying is quoted in Dutch translation by I. van Dijk, Vota Academica, in: Verzamelde Werken, Groningen n. d., Deel II, pp. 70f., without exact reference.

our days: "Now all the Athenians and the strangers sojourning
there spent their time in nothing else but either to tell or to hear
some new thing"[1]? But in tackling such an old subject and in
trying to give some new light the speaker runs the risk of the
verdict: "the new things he said were not true and the true things
were not new". Who will dispute that this rule can often be
applied to what is written on the N. T.? However, this is largely
a subjective opinion, and therefore let me take the risk and
try to bring forward something that is new without bowling too
wide of the wicket.

About 50 years ago the outstanding historian of the ancient
church Adolf Harnack said that the origin of St. John's Gospel
was the greatest riddle of the primitive church[2] and other
scholars of repute expressed the same opinion if with many
variations during the decades that followed[3]. The variety of opinion is extremely great, as may be seen from Howard's masterly
survey in its latest revision by Barrett[4]. The attention has
shifted from the person of the evangelist to the contents of the
book. Gnostic forms of expression, Hellenistic influences, Palestinian background — each of these keywords signifies important
streams of interpretation. Great contributions, far beyond my
praise, have been made in the last thirty years. Is it too bold to
prophesy that in the coming years the big question will be: was
John a disciple of the Qumran-Community[5]? A few months ago
my colleague Quispel brought forward a number of interesting

[1] Acts 17, 21.—According to E. Norden, Agnostos Theos, Leipzig 1913,
p. 333 "vielleicht das ,Gebildetste', was überhaupt im N. T. steht";
E. Haenchen, Die Apostelgeschichte, Göttingen 1956, p. 460, makes some
restrictions.

[2] A. von Harnack, Lehrbuch der Dogmengeschichte[5], Tübingen 1931,
Bd. I, p. 308 (this fifth edition is identical with the fourth).

[3] E. G. K. Bornhäuser, Das Johannesevangelium eine Missionsschrift
für Israel, Gütersloh 1928, p. 15; E. Gaugler, Das Christuszeugnis des
Johannesevangeliums, in: Jesus Christus im Zeugnis der Heiligen Schrift
und der Kirche, München 1936, pp. 34f.; E. Stauffer, Die Theologie des
Neuen Testaments, Geneva 1945, p. 24.

[4] W. F. Howard — C. K. Barrett, The Fourth Gospel in recent criticism
and interpretation[4], London 1955.

[5] Cf. F. M. Braun, L'arrière-fond judaïque du quatrième évangile et la
Communauté de l'Alliance, Revue Biblique 62 (1955) 5—44 (other littera-
ture is mentioned by J. A. T. Robinson, The Baptism of John and the Qumran Community, Harvard Theological Review 50, 1957, 190, nt. 27—191).

observations which again hinted in the direction of Jewish heterodoxy[1]. These burning issues I cannot discuss at the present moment; that would take us somewhat more than three quarters of an hour. The scope of this lecture must be far more restricted, because John—so I call the author without prejudice for simplicity's sake—has himself clearly and unequivocally given an answer which however calls for some comment.

At the outset one more word of apology. If in the course of our discussion not many names of "fathers in learning" are mentioned it is not for lack of respect. On the contrary, I feel deeply indebted to many scholars of past and present generations, of various schools and churches. But after reading a good many books, big and small, essays, articles, papers etc., one is inclined to repeat the words of the Epistle to the Hebrews (11, 32): "and what shall I more say? for the time will fail me if I tell of Gideon, Barak, Samson, Jephtha", ... Bultmann, Dodd, Barrett and all the others. And not possessing the gift of prophecy I had to prepare this lecture without knowing the results of fresh research that are brought before you in these days. However, with the time at our disposal strict concentration will be required— which is by the way a good procedure in dealing with an author who has practised it himself.

In well-known words at the end of the Gospel John has clearly expressed the principle which led him in his writing. It will not be out of place to quote them here, because they will be the pivot of our discussion: "Many other signs therefore did Jesus in the presence of his disciples which are not written in this book; but these are written that ye may believe that Jesus is the Christ, the Son of God, and that believing ye may have life in his name" (20, 30—31).

There are no reasons to assume that these verses refer only to parts of the preceding gospel as we have it now. In view of the strong linguistic unity it seems to me impossible to divide this book into various sources and layers[2].

---

[1] G. Quispel, Het Johannesevangelie en de Gnosis, Nederlands Theologisch Tijdschrift 11 (1957) 173—203.

[2] Because John 20, 31 speaks about "signs" one could think that this text is specially related to a "Semeia-Quelle" (R. Bultmann). See *contra* this division of the Gospel: E. Ruckstuhl, Die literarische Einheit des

John wrote this at the conclusion of his Gospel. There is a marked difference here from Luke who starts by declaring in some beautiful phrases what he wants to offer to his most excellent Theophilus (Luke 1, 1—4). John does it otherwise: he does not outline his plan before the start, but he is like a guide in an unknown mountain area. That man takes us along all sorts of small, winding paths with some beautiful views, to the summit where we have to our great surprise a grand and splendid panorama. Now we look back and see the path by which we came; the partial vistas are seen as a marvellous whole and surveying the complete landscape we appreciate the details in their fullness: that is why we made the hard and difficult climb. The goal at the end dictated the way from its very beginning, but it was not seen from the outset. This is the technique of this evangelist who records the words of Jesus: "What I do thou knowest not now, but thou shalt understand hereafter" (13, 7, cf. 2, 22; 12, 16).

It has always been recognized that John informs his readers that he knows far more about the life and works of Jesus than he tells them in his gospel, but that he deemed this selection sufficient for his purpose. That purpose is twofold; but the latter part flows from the former: it has to do with a certain belief about Jesus and this belief will give to those who accept it life eternal. This belief about Jesus who comes from Nazareth in Galilee, who is a man with father, mother, brothers and friends is formulated in a double manner, viz., that Jesus is a) the Christ, b) the Son of God. This point of identification is the principle statement; without it the second part is impossible.

The unsuspecting student may think that such a clear statement would be the guiding principle of all thinking, speaking and writing on the Fourth Gospel. But on consulting the commentaries and handbooks he will find that he has been deceived. Many times the expositors start with the beginning in ch. 1, are fascinated by the word *Logos* and say John wants to show that Jesus is the incarnate Word, whatever may be the disputed origin and contents of this term. But this is something different from the wording of 20, 31. In reading the latest theology of the New Testament, that of Bultmann, one finds the discussion

Johannesevangeliums, Freiburg (Schweiz) 1951 and B. Noack, Zur johanneischen Tradition, København 1954. — Ch. 21 can of course be excluded.

of the terms "Christ" and "Son of God" somewhere in a corner[1], but they do not function as the steering ideas. The same holds good for Howard's "Christianity according to St. John" which gives a good many fine insights, but where the final word of John himself does not offer the pattern for the reproduction of John's theology.

In surveying the situation as reflected in various books we get roughly speaking the following different answers to our question: what was the purpose of John?

1) John wrote for non-Christians "who are concerned about eternal life and the way to it and may be ready to follow the Christian way if this is presented to them in terms that are intelligibly related to their previous, religious interests and experiences"[2].

2) John wrote for Christians to give them a deeper understanding of their faith: the "spiritual gospel" over against the "carnal" one, as was said in the well-known words of Clement of Alexandria[3]. It is a book of the Christian community which has to express itself in the terms of its new surroundings (Feine — Behm, Michaelis[4]) with some attacks against the disciples of John the Baptist, Jews and Gnostics. Or as Barrett said, it wants to build up the church in the crisis of early eschatology and gnosticism[5] or to show that the historic Jesus is the Christ of the Church and that the Church's interests at the time (sacraments, mission) were already found with the Lord (Cullmann[6]).

3) John wrote to ward off the blows of the Jews who threw fierce slanders at the Christian Messiah; a forerunner of Justin

---

[1] R. Bultmann, Theologie des Neuen Testaments, Tübingen 1953, p. 383; the chapter on the theology of John as a whole has 90 pages, p. 349—439.

[2] C. H. Dodd, The Interpretation of the Fourth Gospel, Cambridge 1953, p. 9.

[3] Clemens Alexandrinus, Hypotyposis, ap. Eusebius, Hist. Eccl. VI 14, 7.

[4] P. Feine — J. Behm, Einleitung in das Neue Testament[9], Heidelberg 1950, p. 116ff.; W. Michaelis, Einleitung in das Neue Testament[2], Bern 1954, p. 117ff.

[5] C. K. Barrett, The Gospel according to St. John, London 1955, p. 114ff.

[6] O. Cullmann, The Early Church, ed. by A. J. B. Higgins, London 1956, p. 186.

Martyr in his Dialogue with Trypho, he did not give an historical account, but showed that the Christian Lord was God's Son and revealed His glory (Wrede, Jülicher, Heitmüller[1]). It often reflects discussions with Jews of the Diaspora[2].

There are of course various combinations, but these are the main positions. The defenders of these diverging points of view derive their arguments from the features the Fourth Gospel displays, largely in contrast with the Synoptics. But we must be allowed to ask whether their definition of the purpose squares with the outspoken opinion of the author himself. Besides that we observe that they are in fact mutually exclusive, so that we must try to make a decision of our own.

It is interesting to notice that this verse 20, 31 has often been the victim of maltreatment. When John says that "Jesus is the Christ, the Son of God" it is immediately followed in scholarly books by the remark that this term "Christ" does not need to be taken seriously. It is of course quite clear that John does not use this word as a proper name (except in two cases 1, 17; 17, 3 which have some peculiarities of their own), that he is aware of some connection with the Jewish Messiah, but that this Christian Messiah is absolutely different from his somewhat vague or highly nationalistic namesake in Judaism; he is not an apocalyptic figure and is the Saviour of the world (4, 42)[3]. One would think that this Christhood of Jesus was the "idée-mère", but that is a mistaken idea. Dodd devoted only a few pages of his great book to this term. This discussion amounts to practically nothing: Jesus is not the Messiah of the Jews[4]. Fortunately there is a proviso: Dodd was only comparing Rabbinic Judaism. In a different context we meet the same thing in Cullmann's recent Christology: he does not even quote our text and in his exposition of the term "Christ" this Gospel which has this word

---

[1] W. Wrede, Charakter und Tendenz des Johannesevangeliums, in: Vorträge und Studien, Tübingen 1907, p. 178ff.; A. Jülicher — E. Fascher, Einleitung in das Neue Testament, Tübingen 1931, p. 418; W. Heitmüller, Die Schriften des Neuen Testaments neu übersetzt und für die Gegenwart erklärt[3], Göttingen 1920, p. 16.

[2] R. H. Strachan, The Fourth Gospel[3], London 1946, p. 50.

[3] E. Gaugler, l. c., p. 37; G. Sevenster, De Christologie van het Nieuwe Testament, Amsterdam 1946, p. 220.

[4] C. H. Dodd, l. c., p. 87—93.

on its banner is virtually ignored[1]. One gets the impression in reading the commentaries that this term "the Christ" has turned up like a bad penny[2]. So it often disappears from the scene without much ado and the statement that Jesus is the "Son of God" is the only one that remains; then one is not hindered by difficult questions about the relation between the Messiah and the Son of God: "Son of God" can be interpreted as a typically Hellenistic term or it can be maintained that it is not the "divine man" of Hellenism nor a metaphorical name of the king, but the real exclusive Son. When, on the other hand, according to Bultmann it was John's aim to say: the revealer reveals that He is the revealer[3], it seems to me that this is a rather grave misrepresentation of our text.

I must confess that I am not quite happy with this result. Are we to assume that John in formulating his purpose was consciously or unconsciously misleading his readers rather after the fashion of detective story writers, who try to lead their readers on the wrong track. In that kind of literature one can find all sorts of false clues throughout the book which lead the interested readers to wrong conclusions and that is just good fun, but on the last pages the writer is absolutely serious and tells the truth. I do not wish to suggest that John wrote such a kind of fiction, but neither do I want him to be taken less seriously than a fiction-writer. It seems wise to take the words of John as they stand and to listen to see if they have not something more than a trivial final word to say.

The main verb in the sentence expressing the purpose is "to believe". That is not astonishing, because it explains why it is so often said, almost after every word or deed of Jesus, that

---

[1] O. Cullmann, Die Christologie des Neuen Testaments, Tübingen 1957, p. 111 ff.

[2] See the commentaries, e. g. Heitmüller, l. c., p. 180: "Der Inhalt dieses Glaubens: Jesus der Sohn Gottes (im johanneischen Sinn)". — It is higly significant to observe the shifting of ideas in a popular book of my predecessor who always gives an excellent summary of current opinion; A. M. Brouwer, De vier Evangelisten, Zutphen 1931, p. 198 wrote: "It was the writer's purpose to make clear that Christ is the incarnate Word, the only-one and as a man ... the Son of God" (my translation and underlining); he repeats this on pp. 201 and 208; the predicative "Christ" has become the subject!

[3] R. Bultmann, Theologie, p. 413.

people did or did not believe[1]. In the final episode when the
Gospel reaches its summit in the adoration of Thomas before his
Lord and God, this word recurs several times: Thomas will not
believe, unless ...; Jesus says to him: "be not faithless, but
believing", and ends with that wonderful beatitude: "because thou
hast seen me, thou hast believed; blessed are they that have not
seen and yet have believed" (20, 24—29, immediately preceding
the final verses). In almost every scene the evangelist describes
he brings out this element. That belief in Jesus gives life eternal
is also a recurrent theme of the Evangelist. His declaration in
20, 31 therefore is a perfect expression of the task he set himself.

But what did he want his readers to believe? "That Jesus is
the Christ, the Son of God." This latter affirmation is amply
illustrated by the Gospel and though there are some slight
differences about its exact meaning, it is not disputed. The unity
of the Father and the Son, the Son's revelation of the Father
to the world are the recurring themes. But it cannot be said
that the former designation "Christ" is so evident a description
of the contents of the Gospel. Therefore we can leave aside what
is generally accepted; it will be good to concentrate our attention
on the term that seems to give some trouble in this connection:
the Christ. It may be that the right understanding of it puts
the whole picture in a different perspective.

"Christ" is the former of the two predicates and that should
prevent us from eliminating or weakening it. Is it not striking
that John begins by declaring this? That he does not confine
himself to the term "Son of God", that he does not choose a
word so current in the Hellenistic world and known to him like
Soter-Saviour (4, 42)? There is no reason whatever to assume
with E. F. Scott that the term "Son of God" was superseding the
name "Christ"[2] or that by this word the idea of "Christ" has
been translated into the vocabulary that was more familiar to
the Hellenistic world. Before making a decision on that point
it will be wise to get a clear idea of that word "Christ".

[1] See the Concordances for the frequency of the verb πιστεύω in John;
πίστις is missing, as is well known. The act of believing is of prime
importance.

[2] E. F. Scott, The Fourth Gospel, its Purpose and Theology[2], Edinburgh 1908, p. 4, cf. p. 182ff., quoted with approval by G. H. C. Macgregor,
The Gospel of John, London 1928, p. 367.

The translation of the Greek words ὅτι ᾽Ιησοῦς ἐστιν ὁ Χριστός
by: "that Jesus is the Christ" cannot, I must confess, be called
satisfactory though it is found in practically all modern translations. Because we are so familiar with the term "Christ", we
often overlook the fact that John stresses in such a remarkable
way the identity between the man Jesus with the title "the
Christ". We are so accustomed to use the loan-word "Christ"
as another name for Jesus that we have almost lost sight of the
fact that it is n o t a proper name, but a title. It is such a standing
term in Christian theology that we forget that there it has
practically lost its meaning or is filled with Christian contents.
But did the same hold good for John and his first readers? Was
this a technical term or was *Christos* conceived in its etymological meaning: "the anointed one"?

Now it is clear that for John this title was not an hieroglyph,
but had preserved its full weight: t h e A n o i n t e d O n e. That is
quite obvious, because he twice (1, 41; 4, 25) uses the Hebrew
term "Messiah"—which has not become a loan-word in early
Christian literature like "amen"—and adds immediately, lest
the listeners might use a meaningless word, the exact translation
in Greek[1]. It is somewhat strange to see that all modern versions
of the N. T. give this reading of the verses: "we have found the
Messiah (which is being interpreted Christ)". But that can hardly
be called a translation! Three verses before 1, 41 the same formula is found in connection with the Jewish word "rabbi" and
there we find "which is to say being interpreted 'Master'"(1, 38).
Who would retain here the Greek word διδάσκαλε? Nobody of
course. But why then is not the same rule applied to vs. 41: "Messiah that is translated the Anointed One"; that is the only exact
r e n d e r i n g of the Greek text. If one wants to keep the relation,
suggested by the Greek, with the name of our Lord "Christ",
there is no other way than that of giving a double translation:
Messiah, Christ, Anointed One. "Christ" was not simply an
alternative for "Jesus" nor was it meaningless; it has kept its
full etymological force.

As a translation of "Messiah" of which John was conscious,
it brings us into the Jewish sphere. For, to be sure, only there

---

[1] It is curious to see that he retained "amen", even reduplicated.
The title "Messiah" is not retained for holiness' sake; for it is translated
and explained.

could this title "the Anointed One" be understood and only there
it mattered. To the Greeks it was quite unintelligible[1]. It is
well known from second-century texts that in order to make
some sense out of the term used by the Christians they interpreted it with the word χρηστός = useful, which had at that
time the same pronunciation[2]. Neither Philo nor Josephus uses
it[3]. Karl Ludwig Schmidt was right in maintaining that this
title is absolutely isolated and unique in the history of religions[4].
But it would be waste of time to give a circumstantial exposition
of the large place this figure of the future Deliverer-King or High
Priest held among the Jews, since he is fully dealt with in every
book on the Theology of the O. T., or of Judaism. As far as the
early Christians are concerned both Vincent Taylor and Cullmann[5] have rightly drawn attention to the fact that this word
was meaningless to the Hellenistic churches and that there it
prolonged its life as a proper name, that is to say, as a fossil.
But that is clearly not the case in the Fourth Gospel; for John
it is still full of life and can serve as the intelligible translation
of a Hebrew word. This seems to me a strong indication that the
gospel has something to do with Jews or Jewish Christians to
whom the title "the Anointed One" was important. John does
not say why the figure he has in view was so called, either because
it was well known to his readers or because the figure itself,
indicated in that way, was familiar. But was it just a "chiffre" or
had it some relation to actual unction? Presently we shall return

---

[1] It does not occur anywhere in Greek religious thought. Interesting in
this connection is the remark of Justin Martyr, Apology 49, 5: "For the
Jews having the prophecies, and being always in expectation of the Christ
to come, did not recognise Him; and not only so, but even treated Him
shamefully. But the Gentiles, who had never heard anything about
Christ, until the apostles set out from Jerusalem and preached concerning Him, and gave them the prophecies, were filled with joy and
faith, and cast away their idols, and dedicated themselves to the Unbe-
gotten God through Christ", being Justin's application of Is. 65, 1—3.

[2] See e. g. Justin Martyr, Apology 4, 1—5; Tertullian, Apologia 3, 5;
Apocryphon Johannis 30, ed. W. Till, p. 101—103.

[3] The title is not found in Leisegang's Index of Philo; Josephus only
uses it in the famous "Testimonia Flaviana" Ant. XVIII 3, 3, § 63 and XX
9, 1, § 200, but these texts are, as is well known, far from being certain.

[4] K. L. Schmidt, Le problème du christianisme primitif, Paris 1938, p. 43.

[5] V. Taylor, The Names of Jesus, London 1953, p. 22 f.; O. Cullmann,
l. c., p. 135.

to that important question. At the moment we take up a subject already alluded to before, namely that we should not attach so much weight to this term since there is a gulf between the Jewish and the Christian conception of the Messiah, the former being narrowly nationalistic, the latter a universal figure.

It has often been remarked that John is the only writer in the N. T., who uses the original word "Messiah" and that he speaks in the same connection of Jesus as "the king of the Jews" (1, 49). But that is of no importance, says Walter Bauer[1], because John in that passage heaps on Jesus all the traditional names current in the Christian church of his day and it should not be asked what was their exact meaning; John was not thinking in Jewish categories, because the Church had completely broken away from Judaism. These arguments do not seem sound to me for the following reasons:

1) John highly valued the term "king of the Jews" as an epithet of Jesus, as may be seen from some other texts in his gospel. In the quotation of Ps. 118 sung at Jesus' triumphal entry into Jerusalem there are added the words "the king of the Jews" (12, 13). In the passion-narrative all the light falls upon the interview of Jesus with Pilate, where Jesus' kingship is under discussion. All the gospels record the inscription on the cross: "Jesus the king of the Jews", but John is the only one who has the story that the Jewish leaders suggested another wording "he has said...", but that Pilate left it as it stood; to John it clearly was a declaration of facts, admitted even by the Roman governor (19, 19 ff.). The designation "king of the Jews" must have meant something to John and his readers.

2) Even if we were to assume that the Church had completely broken away from the Jewish people by the time John wrote, what sort of people would be interested to know that Jesus was the king of the Jews? Would it not have been highly dangerous after the Jewish insurrection of A. D. 70 to speak of the Christian Lord in such terms? What could Christianity win thereby? One cannot lightly pass by these questions and bluntly declare that the term was meaningless to John.

3) Philip is reported to have said: "we have found him of whom Moses in the Law and the prophets did write" (1, 46).

---

[1] W. Bauer, Das Johannesevangelium³, Tübingen 1933, p. 40.

Jesus referred his audience to the Scriptures which bear witness
of Him (5, 39). In many other places the O. T. is alluded to or
directly quoted. Would that be pointless? John must have seen
a strong relation between the O. T. and the Messiah.

4) I cannot help feeling that a great misapprehension plays
a part here. In investigating what the Jews in Jesus' days
expected about the Messiah, the Apocrypha, Pseudepigrapha,
Targumim and rabbinic writings are consulted. But the Old Testament itself is often overlooked, and it was the "living oracles of
God" for all the Jews and not for special groups of sectarians
or learned. It is clear from these sources that there was no
generally accepted doctrine of the eschatological future. In some
circles one hoped for a Messiah, in others it was God Himself
who would deliver His people without an intermediary. The
kingly Messiah of Ps. Sal. 17 is quite different from that second-
rank figure who was expected by the Qumran-community[1].
There was a strictly national conception, but there were also
universal and transcendental tendencies[2]. The king of Ps. 72
will reign over all the earth and the Servant of the Lord in
Deutero-Isaiah is a light for the Gentiles as well (Is. 49, 6f.),
bringing salvation to the ends of the earth although he is essentially connected with Israel. In some cases the Kingdom of God
is really a heavenly kingdom. Before flatly declaring that the
conception found in John about the Anointed One has nothing
to do with the Jewish King-Messiah one must ask whether or
not He has features of the O. T. as well.

That the work of Jesus the Anointed One was in a very real
and living way connected with Jewish expectations may be seen
from a passage, the great importance of which is generally overlooked. At the end of ch. 11 we are told that the "success" of Jesus leads to the advice of the High Priest "that it is expedient for
the people that one man should die". Then follow these words:
"Now this he said not of himself, but being high priest that year
he prophesied that Jesus should die for the nation; and not for

---

[1] M. Black, Messianic Doctrine in the Qumran Scrolls, in: K. Aland —
F. L. Cross (edd.), Studia Patristica, vol. I, Texte und Untersuchungen
Bd. 63, Berlin 1957, p. 441—459; A. S. van der Woude, Die messianischen
Vorstellungen der Gemeinde von Qumran, Assen 1957.
[2] M. A. Beek, Nationale en transcendente motieven in de Joodse
Apokalyptiek van de laatste eeuwen voor Christus, Assen 1941.

the nation only, but that he might also gather together into one
the children of God that are scattered abroad" (11, 51f., cf. vv.
45ff.). This statement is one of the various personal remarks of
the Evangelist[1] and has a direct bearing upon our question.
Here John does not report what others have said or done, but
he himself of his own accord says something about the death
of Jesus and this declaration goes far beyond what the high
priest is reported to have said. That this addition is made, shows
the deep interest in this matter on the part of John. "To gather
together those who are scattered" is a real messianic work. Many
texts in the O. T. and later Jewish literature attest that God or
the Messiah will bring back the Jews out of the Diaspora to the
Holy Land; that is a constant feature of the time of salvation
— an expectation so real to the Jews that even Philo mentions
it[2]. In other words: John has seen this expectation fulfilled, since
Jesus died, but in origin and contents it was Jewish, messianic.

Another remarkable fact is that John himself declares that the
disciples did not understand what happened when Jesus entered
Jerusalem riding on a young ass, but that the messianic character
of the event was seen afterwards: Jesus entered the holy city
as the king promised by Zechariah (12, 16).

But did Jesus not refuse the royal dignity when the Jews
wished to hail him as king after the multiplying of the loaves?
Exactly, and let it be noticed that this feature is not found in
the parallel narratives of the Synoptics, but only in John,
showing once more how interested he was in this aspect of Jesus'
work. The Galileans see in Jesus who has done this the promised
Prophet[3] and they want to crown him, because the multiplication of the loaves is seen as a messianic meal. But why did
Jesus escape? It is not explicitly said, but for the readers of the
Fourth Gospel the answer is not in doubt: he did not seek the
glory of men or "his hour had not yet come" (cf. 5, 41; 7, 6). It
does not say that Jesus did not want, according to John, to be the
king of the Jews, but that he refused this manner of becoming
king. The strongly patriotic Jewish expectations as cherished

---

[1] See 2, 21f. 24f.; 7, 39; 10, 6; 11, 13; 12, 16. 33. 41.

[2] Texts are mentioned in: P. Volz, Die Eschatologie der jüdischen
Gemeinde im neutestamentlichen Zeitalter[2], Tübingen 1934, p. 345f.

[3] John 6, 14; for the designation as "Prophet", see 1, 21. 25; 4, 19;
7, 40. 52; 9, 17.

by the Zealots were not accepted[1]. This negative statement does not however imply that there was no relation with the Messiah foretold to Israel.

The result of this discussion can be summed up like this: although the nationalistic Messianism is not shared by John, he stands on the ground of Jewish messianic belief. Later on we shall return to other messianic features in the portrait of Jesus. But what has been said may be sufficient proof that for John the "Anointed King of Israel" was a living title and not just an empty shell.

We now turn to another point: the wording of the first part of our text. It is quite simple: "that Jesus is the *Χριστός*". There does not seem anything peculiar in it, and therefore it is passed over by most commentators. That is presumably the reason why some interesting parallels which may shed some light upon the purpose of John have, as far as I know, never been adduced or if so, they have not had any effect upon the views on the Gospel. They are not culled from some scarcely known corner of Hellenistic religious thought, but from ... the New Testament itself.

In Acts 17, 2—3 we read: "Paul, as his custom was, went into the synagogue (of Thessalonica) and for three sabbath days reasoned with them (the Jews) from the scriptures opening and alleging that it behoved the Christ to suffer and to rise again from the dead; and that this Jesus whom he said I proclaim unto you, is the Christ" (*ὅτι οὗτός ἐστιν ὁ Χριστός, ὁ Ἰησοῦς, ὃν ἐγὼ καταγγέλλω ὑμῖν*).

In other words Paul has two topics in his discussion with the Jews: a) the Messiah must suffer and rise again; that is a point of doctrine which remained a standing heading in later Christian Testimonies for the Jews[2], and b) the Messiah of the O. T. in that particular form, the suffering and rising Messiah, is the historic Jesus of Nazareth; that is a point of history. These two topics are distinct from one another, as one can see from the sketch of a Pauline sermon in Acts 13, 26ff. The latter item is

---

[1] Though the writer is familiar with them, see: W. R. Inge, John, Gospel of, in: J. Hastings, Dictionary of Christ and the Gospels, Edinburgh 1906, vol. I, p. 877f., the difference is marked.

[2] Cf. J. Rendel Harris, Testimonies, Cambridge 1916—1920, part I, p. 19f., part II, p. 76.

again mentioned in Acts 18,5: in the synagogue of Corinth Paul
was testifying that Jesus was the Christ (εἶναι τὸν Χριστὸν
Ἰησοῦν). The great preacher Apollos, "mighty in the scriptures"
did the same after being better instructed (18, 28): "he helped
them much which had believed through grace, for he powerfully
confuted the Jews publicly showing by the scriptures that
Jesus was the Christ" (εἶναι τὸν Χριστὸν Ἰησοῦν). It is
interesting to see that Acts reports the same immediately after
Paul's conversion: "and straightway in the synagogues he
proclaimed Jesus that he is the Son of God ... he confounded
the Jews that dwelt at Damascus proving that this is the
Christ" (9, 20. 22), this last case offering an interesting combination of the very same terms used by John 20, 31.

According to this picture of Paul's missionary activity the
main topic to be discussed with the Jews in the synagogues
where he went to win them for his Lord, was "that Jesus is the
Christ". He argues from the Scriptures, i. e. texts from the
Old Testament to which John 5, 39 also directed the Jews.
That this demonstration was not so harmless in various respects,
was not purely academic, but had some consequences, appears
from the sequence in Acts 17, namely vs. 7: there the Jews
accuse the Christians before the general public of revolutionary
activities against the Roman emperor, because the Christians
say that "there is another king, one Jesus". The identification
of the Messiah (the Christ) with Jesus implies that he is a king[1].
Luke offers this small but highly interesting piece of information in his usual terse manner; it suggests however some very
heated debates and the living connection between Messiahship
and kingship.

I for one do not see any reason to doubt the trustworthiness
of this Lucan account. One cannot play off the letters of Paul
against Acts, because the epistles were destined for Christians.
But even if this account were a pure invention of Luke it shows
what was the big issue between Jews and Christians. Pure Hel-

---

[1] Cf. supra p. 177 for the connexion of these ideas "Christ" and
"King" in John; as far as the Jewish conception of the Messiah is concerned, the combination is usual. The revolutionary aspect lies of
course in the fact that basileus is both "king" and "emperor", there
being no difference as with us. It is strang eto see that this interesting
piece of evidence is so overlooked.

lenists needed some other way of approach. "That Jesus is the
Christ", this Johannine phrase is a formula which has
its roots in the Christian mission among the Jews.

This conclusion is confirmed by some texts from the 2nd
century which reflect again Jewish-Christian discussions. In the
famous passage of Hegesippus on James, the Lord's brother, it
is said that some of the Jews in Jerusalem became believers
"that Jesus is the Christ"; the leaders of the Jews want
James to persuade the people "not to go astray about Jesus
as though he were the Christ"[1]. The man who was hailed
Messiah by Rabbi Akiba, Bar Kochba, urged the Christians to
deny that Jesus is the Christ and to blaspheme; if they
would not, he had them put to death[2].

Most important in this connection is the *Dialogue* of Justin
Martyr with the Jew Trypho (middle 2nd cent.). In that discussion
between Synagogue and Church Trypho speaks about Christians
who keep the Law of Moses and believe in the crucified Jesus, having acknowledged that "He is the Anointed One (Christ)
of God" (46,1; 47,1). But even more important is an utterance
of Trypho himself: he admits that it has been clearly proved
by the Scriptures that it behoved the Christ (the Messiah) to
suffer and that he will return with glory etc. (the position of
Justin), but he then proceeds to the next question: "prove now that
he (οὗτος, viz. Jesus) it is" (39, 7; cf. p. 395). Later on the same
request is made. Notwithstanding that repeated appeal Justin,
as Lukyn Williams rightly put it, "nowhere does do so in so
many words. He is content to indicate the similarity of Old
Testament predictions of the Messiah to events in Jesus' life"[3].
And it was not easy to do that.

From this evidence we gather that the phrase "that Jesus is
the Anointed One" belongs to the standard topics that were
at stake between Church and Synagogue, the decisive one, and
that it was not used by the Christians for apologetic motives, but
to win Jews for this Jesus as the Messiah foretold and expected.
If this identity of Jesus with the Messiah could be substantiated

---

[1] Hegesippus, ap. Eusebius, Hist. Eccl. II 23, 8—10. — The meaning
of 1 John 2, 22 cannot be discussed here.

[2] Justin Martyr, Apol. 31, 6.

[3] A. Lukyn Williams, Justin Martyr Dialogue with Trypho, London
1930, p. xxxvi.

the Jews would accept Him (that holds good for Justin too who in this case is falsely called an "apologetic" writer). What Justin did not do properly, John had undertaken long before, because that was, as he explicitly states, his aim.

In this way it is also possible to explain a fact that has long puzzled me. Since the evangelist had in view Jews, one does not find in his gospel reactions against pagan practices like idolatry (except in so far they may fall under the very general heading "the world" which comprises everything), while on the other hand mistaken conceptions of the Jews are severely criticized.

The comparison between John and Justin's Dialogue brings to light two more interesting characteristics of this gospel:

1) Justin deals—even if allowance is made for all his repetitions—with a good many aspects of the New Covenant: the Christian attitude towards the Law, Circumcision, Sabbath etc. That is not found in John. The evangelist is not all-comprising, but has only one theme which he develops in recurring variations: Jesus is the Anointed One, the Son of God. He shows a tremendous concentration on this sole issue: *Solus Christus*! It is important to take this into account, because one has often wondered that so many themes which are mentioned in the Synoptics and Paul are not found here. He knows e. g. the conception of the Kingdom of God (3, 3), but it has no central place. Why not? Not because such notions were unknown to him or did not interest him, but because he absolutely stuck to his programme and made everything subordinate to it.

2) Justin's book consists of a string of quotations from the O. T., fully exploited by Rendel Harris for his theory of the Testimony-book. But in John—though he has some testimonies —they are few in number, most of them in the passion-narrative[1]. That is the more striking, because he often refers to the O. T. in general and knows about the fulfilment of the Scriptures[2]. But John clearly did not use this method. What has this to say?

---

[1] Cf. Rendel Harris, l. c., part II, p. 70: "we have to mark this paucity of Old Testament references".

[2] "Fulfilment": John 12, 38; 13, 18; 15, 25; 17, 12; 18, 9. 32; 19, 24; 19, 36; cf. also the texts where he speaks about the Law, the Scripture: "it is written" etc.

It was an enormous task the Christian missionaries undertook: to show not only that the Messiah suffered—which was a change the Jewish portrait of the Messiah — but that he was identical with the definite man Jesus of Nazareth, son of Joseph (1, 45) and Mary (2, 1), the rabbi. This was not a new theory about the heavenly messenger, but a historical fact. It should be realized that all that contemporary Judaism has to say about the Messiah in its various circles and books is concerned with a figure of the future, of thoughts, dreams and promises, the ideal, but imaginary deliverer, king or prophet or priest, but that it never was a man of flesh and blood[1]. Now the Christians came with the message that the Messiah had been on earth in the simple form of a Galilean rabbi. That was something unknown and unheard of and we can hardly realize the difficulty. How could this identity be established? The attempt was made by means of the Scripture-texts. But helpful though that proved in some cases, especially for those already convinced, the man who used these testimonies in debate with the unbelievers was met by completely different explanations of the same texts from the side of his opponents[2] and could hear the reproach: "All the words of the prophecy which, Sir, you adduce, are ambiguous and contain nothing decisive in proof of your argument" (*Dial.* 51, 1).

It has been remarked that Jesus' discussions with the Jews are wholly unhistorical. They sound, especially in chs. 5 and 8, like a law-suit[3]. One of John's favourite words is "witness"; the figure of John the Baptist is completely reduced to that activity[4]. Not Jesus' own declaration is valid (5, 31); he must

---

[1] We cannot be sure whether movements as those described e. g. by Josephus, Ant. XX 5, 1 and 8, 6 were headed by a man who considered himself the "Messiah". Josephus speaks about "prophets" but may have had his reasons for that. — Barkochba was hailed as the Messiah by R. Akiba, see: E. Schürer, Geschichte des jüdischen Volkes im Zeitalter Jesu Christi[3-4], Leipzig 1901, Bd. I, p. 682ff., but that was an exceptional case and not generally accepted by the Jews. In general one held that the "days of the Messiah" would be in the future.

[2] See e. g. Justin Martyr, Dial. c. Tryph. 33, 1 and 85, 1 and the note of Lukyn Williams, l. c., p. 72, nt. 3.

[3] W. Wrede, l. c., p. 209. Wrede gives much relevant material which could not be incorporated in this article; his line of argument is quite different from that followed in this paper. Important though his work is, he has not I would think put things in their proper setting.

[4] Cf. 1, 19ff. and 3, 26ff.

have affirmation from others. In 8, 17 he quotes the rule from the O. T. law: "the witness of two men is true" (Deut. 19, 15) and this rule can be discovered in several places (ch. 1 double witness of the disciples; ch. 5 witness of John the Baptist and the Father)[1]. There is another interesting fact. In John's Gospel we find a very remarkable and astonishing use of the double "Amen", for which no explanation is offered. In the Synoptic Gospels "Amen" stands in contrast with the Jewish usage at the beginning of a saying of Jesus[2]. With the double "Amen"—its place in John is obscured by the translation "verily"—Jesus gives a strong declaration, practically amounting to an oath. Why? Would not such a pronouncement be specially impressive for a Jew?

In the light of the foregoing observation these facts can be fully understood: in the synagogue there was a law-suit with the issue "is Jesus the Messiah or not?"[3]. The testimonies of the O. T. were of doubtful interpretation. John used independent witnesses. Justin said after a short digression in reply: "How is there still room for doubt when you can be persuaded by facts ($\xi\varrho\gamma\omega$, 51, 2)." That reminds us of the well-known classical contrast between "word" and "deed", where the latter is decisive. But it also brings home to us some sayings of the Fourth Gospel e. g. "Believest thou not that I am in the Father, and the Father in me? The words that I say unto you I speak not from myself; but the Father abiding in me doeth his works. Believe me that I am in the Father and the Father in me; or else believe me for the very works' sake" (14, 10—11).

This is the appropriate moment to introduce another favorite word of John which is also important in the text 20, 30 f., viz. "signs". The definition of Dodd: "symbols of an unseen reality"[4] sounds too Platonic. The use of the word must be seen in relation to the missionary activity of the early Church[5] and against the

---

[1] One of my pupils, the Rev. H. van Vliet (Kerkrade-Chèvremont) has finished a thesis on this subject which will be published in 1958. — See the concordance s. v. $\mu\acute{\alpha}\varrho\tau\upsilon\varsigma$ etc.

[2] See J. Jeremias, Kennzeichen der ipsissima vox Jesu, in: Synoptische Studien, Festschrift für A. Wikenhauser, München 1953, p. 89—93.

[3] Cf. pp. 395 ff.

[4] C. H. Dodd, l. c., p. 444.

[5] The combination "signs and wonders" often occurs in Acts; it is there a confirmation of the preaching of the Gospel, e. g. 14, 3 and Hebr. 2, 4; important is also 2 Cor. 12, 12.

background of the O. T. The "signs" which Jesus does have a great influence upon the multitude and work faith in Him (11, 47). They hail Jesus as the king of the Jews because they have heard that he raised Lazarus from the dead, "for they had heard this sign" (12, 18). That this is closely linked up with the messianic work is not only seen here, but is also evident from the people's expectation: "When the Christ shall come, will he do more signs than these which this man has done?" (7,31). From the signs they conclude that he is the Messiah. These signs, Nicodemus confesses, nobody could do "except God be with him" (3, 2, an expression of very special divine assistance[1]). Here John makes us clearly understand that Jesus has done far more than is related in the gospel, but that this is sufficient (cf. also 6, 2). People ask for Jesus' authority by which He cleansed the Temple in the words: "What signs do you do?" What are these signs? The healing of a blind man, the raising of Lazarus and other miracles. Jesus did not use the word himself, but for Him they are the "works of God" which no man can do[2]. The raising of Lazarus is done at that moment in order that people may believe that the Father has sent Him (11, 42). The man's blindness is not the result of preceding sin, but is so "that the works of God should be made manifest in him" (9, 4). "For the works which the Father has given me to accomplish, the very works that I do, bear witness of me that the Father has sent me" (5, 36). They are proof that Jesus is specially commissioned by God to do His work, that He is the Messiah. And the great "It is accomplished" is heard, when He has given his life for the life of the world, as the king of Israel. Just as in the O. T. Moses must do some signs that he may be believed as the prophet, sent by God[3], so it is here. Stress is not laid upon the element of wonder in itself[4], but upon the revelation of Jesus' glory (2, 11). Bultmann

---

[1] See my forthcoming article: "Dominus Vobiscum", the background and meaning of a liturgical formula.

[2] Cf. 15, 24; this point has been recently dealt with by L. Cerfaux, Les miracles, signes messianiques de Jésus et œuvres de Dieu, selon l'Evangile de S. Jean, in: L'attente du Messie, Bruges 1954, p. 131—138.

[3] Exod. 3, 12 (God said to Moses): "Certainly I will be with thee; and this shall be the token (σημεῖον) unto thee, that I have sent thee", and the "signs" mentioned in the following passages.

[4] The combination "signs and wonders" is found only once, 4, 48, but this is a word of reproach in the mouth of Jesus against the Jews:

says that they do not accredit Jesus because they require faith[1]. That does not seem a right conclusion. To be sure, they require faith, but for John it was important that they were done and that it was impossible to deny that they had been done. They are proofs which can be accepted in a completely earthly manner (6, 27) or rejected altogether or accepted for what they were: the works of God. They authenticate Him, if one accepts "Law and Prophets". Jesus heals a lame man and a blind man; he raises a dead man. Was it not written: "Then the eyes of the blind shall be opened and the ears of the deaf shall be unstopped; then shall the lame man leap as a hart" (Is. 35, 5—6)? He who has received all things from his Father, has also power to raise the dead (a Jewish name for God is "He who quickens the dead"[2]). He is the one who sets free (Is. 61, 1, cf. John 8, 36). As king-Messiah he is the Good Shepherd (ch. 10, cf. Ezek. 34). He brings light to those in darkness (12, 46 ff., cf. Is. 9, 2; 60, 1). Jesus the fountain of living water (ch. 4) gives drink to His people (Is. 43, 20).

These works are proof of Jesus' Messiahship. As such He is recognized by the Samaritan woman, "because He told me everything" (4, 39). That is the prophetic capacity of the Anointed One who knows everything. There is in John a certain distinction between the Prophet and the Messiah (cf. 1, 21), but it should not be forgotten that the Messiah has also prophetic features[3]. He surpasses Moses in the multiplying of the loaves (ch. 6). Just as the prophets are sent by God, so is He. From the messianic point of view we must also see e. g. the changing of water into wine (2, 1 ff.); that has nothing to do with Dionysus[4], but signalizes that the purifying water of the Jewish cult has

---

"Except ye see signs and wonders, ye will in no wise believe." As compared with the usual combination of the two words, the simple use of "signs" in John is significant.

[1] R. Bultmann, Theologie, p. 406f.

[2] Cf. H. L. Strack — P. Billerbeck, Kommentar zum N. T. aus Talmud und Midrasch, München 1922, Bd. I, p. 523f., 593; — The name "He who quickens the dead" (Rom. 4, 17; 2 Cor. 1, 9) is found in the Jewish Daily Prayer, the "Eighteen Benedictions" 2.

[3] Billerbeck, l. c., Bd. II, p. 479f. — In the "Gospel according to the Hebrews" fr. 10 (ed. Klostermann, p. 8) it is said about the prophets μετὰ τὸ χρισθῆναι αὐτοὺς ἐν πνεύματι ἁγίῳ.

[4] See Barrett, St. John, pp. 157f.; Dodd, l. c., pp. 297ff.

been changed into the wine of the messianic meal. Priestly features of the Messiah are missing altogether. He is the Son of David, whose origin the Jews do not know, thinking that He comes from Nazareth and refuting his messianic claim by speaking of Bethlehem, where He was really born (7, 40ff.)[1].

Not only where men speak about Him as being the Messiah, not only where He is addressed as such, but in every single story He is portrayed as the Promised One with colours from the O. T. palette. But the Kingdom of Him who reigns in heaven is completely heavenly, otherworldly; therefore Jesus' kingdom is not of this world and therefore John did not like the apocalyptics revel in all sorts of speculations of the future. Only after the resurrection the disciples understood it: then they saw His glory. John does not speak about the fact that it behoved the Anointed One to die (first point mentioned on p. 180). The sufferings of the Messiah were taken for granted when Jesus was the Messiah, for they belonged to the story of Jesus' life. But also the Cross is seen in the light of the glory and power: Jesus is lifted up (3, 14)[2]. When Jesus is lifted up from the earth, He draws all men unto Himself (12, 32). The expectation is not bound to the earth in any form, but looks to the heavenly kingdom. The scattered children of God, i. e. the members of the chosen People (11, 52), are not gathered to the Holy Land, as in Jewish eschatology, but together. Not Garizim nor Jerusalem are the places of adoration, but the Father seeks those who worship Him in spirit and truth (4, 20ff.). Members of the chosen People are not those who are so by birth, have Abraham as their father, but those who by faith in Jesus have become such, and that is a new birth (1, 13; ch. 3; 8, 33ff.).

The limitations imposed on this paper by the time at our disposal prevent us from entering into a full investigation of Johannine Christology and so we must leave it here. There is

[1] Dodd, l. c., p. 297 says that John 2, 1—11 offers "a particularly striking example of a feature of this gospel which will frequently recur. We may call it the Johannine irony"; cf. also the paper of H. Clavier in Studia Evangelica, p. 261—276.

[2] The two meanings of "to be lifted up" in John have often been commented upon, see e. g. W. Bauer, l. c., p. 56f.; Barrett, l. c., p. 178f.; in general: O. Cullmann, Der johanneische Gebrauch doppeldeutiger Ausdrücke als Schlüssel zum Verständnis des 4. Evangeliums, Theologische Zeitschrift 4 (1948) 360—372.

only one more point left in our text which calls for some comment. It is said there "that Jesus is the Anointed One, the Son of God". Is this combination possible? Great scholars like Dalman and Bousset have denied that the Messiah in Judaism is called "Son of God"; some texts which seem to have the combination like those in 4 Ezra being of doubtful value on textual grounds. Others like Cullmann do not think it impossible[1]. This controversy is as a matter of fact irrelevant for the present discussion of John. This evangelist is fully aware that exactly this point is a stumbling-block unto the Jews. What is relevant is that in John 5 Jesus has done a messianic work (the healing of a crippled man) and He is allowed to do it, because He is the Son of the Father. "For this cause therefore the Jews sought the more to kill him, because ... he called God his own father, making himself equal with God" (5, 18). In 10, 33ff. we are told that the Jews sought to stone Jesus for blasphemy (according to the Law, Lev. 24, 16). But Jesus refutes them with the quotation from Ps. 82, 6: those to whom the word of God came are sons of God. If the Scripture is eternal, they cannot object to Him, because He is not only the hearer of the word, but the messenger, prophet, Messiah. The special concern of John is precisely that Jesus the Messiah is not an ordinary man, a shadowy figure, not an angel, but the Son of God. If it was possible to prove and to persuade the Jews that Jesus by His works was the Messiah, then the further step could be taken: that He is the Son of God. That was not quite impossible on Jewish suppositions. The Christian proof-texts for that contention were Ps. 2, 7; 2 Sam. 7, 14; cf. Hebr. 1, 5[2]. And if the Messiah was really the Son of God, then the appeal of this gospel was the more urgent.

What were the grounds of the certainty that Jesus was the Anointed One? John does not explain the name as Luke twice

---

[1] O. Cullmann, Christologie, p. 280 and note 4 with references to Dalman and Bousset.

[2] Cf. p. 181. Acts 9, 20. 22; Luke 4, 41 the demons went out crying: ὅτι σὺ εἶ ὁ υἱὸς τοῦ θεοῦ, but Jesus rebuked them and did not suffer them to tell ὅτι ᾔδεισαν τὸν Χριστὸν αὐτὸν εἶναι. — Interesting are also the data of Origen who says speaking about Dositheus, the Samaritan, in Contra Celsum I 57: that he pretended ὅτι αὐτὸς εἴη ὁ προφητευόμενος ὑπὸ Μωυσέως Χριστός (= Deut. 18, 15 the Prophet), and in C. C. VII 11 καὶ αὐτὸς υἱὸς

did for his Hellenistic readers (Luke 4, 18; Acts 10, 38). John
assumes that his readers will understand it (it was not a proper
name, but a title full of meaning, cf. p. 175ff.), because the idea of
the Anointed One was familiar to them. It is remarkable that he
speaks in ch. 1 without further notice about the Messiah and
King of Israel. The indication of Luke shows us the way: He was
anointed with the Holy Spirit. This is expressed by John 1, 39:
"John bare witness, saying, I have beheld the Spirit descending
as a dove out of heaven (= from God), and it abode upon him."
On the Messiah rests according to Is. 11, 2 the Spirit of the
Lord[1]. Because it stays with Jesus he can do the signs which
John did not (10, 41); He is the Messiah filled with the Spirit
(7, 38ff.) who can promise the Spirit who leads into the full
truth as a Comforter to His disciples. God is Spirit (4, 24) and
the Son has the Spirit; and no one can enter into the Kingdom of
God in which Jesus is the Messiah, unless born of the Spirit
(3, 6). Let it be noticed that the divine power of the Spirit is
recognized as something extraordinary in Jesus by the Jews.
In dealing with the portrait of Christ in John it is generally
overlooked that Jesus is attacked, because He has a demon. This
expression means more than: "you are mad"[2], as will be seen
from 8, 48ff. and 10, 20f. In the former place the charge is
refuted by reference to the work Jesus did in opening the eyes
of the blind: He honours the Father and proves in that way that
he is a real prophet whose characteristic is that he directs all
attention to God[3]. But that such a charge could be formulated
points to something "peculiar" in Jesus, and I cannot help
thinking that it goes back to the true situation in Jesus' life.

John wrote of these signs in order that his readers might believe
that Jesus was the Anointed One, the Son of God. Facts are used
to prove that the man of Galilee was the Messiah promised to
the Fathers, in the most intimate connection with the Father

τοῦ θεοῦ (see the note in Chadwick's translation, Cambridge 1953, p. 325
note 1) where we have the same connection, but in a rival case.
    [1] See the texts referred to by Billerbeck, l. c., Bd. IV 2, p. 1297,
Register on Is. 11, 2.
    [2] So Barrett, l. c., p. 263.
    [3] In Deut. 13, 5 it is a sign of the false prophet to lead the people
astray.

whom nobody has ever seen (1, 18). The facts he describes are
followed by declarations of Jesus. John knows of attacks
against this claim of his Master, but the central issue is the
Messiahship. These facts happened in Palestine. Who else in the
Roman world could be interested in the question whether the
Messiah had appeared in Jesus of Nazareth except Jews or people
very strongly attached to Judaism, the "God-fearers" of the
synagogues? The whole background of this gospel is packed
with Palestinian stories and conceptions; it smells of the soil of
Palestine[1]. And yet there is also much that is strange to Palestine[2]. How can this combination be explained?

We saw that the way in which John formulated his purpose
brings us into the sphere of the synagogue where Christians
come with their message. This fact is corroborated by some other
facts from the same surroundings: a) Jesus is continually called
by the Jewish title "rabbi" (more frequently than in the other
gospels; Luke avoids it) and a conspicuous place is given to that
"teacher of Israel" Nicodemus (ch. 3; 7, 50; 19, 39); b) Jesus
speaks in 15, 18ff. about the hatred of the world against his followers and promises the Spirit that will bear witness so that thereby they can witness; there is a chance that they may stumble, i. e.
lose sight of his Messiahship, and then Jesus continues: "They
shall put you out of the synagogues: yea the hour cometh that
whosoever killeth you will think that he offereth service to God"
(16, 1f.). How is it possible that the "hatred of the world" takes
the form of "putting out of the synagogue"? In the "Acts of the
Martyrs" we read of quite different forms of punishment. The
answer must be: because John had close relations with the synagogue; see also 9, 22 "for the Jews had agreed that if any man
should confess him to be the Christ, he should be put out
of the synagogue" (pp. 180ff.) and 12, 42; c) Jesus says that He has
been teaching openly in the Temple and the synagogues (18, 20)
and this again represents the "world" (see first half of the
verse).

---

[1] W. F. Albright, Recent discoveries in Palestine and the Gospel of
St. John, in: The background of the New Testament and its eschatology,
essays in honour of Charles Harold Dodd, Cambridge 1956, pp. 153—171,
has stressed this quite recently.

[2] This is always brought to the fore by the Hellenistic and Gnostic
interpretation, and cannot be dismissed.

This synagogue with which John had relations did not exist
in Palestine, but in the Diaspora, because: a) John explains
various usages of the Jews such as their way of purification (2, 6),
of burying (19, 40)[1]; that can only have been done for people
who live outside Palestine; b) the language of John has not only
semitic elements—to give a cautious presentation of a much
disputed matter—, but also typically Greek expressions, such
as $\delta o \xi \acute{a} \zeta \omega$ = "to honour" and "to have an opinion"; for
"world" which is not a direct translation of ʿolam; and on the
whole his Greek can be called fairly good; c) in the interesting
eschatological passage 11, 52 (see pp. 178f.) the "scattered ones"
are not only specially mentioned, but added and this shows the
author's concern for them; probably one may see the same
group alluded to in 10, 16 "and other sheep I have which are
not of this fold; them also I must bring . . . and they shall become
one flock and one fold" (see also p. 188).

If we are justified in locating this Gospel in a Diaspora-syna-
gogue, it is striking to see how beautifully it dovetails with the
picture of the relations between synagogue and Christian-
mission in Acts. Besides the theme of the book, words like
"witness" and "signs", the charge about the Christ-King[2] one
notices the schisms among the Jews (7, 43; 9, 16; 10, 19 with the
stories in Acts 13ff.), the way in which Paul in one place after
another fails to win the synagogue, is the victim of the zeal of
the Jews, becomes an "aposynagogos". In Acts also we find an
explanation of the curious fact that has long puzzled the commentators. John speaks about the Jews as the opponents of Jesus
in such a way that it has often given the impression that He had
completely broken with the Jewish people[3]. On the other hand
it cannot be forgotten that he also mentions cases of Jews who
followed Jesus and that he sees Jesus' death as profitable for
the Jewish people (11, 52). The Judeans and the rulers of the Jews
especially lay snares for Jesus. Now, in the sketch of a "Pauline"
sermon given in Acts 13, 16ff. the turning-point falls in vs. 26f.
and there it is said that the word of salvation in the promises of
God to Israel, fulfilled in Jesus, has come to the Diaspora "for
they that dwell in Jerusalem and their rulers, because they

---

[1] A list of them is given by Barrett, l. c., pp. 102 ff.

[2] See p. 181.

[3] Cf. the material in Bauer, l. c., p. 31.

knew him not nor the voices of the prophets which are read every sabbath, fulfilled them by condemning Jesus" etc. There is a distinction made between the Jews in Jerusalem and in the Diaspora, and that would account for the particular presentation in John.

That synagogue of the Diaspora must be sought in the Greek sphere. When Jesus says to the Jews that He will go where they cannot come, their misunderstanding led them to ask: "Whither will this man go that we shall not find Him? Will He go unto the Dispersion among the Greeks, and teach the Greeks?" Why this combination: dispersion . . . among the Greeks? The Jewish Diaspora was spread over all the world: it would have been possible to speak about the Dispersion in general; why is not Babylon, Egypt or Rome mentioned? There is only one explanation possible: because the writer was specially interested in this part of the world, and it is highly probable that we have here a typically Johannine piece of irony: what these Jews thought impossible, has happened, when the Christian missionaries came to that part of the world that was specifically Hellenic. This interest in the dealings of the Greeks is also witnessed in 12, 20: "Now there were certain Greeks among those that went up to worship at the feast; these therefore came to Philip . . . and asked him, saying: Sir, we would see Jesus." These were Greek pilgrims, Jews or at least very much interested in Judaism; were they relatives of those who read the gospel? This attention to the Greeks points to either Greece or Asia Minor[1].

---

[1] The Ἕλληνες = Greeks cannot be taken here in the general sense of "pagans" or the Greek-speaking population of the Empire, because it is a special form of the Dispersion which in itself could be anywhere; see H. Windisch, Ἕλλην, in: G. Kittel, Theologisches Wörterbuch zum Neuen Testament, Stuttgart 1935, Bd. II, p. 506: "Gemeint sind aber tatsächlich die Gegenden dieser Hellenen, denn vermutet wird, er wolle die Hellenen . . . ‚lehren' ". — Cullmann has drawn attention to the special interest of the Fourth Gospel to the Samaritans (Samaria and the Origins of the Christian Mission, in: The Early Church, pp. 185—192). This may reflect a general interest of John in missions and in particular his knowledge about facts related in Acts 8. But on the question about the origin of the Gospel it has less bearing than the somewhat peculiar words about the Hellenes. It may be added that inscriptions of Samaritans have been found in Greece (Athens, see Schürer, a. a. O., Bd. III, p. 56) and that the famous Justin who lived for a time in Ephesus was born in Nablous, is well known.

Are we allowed to infer from the special attention given to Philip (1, 43; 6, 5f.; 12, 20f.; 14, 8f.) that the readers had close relations with him? It is he who brings the Greeks to Jesus. There is a tradition, handed down by Polycrates of Ephesus (end of 2nd cent.), that the apostle Philip had come to Asia Minor and was buried in Hierapolis; an inscription of a church dedicated to "the holy apostle and theologian Philip" was discovered in that place long ago by Ramsay[1]. J. B. Lightfoot defended the trustworthiness of this tradition, but it was rejected by scholars like Zahn, Harnack and W. Bauer who decided for another line of tradition, saying that it was Philip the evangelist (Acts 6, 8; 21, 7) who came to Hierapolis[2]. The question of these different traditions cannot be settled now, but it is noteworthy that such a connection between the apostle Philip and Asia Minor is mentioned.

However this may be, there is another item which points to Asia Minor. Since Baldensperger it has become commonly agreed that the rôle played by John the Baptist in this gospel stamps him so much as the inferior of Jesus that John must have known people who upheld rival claims for the Baptist. Acts 19, 3ff. has a dark piece of information about disciples of this John in Ephesus.

If these considerations are sound, they make us think that the place where John had his disputes with the synagogues was somewhere in Asia Minor and that the old tradition of Irenaeus, saying that the Fourth Gospel originated in Ephesus may be completely right[3]. Led back to this traditional view I may say — to avoid misunderstanding — that until quite recently I

---

[1] See G. Milligan, Philip, in: J. Hastings, Dictionary of Christ and the Gospels, vol. II, p. 359; the text of Polycrates is ap. Eusebius, Hist. Eccl. III 31, 2f.

[2] J. B. Lightfoot, Saint Paul's Epistles to the Colossians and to Philemon, London 1897, p. 45ff.; Th. Zahn, Forschungen zur Geschichte des neutestamentlichen Kanons und der altkirchlichen Literatur, VI. Theil, Leipzig 1900, p. 158—175; A. von Harnack, Die Mission und Ausbreitung des Christentums in den ersten drei Jahrhunderten[4], Leipzig 1924, Bd. II, p. 770; W. Bauer, Nachrichten über die Apostel, in: E. Hennecke, Neutestamentliche Apokryphen[2], Tübingen 1924, p. 101f.

[3] Irenaeus, Adv. Haer. II 22, 5 and III 1, 1—4. This traditional view has often been rejected during the last century. It would be out of place to go over the ground again and to pass in review the conflicting arguments, for which see the various Introductions to the N. T.

held the view that John was written in Syria and I had no inclination to become a defender of the traditional standpoint, but a fresh investigation the successive steps of which have been reproduced on the preceding pages clearly pointed in the direction of Ephesus.

We come to our conclusion: **the purpose of the Fourth Gospel was to bring the visitors of a synagogue in the Diaspora (Jews and Godfearers) to belief in Jesus as the Messiah of Israel.** Thus we have found the "Sitz im Leben" of this puzzling book and it appears not to be so isolated as it has often been thought. It was a missionary book for the Jews (*pace* my friend Riesenfeld). This is the same thesis that was defended 30 years ago by Karl Bornhäuser[1]. His presentation of the case did not prove convincing; not much attention has been paid to it and it was generally rejected. His arguments I cannot accept. But the result, reached along completely different lines, is largely the same. I hope that the line of argument in this paper will stand a critical examination.

John did not write for Christians in the first place, except perhaps in chs. 13—17 which show a somewhat different character, nor did he envisage pagan readers. His book was not an apology to defend the Christian church, but a mission-book which sought to win[2]. For this purpose: to make clear that Jesus is the Messiah, he worked over the material he had received.

I am fully aware that the step we have made is only the first step in dealing with the first part of John's purpose. But should not first things be put first? That we have tried to do. Other steps will have to follow, in order to explore more fully the implications of

---

[1] K. Bornhäuser, Das Johannesevangelium, eine Missionsschrift für Israel, Gütersloh 1928.

[2] P. Winter, Zum Verständnis des Johannisevangeliums, Vox Theologica 25 (1955) [also Theologische Literaturzeitung 1955, 3], p. 155 in a review of Dodd's Interpretation was quite right in asking: "Soll man es als einen Zufall ansehen, daß die im Vierten Evangelium auf Jesus angewendeten Symbole 'Lamm', 'Weinstock', 'Licht der Völker' (oder 'der Welt') auf Vorbilder zurückgehen, die im A. T. durchweg auf Israel angewandt sind?" and in expecting here the answer: that is purpose. But his inference that the Fourth Gospel was directed against a work of Jewish missionary literature is not borne out by facts and is nothing more than an unnecessary guess.

this view for the understanding and exegesis of this Gospel. The historical exactness or inexactness of its picture e. g. has not been decided; the value of the various parts of John must be fixed in each separate case. It may be that the relation of John to the Synoptics will appear in this light somewhat different from the usual conception. It is tempting to make a commentary from this point of view. But does the evangelist himself not say that far more could be said? I have had to content myself to-night with some brief remarks.

John wished to do one thing. That is the reason why on close inspection his gospel looks so frayed. It leaves many open questions and does not iron out everything. It is like an album with a number of different carefully selected drawings of the same person in various situations, and John tells about them, about Him. And the wonderful thing in reading this gospel is always the deep impression that its author has combined these often conflicting bits of information into a marvellous unity. It leaves behind that radiant image of Jesus the Messiah, the Son of God in Whom to believe is life eternal.

> Jesus, these eyes have never seen
> That radiant form of Thine;
> The veil of sense hangs dark between
> Thy blessed face and mine.
>
> Yet, though I have not seen, and still
> Must rest in faith alone,
> I love thee, dearest Lord, and will,
> Unseen, but not unknown.

Christ's Foreknowledge of His Crucifixion

D. E. H. WHITELEY, Oxford

It may at first sight appear to be a piece of superfluous mysti-
fication to ask whether Christ foresaw His own death. In St.
Mark's Gospel, immediately after St. Peter's confession at
Caesarea Philippi, we read: "And he began to teach them that the
Son of Man must suffer many things, and be rejected by the
Elders, and the chief priests, and the scribes, and be killed, and
after three days rise again" (8, 31); this, of course, is not an isolated
passage, but has numerous parallels in all four gospels[1]. Again, to
suppose that Our Lord did not possess foreknowledge of His death
might well seem inconsistent with a belief in His Divinity.

On the other hand, we are bound to consider the possibility that
these predictions are to be regarded as prophecies after the event.
In Acts 2, 23 we read: "Him, being delivered up by the determinate counsel and foreknowledge of God, ye by the hand of
lawless men did crucify and slay." That the crucifixion was part
of God's foreordained plan is a standard theme of the Apostolic
Church[2]. Even if belief in a suffering Messiah did occur in the
Judaism of the First Century A. D., as some[3] have maintained,
it was certainly not widespread. Since the early Christians
rightly saw the hand of God in the Resurrection, they may have
supposed, perhaps incorrectly, that the Crucifixion was due
solely to God's antecedent will; in this case their belief would have
been emphasized in preaching because it provided an answer to
the scandal of a crucified Messiah. Further, the accounts of the
Agony in the Garden of Gethsemane are not easy to reconcile

---

[1] E. g., Mk. 9, 30—32; 9, 12; 10, 32—34; 10, 45; 12, 1—12; 14, 7 and
parallels; Matt. 26, 2; Luke 9, 31; 12, 49; 13, 33; 13, 34 = Matt. 13, 37;
14, 26 = Matt. 10, 37; 17, 25.

[2] E. g., Acts 2, 23; 3, 18; 4, 28; 13, 29; I Cor. 15, 3; I Pet. 1, 11.

[3] The evidence is to be found in Strack-Billerbeck, Kommentar zum
Neuen Testament aus Talmud und Midrasch II, 1924, pp. 273—299.

with the theory that Christ at all times regarded His death as inevitable; nor is the cry of dereliction: "My God, my God, why hast thou forsaken me?" (Mark 15, 34). The lament over Jerusalem[1] does not suggest that Our Lord had always believed His rejection to be a foregone conclusion. In any event, no account is satisfactory which reduces those responsible for the crucifixion, indeed even Christ Himself κατὰ τὴν ἀνθρωπότητα, to the status of mere puppets in the hand of Fate. It has been said of the Incarnation, Crucifixion and Resurrection of Christ that "What has happened is only the emergence into history of what was eternally laid up in the determination of God". Language of this nature, unless very carefully qualified, can lead to a situation in which God's acts of redemption are not taken seriously as acts in history. It cannot be right to water down the perfect humanity of Christ or the reality of His involvement in the world He came to save.

Enough has been said to make it clear that there is a genuine problem to consider. In this paper it will be maintained first, that Christ probably did foresee His own death, although this cannot be viewed as absolutely certain; secondly, that He may have regarded His death as conditionally predestined; and thirdly, that Christ did offer to His contemporaries a real opportunity of repentance and salvation, that He did not merely "go through the motions" of offering salvation, knowing full well that it would inevitably be rejected, in order to demonstrate the justice of their condemnation.

The meaning of the term "conditional predestination" may be illustrated from a Rabbinic solution of the difficulty posed by the contradiction between Genesis 15,13 and Genesis 15, 16. The former verse reads: "And he said unto Abraham, know of a surety that thy seed shall be a stranger in a land that is not theirs, and shall serve them; and they shall afflict them four hundred years." The latter verse includes the words: "And in the fourth generation they shall come hither again." Both these prophecies are made absolutely, no condition being expressed. The solution proposed is that if the Israelites repent they are to be delivered after four generations, if not, after four hundred years[2]. It may

---

[1] Matt. 23, 37—39 = Luke 13, 34. 35.

[2] Strack-Billerbeck, Kommentar zum Neuen Testament aus Talmud und Midrasch II, 1924, p. 670.

be that Christ regarded His death as predestined conditionally upon His rejection by the Jews. He probably thought towards the end of His life that they were unlikely to accept Him. In this case He went up to Jerusalem for the last time fully prepared to die, and no doubt expecting that the fulfilment of God's purpose would indeed take the form of His rejection and death. Nevertheless, the last chance which He offered to His own race during the final week was still a "live option".

Nothing that has been said or will be said in this paper is intended to contravert the inevitability of Christ's death. But this was not due solely to God's will; it was due in part to contingent events, foreseen by God but nevertheless acts of freedom, namely the sin of men in freely rejecting Christ.

It may be urged that it is not legitimate to introduce doctrinal considerations at a Conference on the Four Gospels. But Christian doctrines are not the arbitrary creation of dogmatic theologians; they are based upon the Bible, including the Gospels: such phrases as "the Divinity of Christ" and "the Humanity of Christ" may be regarded as portmanteau expressions referring to bodies of New Testament evidence. Again, theologians and philosophers now have to shout to each other across a wide chasm, and it would be a further tragedy if any similar division should grow up within the field of theology between Biblical scholars and dogmatic theologians. No attempt will be made in this paper to treat of the Atonement, but it will be necessary to speak very briefly about the Incarnation, and at somewhat greater length about Predestination.

There is no insuperable difficulty with regard to the Incarnation so long as we confine ourselves to formal statements. It is true that Christ had two natures and not one; it is also true that there is in Him no duality of persons, but One Person. Such statements may be compared with the ground-plan of a College. From a ground-plan of Christ Church we can learn that the Meadow Buildings are east of the Hall, and that the Cathedral is approached from Tom Quad, and not from Peckwater. But a mere ground-plan, though it may be accurate so far as it goes, does not do justice to the architecture of Christ Church. In the same way a formula like: "Who, although he be God and Man: yet he is not two, but one Christ" is perfectly accurate so far as it goes, but does not give us a full delineation either of the Humanity or of the

Divinity of Christ, and is not intended to do so. Unfortunately, it is not possible to present an account of Christ which will do justice to both of His natures. We may distinguish two manners of representing Christ on the cross: the one portrays a tortured human body hanging from the cross; the other shows us the victorious King, reigning from the Tree. Each of these representations preserves an element of the total truth which we must not overlook, and it is not possible in any form of visual art to portray Christ in a manner which does justice to both. In the same way, if we give an account of Christ which attempts to do justice, subject to our human limitations, to the Divinity, we shall do less than justice to His Humanity and vice versa. If we desire a balanced exposition, we must be content with the bare formulae of the credal documents, which present us with something corresponding to a ground-plan of a building. In this paper we shall attempt to do justice, within the limits of our subject, to His Humanity only, but without any intention of denying by implication either His Divinity or the unity of His Person.

The predictions of the Passion seem to claim for Christ not merely foreknowledge, but foreknowledge of a predestined event. If we believe that God is not subject to limitations of space, time and matter, there is no difficulty in ascribing to Him immediate knowledge of contingent events which to us are still in the future. But two difficulties, not I believe insuperable, immediately arise when we assert that Christ enjoyed foreknowledge of the Crucifixion. First, human beings do not in general know the future; we are compelled to walk by faith and not by sight. If Christ possessed certain foreknowledge of His death, and still more if He foresaw with certainty His own Resurrection, then it is hardly true to say that He was tempted in all things like as we are, yet without sin. Of course, it is not legitimate to press this verse from Hebrews too far or to understand it in an excessively absolute fashion. Secondly, the Evangelists do not appear to view the Crucifixion as a contingent, but as a predestined event: the Son of Man must (δεῖ) suffer many things.

Predestination must therefore receive further consideration. First, predestinarian language and thought were common in Western Asia[1] during the first millenium B. C., especially in the

---

[1] S. Mowinckel, He that Cometh, tr. G. W. Anderson, 1956, pp. 35f.

Old Testament and above all in the Apocalyptic literature. It may be urged that God guided the minds of the Old Testament writers, and that the images and mental framework of Judaism were a mould prepared beforehand by God to receive the molten metal of His full self-revelation in Christ. I have no wish to deny that God guided the minds of those men to whom we owe the Old Testament, prophets, priests and redactors, possibly even in some degree the minds of their intellectual ancestors in Canaan and Mesopotamia. But it is not easy to suppose that Judaism was guided infallibly: Christ had so much to put right. When we consider the use made by Christ of such figures as "Messiah", "Son of Man", "Son of God", etc., we are aware of the fact that He did not find wholly suitable images ready to His hand; they had to be transformed and enhanced, just as the Israelites had transmuted what they took over from their predecessors in Canaan and elsewhere. Many of the bricks in the temple of Hebrew religion may be of Canaanite origin, but the temple which Israel erected from the ruins of Canaanite religion was a Yahwist temple. In the same way we must be careful not to explain Christianity in terms of its origins to such an extent that we overlook its originality. For this reason, we can not assume that the mould of Old Testament thought was infallibly inspired by God. It may be that the predestinarian language which suggests a mechanised fatalism, was in part a legacy from its Jewish past which the New Testament took over somewhat uncritically.

Again, it is legitimate to ask with regard to any theological assertion to what extent it is a statement of fact, and to what extent it expresses an attitude. There are, indeed, philosophers such as J. Wisdom[1] and R. B. Braithwaite[2] who would appear to regard the fundamental tenets of Christianity as mere expressions of attitude. B. Mitchell[3] and E. L. Mascall[4] are surely justified in contending that so to empty Theology of its factual content is not legitimate for a Christian. Yet it remains possible that theological assertions are partly assertions of attitude. It is here suggested that the doctrine of Predestination is in part a statement of

[1] Cp. his article entitled "Gods", Logic and Language, ed. A. G. N. Flew, first series 1951, pp. 187—206.

[2] An Empiricist's View on the Nature of Religious Belief, 1955.

[3] Faith and Logic, 1957, p. 159.

[4] Words and Images, 1957, esp. pp. 14—28 and 46—62.

attitude, the attitude of the man of faith who accepts all life's
blows and gifts "as from the Lord", the man to whom all that
happens is sacramental, to whom every event veils and reveals
a single reality, namely God Himself.

However, the doctrine of Predestination is not concerned with
attitudes alone: it has a factual content. But this factual content
must not be understood as if God were an engineer. Much of the
offence of the doctrine is due to the fact that we understand it in
a mechanistic fashion as a system of depersonalized mechanical
necessities. The Bible teaching on predestination certainly includes an element of necessitation, but it includes far more. In
the words of Mowinckel: " 'Elect' or 'chosen' in the Old Testament
indicates that the person in question stands in a specially close
relationship to Yahweh, partly as the object of His particular care,
love, guidance and protection, partly as His chosen instrument
to fulfil some task and carry out His will." [1] Unfortunately, theologians have strained out the personal element; they have tried to
understand the metaphysical images, to quote A. M. Farrer, by
"getting behind them to a non-metaphorical understanding of
fact"[2]. Worse still, this understanding has been constructed on
the basis of mechanistic concepts.

Yet we cannot evade the question "Is God's purpose for the
world to be achieved or is it not?" And if we are Christians we
are bound to say that God's purpose will be achieved, that God
is powerful over all, παντοκράτωρ. In other words, no Christian
theology worthy of the name can avoid an element of Predestination. But this does not compel us to affirm that every event is
uniquely determined by the will of God. Such language may be
legitimate as a means of expressing adoration to God, but ought
not to be employed as a statement about God's ordering of
mundane events.

If, on the other hand, we extend divine predestination to cover
all events, and understand our statements not as devotional
language but as factual statements concerning the world, we lay
ourselves open to serious difficulties. These difficulties have been
placed in a sharp focus by Professor Antony Flew in an article
entitled "Divine Omnipotence and Human Freedom", which is

---

[1] He that Cometh, p. 365.
[2] The Glass of Vision, 1948, p. 62.

best regarded as a *reductio ad absurdum* of a false understanding of God's omnipotence. Christian apologists who are called upon to reconcile the fact of sin with the doctrine of God's omnipotence normally say that free-will, which makes sin possible, is a necessary precondition of moral growth. Flew replies that it is possible for a man to act with a sense of being free when under the influence of post-hypnotic suggestion[1]. He canvasses a description of God as the Great Hypnotist[2], and suggests that a God who was truly omnipotent could produce morally perfect beings by means of something like post-hypnotic suggestion, thus avoiding the necessity for free-will and the sin which free-will makes possible. Against this contention I should like to quote with general approval the words of L. Hodgson[3]: "To demand that God should be able to make good men by some other method than that on which He is actually engaged, by some method more or less analogous to that of the maker of clockwork toys, is like demanding that He should be able to make square circles." Hodgson would seem to suggest that the impossibility is logical, but surely it is not; it would not involve us in violating the law of non-contradiction, in asserting that the same proposition is both true and false. I would suggest that human free-will, which makes sin possible, is a causally necessary means to human perfection. Flew would not accept this contention, for he says that: "The notion of causally necessary means to ends, as opposed to that of logically necessary preconditions, cannot apply to creative omnipotence."[4] This notion cannot indeed apply to the abstract, mechanistic theory of God's omnipotence against which he is contending and of which he has produced an effective *reductio ad absurdum*. On the other hand, it is compatible with the assertion that God is παντοκράτωρ and, I believe, with a proper understanding of the Bible. It may be felt that I have devoted too much time to philosophical considerations; but it is surely essential to avoid studying the New Testament in isolation from the problems of Christian doctrine, and, more specifically to avoid in our interpretation of the Gospels an understanding of Predestination which can not be reconciled with the fact of human sin.

---

[1] Op. cit., p. 161.

[2] Op. cit., p. 163.

[3] L. Hodgson, For Faith and Freedom, 1956, p. 183.

[4] Op. cit., p. 147.

If we are to account for human sin, we must not allow Predestination to encroach too much upon human freedom, and if we say that Christ lived a truly human life, and was at one with the race He came to save, we must beware of allowing Predestination to bulk too large in the account we give of His life on earth.

When we turn to the Gospels we find a variety of conflicting opinions held by scholars of high standing. The difficulty is that on many of the most important points the evidence of the New Testament itself is not conclusive. Since we all desire certainty, whether negative or positive, there is a great temptation to import surreptitiously a concealed presupposition, which appears to justify itself since it offers a solution to many problems and introduces order into chaos. If, for example, we tacitly accept the presupposition that prophecy is impossible, then all the predictions of the Passion are *vaticinia post eventum* and our quest is ended. I would not maintain the predictions are entirely free from *ex post facto* features, but would rather accept the contention of W. Manson[1] that Christ did foretell His death, although "the details of the predictions have in several cases been supplied from the Passion-history"[2]. In this case we are committed to the view that Our Lord's predictions were partly genuine prophecy and partly prophecy after the event, and that we are not able to draw a line between the two with precision. Such a "facing-both-ways" conclusion lacks the appeal either of a literalist solution which accepts all as genuine prophecy or of a sceptical verdict which consigns them all to the *post eventum* category.

We maintain, then, that the three Predictions of the Passion have a dominical origin, although the phraseology in which they are expressed owes something to the Evangelists, as, no doubt does their position in the structure of the Gospel, and possibly even their number. The belief that prediction is impossible rests upon presuppositions which I am not able to accept. The authenticity of the predictions is not incompatible with free-will or with Our Lord's humanity unless we assume a soulless, mechanical theory of predestination which it is the main object of this paper to attack. The remaining obstacle in the way of accepting them is their obvious apologetic value in the apostolic church. Our evidence for the life and teaching of Christ resides, for all practical

---

[1] *Jesus the Messiah*, 1943, pp. 128 f.

[2] Op. cit., p. 129.

purposes, solely in the Christian tradition preserved for us in the New Testament. Accordingly, it is always possible in principle to ascribe to later tradition any of the pericopae found in the Gospels and to deny them a place in the life of Christ Himself. But though this is always possible in principle, and though it is often impossible to prove conclusively that a particular saying or action ascribed to Christ is in fact authentic, a point arises where this sceptical procedure becomes frankly ridiculous. It is reasonable to suppose that St. Mark, for example, schematized his material on the basis of his theological beliefs. But this does not involve us in believing that his gospel was his own arbitrary creation. It is highly probable that much in the Gospels is based not upon history, but upon the apologetic needs and other interests of the Church. But it is only reasonable to regard the beliefs of the Early Church as a growth from, and a development of the teaching of Christ and not as the creation of the Church itself. The belief that Christ was foreordained to die probably does loom larger, for obvious apologetic reasons, in the thought of the Early Church than it did in the teaching of Christ Himself, but it is surely an exaggeration of something which was already present in the mind of Christ during His earthly ministry rather than an irresponsible fabrication. It is always important to distinguish two separate questions: What is a man's motive for making a statement; and what is the truth of the statement which he makes? Granted that the early Christians were motivated by a desire to counter the difficulty raised by the fact that their Messiah had been crucified, it does not follow that they had to counter this difficulty by telling a lie; why should they not, for apologetic reasons, have told the truth?

Granted that the predictions were moulded by the Church to suit its apologetic needs, there remains a core which has resisted this process. We may take as an example Luke 17, 25 "But first must he suffer many things and be rejected of this generation". M. Goguel comments[1], "It is certainly older than the threefold prediction, which is inconsistent with the ideas of primitive Christianity, since what is spoken of there is suffering and rejection, not death, and since there is no question of resurrection". It is noteworthy that those passages which speak of Christ's death do

---

[1] Jésus, 2nd ed. 1950, p. 123.

not specify crucifixion. Prior to the Passion narratives themselves, the words σταυρός and σταυρόω are found in the Synoptic
Gospels, with the exception of one significant verse, only in
passages which speak of Christ's disciples taking up their cross
and following Him[1]; they do not occur in those sayings which
foretell the death of Christ. The significant exception is provided
by the third prediction of the Passion. Mark reads: "And they
shall mock him, and shall spit upon him, and shall scourge him,
and shall kill him; and after three days he shall rise again"
(10, 34). But in Matthew (20, 18.19) we find a *post eventum* modi-
fication of the *ante eventum* prophecy which is recorded in Mark:
"And they shall condemn him to death, and shall deliver him
unto the Gentiles to mock and to scourge and to crucify;
and the third day he shall be raised up." St. Luke includes the
handing over to the Gentiles, which accords with the facts more
closely than the Marcan version and is therefore probably *post
eventum*, but says nothing about crucifixion (18, 32. 33). Apart
from this single instance, crucifixion is not mentioned in the
predictions. This fact gains in importance when we recollect that
what offended non-Christians was not merely the fact that Christ
had been slain, but the shameful manner of His death. We remember I Cor. 1, 23 "But we preach Christ crucified, unto Jews a
stumbling-block and unto Gentiles foolishness", and Gal. 3, 13,
"Cursed is everyone that hangeth upon a tree"[2]. The fact that in
every passage except one the synoptists have refrained from
justifying the actual instrument of execution, the cross which
gave so much offence, by means of predictions referring back to
God's predestined purpose and to the Old Testament is a
tribute to their reliability. It is not necessary to labour this
point, since among contemporary scholars it is generally agreed
that Christ foresaw His death, and regarded it as part of the
divine plan.

It is otherwise in the case of our next thesis, which is that
Christ regarded His death as predestined conditionally, and that
even in Gethsemane He still had a real hope that the cup might
pass away. To this thesis the main weight of New Testament
scholarship is opposed. E. Stauffer, for example, writes "But the
way of the Lord, which God had ordained before-hand from the

[1] Matt. 10, 38; 16, 24; Mk. 8, 34; Lk. 9, 23; 14, 27.
[2] Cp. I Cor. 1, 18; Phil. 2, 8; Heb. 12, 2.

beginning, is foretold in scripture chiefly as a way of suffering ...
The scripture is a guarantee that along this road there are
neither accidents nor chances. Like a star that shines in the
night sky, Jesus pursues his prescribed path ... In Gethsemane
He prepared himself for the fateful hour of his own life, and indeed
of all history."[1] The historicity of the Agony in the Garden is
dismissed by C. Guignebert[2] and seriously challenged by Goguel[3].
E. Klostermann[4] scouts the idea that Christ remained within the
range of hearing of the three disciples, so that they could be
witnesses of His wrestling in prayer. He makes the acid comment
that the writer knows what Jesus said in prayer even when the
disciples are asleep. The objections which may be raised against
the historicity of the Gethsemane episode are first that Christ
would not pray to escape from the task prescribed for Him by
God; secondly, that our accounts lack continuity, with the result
that it is difficult to reconstruct the sequence of events without
having to supply details not recorded by the Evangelists; and
thirdly, that the only possible witnesses are said to have been
asleep at the time. In reply to the first objection it will suffice
to quote the words of Dr. Farrer: "Christ had foretold his
betrayal and death several times before he ever prayed in
Gethsemane. But to deny him recourse to prayer because of
predestination is to turn a faith in Providence into a soulless
fatalism."[5] As an example of the somewhat incoherent manner
in which the scene is depicted, we may take the point made by
Goguel[6]: "In the Gethsemane episode the detail of the inner
circle of three who were taken further than their fellow apostles
could well have been added later, since, when Jesus returned to the
place where he had left them, it has not been stated that they
returned together to rejoin the eight others, and yet the eleven
seem to be present at the moment of the arrest" (since it is
recorded that they all left him and fled). Goguel's point is a valid
refutation of the contention that Mark provides us with a full,
orderly and complete account of everything that occurred. But

---

[1] New Testament Theology, tr. J. Marsh, 1955, pp. 26—27.
[2] Jesus, tr. S. H. Hooke, 1935, p. 458.
[3] Op. cit., p. 274.
[4] Das Markus-Evangelium, 4th ed. 1950, p. 150.
[5] A Study in St. Mark, 1951, p. 197.
[6] Op. cit., p. 274.

it is not here suggested that St. Mark wrote history of such a kind. I am prepared to agree with Guignebert[1] and many others that the Gethsemane episode may have played a part in the liturgical re-enactment of the Passion. But there is in principle no reason why the fact that an account owes its preservation to liturgical use should be held to disprove its historicity. The liturgical use accounts for the absence of connecting passages to which Goguel draws our attention but does not in itself militate against the substantial historicity of the Gospel account, especially since there are solid grounds for accepting it.

With regard to the sleep of the three apostles, some interesting suggestions have been made by Professor Daube[2]. They are based upon Mishna Pesahim 10, 8[3], in which it is laid down that the Passover meal is terminated and may not be resumed if all those taking part fall asleep. A second-century Rabbi adds that if they merely doze, the meal is not terminated. A fifth-century Rabbi adds that a man may be said to be merely dozing "if, when addressed, he replies but does not know how to answer sensibly"[4]. Daube points out that this reminds us of Mark 14, 40, "For their eyes were very heavy, and they wist not what to answer him". His main contention is that this Rabbinic evidence explains why such emphasis is laid upon the sleep of the disciples: Jesus wished them to keep awake, so that the Passover meal should not be terminated.

I should like to advance three very tentative proposals, for which, of course, Professor Daube cannot be held responsible. In Mark 14, 40 "And again he came, and found them sleeping, for ($\gamma \grave{\alpha} \varrho$) their eyes were very heavy and they wist not what to answer him", the $\gamma \grave{\alpha} \varrho$ may well be epexegetic. In this case we can explain the verse, "He found them sleeping, that is to say, their eyes were very heavy, and they were not able to answer him intelligibly". This does suggest that the disciples were dozing rather than sleeping soundly. In any case, we are not told that all three were sound asleep the whole time. If even one was awake for part of the time he could have overheard the prayer, grasped

---

[1] Op. cit., p. 458.

[2] D. Daube, The New Testament and Rabbinic Judaism, 1956, pp. 332—5.

[3] Tr. Danby, p. 151.

[4] R. Ashi, Bab. Pes. 120b.

its tenor and passed it down to St. Mark by way of the Passion narrative. Secondly, it may be that Christ hoped for a great saving act of God, an antitype to His act of salvation at the first Passover, and that this was His reason for wishing to prolong the feast by keeping His companions awake. Thirdly, this would account for His surprise[1] (ἤρξατο ἐκθαμβεῖσθαι). He may have expected a divine act which would turn the hearts of the disobedient to the wisdom of the just, and it is possible that He was amazed at its non-occurrence. This speculation — for it is no more — is not inconsistent with the fact that He foretold His death. He probably saw ahead two paths, the path of rejection and death and the path of acceptance by the Jews. God had predestined both of these paths, but had not predestined which one He had to follow. Christ probably thought it more likely that He would have to follow the path which lead through death, but it was not until Gethsemane that the alternative was ruled out. Yet when Christ realised that the alternative had been ruled out, He accepted the cup in complete obedience.

It is illuminating to contrast the Marcan account of Gethsemane with the idealized description of the Martyrdom of the seven brethren recorded in II Maccabees 7. The seven faced their death with stoical courage. It is difficult to see how the Gethsemane account could have arisen unless it were true. This point has been argued forcibly by Vincent Taylor[2] and many others. We do not know of any body of Christians who could have fabricated such an account. It would, of course, be a valuable weapon against the false views propounded in the Gospel of Peter: "But he kept silence as one feeling no pain."[3] Yet there is no evidence for errors of this type in the middle of the first century A. D. It is true that in Hebrews 4, 14—16 and above all 5, 7—10, we find an echo of something like the Gethsemane tradition which serves a purpose in the argument of the book, being employed to show that Christ our great high-priest is one with us. Yet the ideals of the epistle with regard to martyrdom, as expressed in Ch. 11, recall II Maccabees rather than St. Mark's account of Gethsemane. It would seem that the author of the epistle was quite

---

[1] H. B. Swete, The Gospel according to St. Mark, 2nd ed. 1902, ad loc.
[2] The Gospel according to St. Mark, 1952, ad. loc.
[3] The Apocryphal New Testament, ed. and tr. M. R. James, 1924, p. 91.

incapable of inventing his "Gethsemane passage" but availed himself of a tradition which came to him from his predecessors in the faith. Our knowledge of early Christianity is far from being exhaustive, so no argument from silence can be conclusive in a matter of this nature. But since we can point to no body of Christians who might have invented a story of this kind, and since to most it must have been an embarrassment, we are justified in concluding that the Gospel accounts of Gethsemane, although their phraseology owes something to liturgical παράδοσις, are probably based upon solid history.

It has been suggested in this paper that Christ viewed His predictions of the Passion on a basis of "conditional predestination". There is to be found in the Bible and in later Judaism a strand of conditional predestination, that is to say, of passages in which conditional prophecies, or prophecies which are so regarded, are expressed in absolute language. Nathan says to David "The child also that is born to thee shall surely die" (II Sam. 12, 14). No language could be more absolute; yet David's attitude is expressed by the words: "Who knoweth whether the Lord will not be gracious unto me, that the child may live?" (II Sam 12, 22). Isaiah said to Hezekiah, "Thou shalt die and not live" (II Kings 20, 1), which again is absolute language. But in the event God heard Hezekiah's prayer and added fifteen years to his life. The *locus classicus* for this type of thought is of course Jer. 18, 5—12. The Book of Jonah would appear to rest upon similar presuppositions. In all these cases, except the first, prophecy is conditional upon the free response of human beings. The promise of Christ to the apostles that they should sit on twelve thrones judging the twelve tribes of Israel is expressed unconditionally in spite of the fact that it is addressed to a group which included the traitor Judas. The Rabbinic doctrine of Predestination was softened by the possibility that God's decrees might be modified through prayer or righteous acts[1].

In view of these facts it seems possible that Christ may have foretold His death, perhaps in absolute terms, without regarding it as predetermined in a mechanical fashion. Since He did in fact die and rise again it is natural that the New Testament writers

---

[1] J. Bonsirven, Le Judaisme Palestinien au temps de Jésus-Christ, 1935, vol. I, p. 191; cp. H. H. Rowley, The Biblical Doctrine of Election, 1950, p. 170.

should stress this element in His teaching, especially for apologetic reasons. In addition, they rightly regarded all that He did as a fulfilment of God's purpose, and it is easy to employ deterministic language when speaking about God's purpose. On the other hand, in the Gethsemane account and elsewhere[1] we find evidence that Christ did not view His death as mechanically predetermined. This element would not be likely to bulk as largely in Christian tradition as it did in Our Lord's own teaching, since it envisaged a possibility which has not in fact been fulfilled.

This hypothesis cannot be regarded as certain. It is possible to regard all prophecies of the passion as *vaticinia post eventum*, but only at the cost of doing violence to the New Testament. It is also possible to regard the predictions as based upon a soulless mechanical doctrine of Predestination, but if we do so we encounter grave theological and philosophical difficulties and are obliged to give less than their natural value to the Gethsemane episode and similar passages. The hypothesis of "conditional predestination" cannot claim to be more than an hypothesis, but it does at least avoid these formidable difficulties.

---

[1] Cp. C. J. Cadoux, The Historic Mission of Jesus, 1941, pp. 183—193.

The Gospel-Epistle Relationship in Canon and Liturgy

R. R. WILLIAMS, Bishop of Leicester

In the nineteenth and early twentieth centuries, in what might be called the pre-Hoskyns period of New Testament criticism, the difference between the general spirit of the Gospels and the general spirit of the Epistles was freely recognised. On the whole the Epistles were felt to represent a decline from the Gospels. The teaching of the Gospels was felt to be simple and direct; that of the Epistles to be complicated and obscure. The Gospels were thought to be mainly ethical; the Epistles doctrinal, their theological content being looked upon as an artificial superstructure bearing little relation to the spontaneous and natural outlook of the Gospels. The Gospels were thought of as the original, primary documents of the Christian Church, the Epistles as secondary, marking a stage on the way to the catholicising of the Church in the third and fourth centuries. There were of course many variations in the way this thesis was held and presented. Harnack, who is usually quoted as the typical exponent of this view, did not hold a theory of decline as between Gospel and Epistle, but rather felt that St. Paul had carried out a necessary process of selection from the Gospel material whereby Christianity had been released from its excessive Judaistic character and liberated so that it could become a world faith, but the difference between Gospel and Epistle is something that he would gladly have admitted.

Since Hoskyns, especially since the publication of *The Riddle of the New Testament*, all this has changed. Hoskyns — and he of course had precursors as well as successors — held that all the New Testament documents, when submitted to the most rigorous critical and historical tests, converge on a single point, the supernatural act of God in the Incarnation of the Son of God, and his redemptive work, before which every man has to come to a decision of stupendous significance. This he found in the Gospels equally as in the Epistles. The Gospels were shown to present not an amiable moral teacher, but a portent, a staggering intruder from another world, challenging His contemporaries and their successors to answer the question "What think ye of Christ?" Under this impetus, many scholars have written books and articles to illustrate the underlying unity of the New Testament documents. A. M. Hunter devoted to this subject his book *The Unity of the New Testament*, C. H. Dodd in *New Testament Studies* contributes a chapter on the essential unity of St. Matthew's Gospel with the Pauline theology, something that would have been considered a *tour de force* a few years previously. J. C. Fenton in *Studies in the Gospels* (Essays in memory of R. H. Lightfoot) writes on *Paul and Mark*, striving to show that Mark is full of characteristic Pauline concepts. C. P. M. Jones does the same thing for Luke and Hebrews.

All this may be carried so far as to obscure some very great differences in the approach of evangelist and apostle. I desire to show the differences which still separate the writers of these two kinds of literature, and to pose the question as to how such very different kinds of writing came to be bracketed together in the second century Church, and to remain so ever since. By A. D. 170, at the very latest, Gospels and Epistles were felt to make up together — with some other works — the Canon of the New Testament. Almost as soon as we can trace the substance of the Liturgy, Gospels and Epistles are read side by side. For purposes of Canon and Liturgy they were felt to be complementary, in spite of any apparent differences or divergencies in their outlook. How that may have come to be is our question, but before we approach it, in view of the "post-Hoskyns" stress on unity, it is necessary to consider once more the differences between Gospels and Epistles.

It is at once apparent that a Gospel and an Epistle are quite different kinds of literature. The Gospel is dealing with the past; the Epistle with the present — at least this is superficially true. The evangelist may have a present purpose — to convert, to edify, to encourage, — but he does it by means of recreating the past, presenting a record of the birth, life, teaching, miracles, passion, and resurrection of a historical figure, who lived perhaps thirty, forty, fifty years before. The Apostle gives his message direct to his readers — dealing with their problems, and giving his contemporary, authoritative advice and exhortation. He may know a good deal of the evangelical tradition — here and there he may refer to it, or even quote it — but in the main he goes straight to his subject. The two literatures must have originated in a different need, possibly in different geographical environments.

Following on from this, it is only to be expected that the local colour and background of the two types of literature is very different. The Gospels, though written in Greek, are naturally strongly Palestinian in general character. In the Gospels we meet with rabbis, priests, Pharisees, Sadducees; we move in fields and villages; we visit Temple and Synagogue. We are aware all the time of the social customs of Palestine, its weddings and funerals, its journeyings and homecomings, we even sense the architecture of its houses. All this is forgotten in the Epistles. In so far as any local colour is available — and the first impression created is one of its absence rather than its presence — it is that of the Graeco-Roman world of the Eastern Mediterranean. We come across the heathen temples of Corinth, the games, the triumphal processions of victorious Caesars, the palace guard, the divisions between bond and free, Greek and barbarian. We are in a new world, and it is not the same world, as that in which the life of Jesus had its setting.

Further, the historical perspective implied in the two literatures is very different, and this is perhaps the most significant of all the divergences. In the Epistles, the historical interest in Christ is centred on the great decisive events, considered in their theological meaning — His Incarnation, His Death, Resurrection and Ascension. This is so obvious as hardly to need illustration, but a reference to I Cor. 15, 1—8, or to Phil. 2, 5—11 shows at once what is meant. The apostle does not so much look back to Christ as up to Him. The evangelist on the other hand looks back not only to the broad outline of the Gospel events — he has this outline as a framework — but he looks back to the detailed events and episodes, to the actual miracles, the parables one by one, the training of the twelve, the story of the Passion told in great detail.

Every Anglican priest must be aware of this "switch" in perspective when he turns from the Epistle to the Gospel in the Holy Communion service. In the Epistle, the work of Christ is surveyed as a whole, through a telescope. In the Gospel it is surveyed in detail, through a microscope. The microscopic cross section needs much more in the way of skilled interpretation than the telescopic panorama. It is a common belief that the Epistles are hard — this view has been held since the time of the author of II Peter — and that the Gospels are easy. This is quite a misunderstanding. The actual words of the Epistles may be abstract and technical, but the meaning is direct, contemporary, immediate. The words of the Gospels may be easy, but to grasp their significance involves (1) a knowledge of the geographical and historical background of the passage — e. g. what virgins did at weddings, how people thought about lepers, how a man could come down through a roof — and (2) — this is harder — how an individual episode, a miracle or parable fits into the context of the work of Christ as seen from our historical viewpoint, two thousand years or so after the Crucifixion.

This leads on to the last major difference to which I shall refer, the difference in doctrinal outlook. For the moment we may confine our attention to the Synoptic Gospels and the Pauline Epistles. If we included the Fourth Gospel on one side and St. James on the other we should find the gap between the two groups narrowed, but it is quite measurable between, shall we say, Romans and parts of St. Matthew. In a sentence, could we not say that while St. Paul's motto is "not of works", there are large sections of the Gospels where good works, in one form or another, are strongly insisted upon? We might think of the teaching of St. John the Baptist, "Bring forth fruits meet for repentance", and much of the teaching of the Lord. Parables like those of the wicked servant, or the sheep and the goats, much of the Sermon on the Mount, or the teaching against Pharisees, seem at first sight to present a direct moral challenge to improved and re-orientated living. If we had not the Epistles we could hardly have anticipated, from the Synoptic Gospels, such a concentration upon faith in Christ Crucified as we find in, say, Galatians, although having the Pauline Epistles in our hand, it is not impossible to find points of contact. We can illustrate this from the Gospel and Epistle for this week, that for the 13th

Sunday after Trinity. The Epistle ends "The Scripture hath
concluded all under sin that the promise by faith of Jesus Christ
might be given to them that believe". The Gospel says that the
way to obtain eternal life is to love God and one's neighbour, and
of the latter love the example is given of the behaviour of the
good Samaritan. The parsons and theologians can harmonise
these two points of view — in any case we are forbidden by the
20th Article to expound one place of Scripture so that it be
repugnant to another! — but the simple worshipper could be
forgiven if he were somewhat confused. Stories like that of the
Prodigal Son, the Pharisee and the Publican and the woman in
Simon's house, which come much nearer to the Pauline outlook
on justification by faith, only throw into greater relief the great
mass of the Gospel material.

This then is the picture. At the same time as the Pauline Epistles
were being treasured, and about the same time as they were
being collected and "published" — if we take a common modern
view — there were appearing the volumes which we now call
the Gospels. It is surely very probable that these very divergent
types of literature grew up in different circles, probably in different parts of the Mediterranean world. If this is not true of the
Gospels as we know them, it surely must have been true of the
processes whereby the Gospel sources were treasured, gathered,
and edited.

The view that the Epistles held their own, almost unrivalled by
the Gospel-type of literature, till well into the Second Century is
supported by such evidence as is forthcoming from the Apostolic
Fathers. In these writers what we find is (1) a frequent emphasis
on the *Kerygma*, the broad outline of the Gospel story, much as
we find in the Pauline Epistles, (2) occasional "tags" if I may
call them so from the Gospels, brought in to illustrate and drive
home some particular moral or spiritual lesson. This applies to
all the Apostolic Fathers with the exception of the *Didache*, which
must be considered separately. It will be profitable to set out
the evidence for this point in some detail.

In 1905 a book was produced by a Committee of the Oxford
Society of Historical Theology called *The New Testament in the
Apostolic Fathers*. The main interest of its writers was to examine,
by minute literary tests, the number and exactitude of references to New Testament passages in the Apostolic Fathers.

They classed the quotations or allusions they found as A, B, C, D — A being the quotations which were more or less unmistakable, B those which were fairly certain, C and D those which were felt to be more and more doubtful. It is significant that of their six A's all are from the Epistles; of their fourteen B's, twelve are from the Epistles. Clearly the Epistles had reached a stage where they were frequently quoted, with some degree of authority, and the Gospels had not yet reached this stage.

Let us review the use of the Gospels in these Fathers, as far as we can trace it.

Clement of Rome (13, 1) when insisting on lowliness of mind, says, "especially remembering the words of the Lord Jesus, which he spake, teaching gentleness and long suffering". Then follow words very similar to Mt. 5, 7 and Lk. 6, 31. 36—38, but words which fall short of direct quotation. They may come from some written or unwritten catechesis. A very similar quotation is found in the Epistle of Polycarp (Pol. 2, 3) and Lightfoot thinks that Polycarp is here more or less quoting Clement. In Barnabas 5, 9 there is an allusion to Mt. 9, 11—13 — about Jesus not calling righteous but sinners — and in 4, 14 the words occur "as it is written 'Many are called, but few chosen'" (Mt. 22, 14).

In the letters of Ignatius there are five possible references to the Gospels of which the most interesting is Smyrneans 1, 1 where it is stated that our Lord was "baptised to fulfil all righteousness", a fairly close reference to Mt. 3, 15. In Eph. 17, 1, Ignatius says "The Lord received the ointment upon the head" apparently referring to Mt. 26, 7 — this is about the only direct reference in the Apostolic Fathers to an actual incident in the Gospel story, other than the great crises of birth, death and resurrection.

Polycarp (7, 2) does refer to the words of Jesus "The spirit is willing but the flesh is weak" (Mt. 26, 41).

There are a few other allusions, but these are the chief. It is clear that the Gospels had not yet established themselves in the Christian world as a whole as a frequent source of reference and fount of authority. We may contrast the words of Clement in reference to I Corinthians (47, 1) "Take up the Epistle of the Blessed Paul, the Apostle, What first did he write to you in the

beginning of the Gospel?" ("The Gospel" here means the story
of the Gospel-created church, as in Phil. 4, 15.)

The *Didache*, it is true, presents a different picture. Here we find
the two commandments (1, 2), the negative form of the golden
rule, the Trinitarian formula (7, 1), the Lord's Prayer ("as the
Lord commanded in His Gospel", 8, 1), and "the ordinance of the
Gospel" in reference to the maintenance of apostles and prophets (11, 3). It is rather interesting that the *Didache* — a church
order of the Pastoral Epistle type — is so much more strongly
tinctured with Gospel material than the epistolary literature of
Clement and Ignatius. One might conjecture that in circles
where they wished to preserve the structure of the community
on primitive lines, they also preserved the tradition of the words
and works of the historic Jesus. It would not be surprising if this
happened in Syria, and this would be a natural site for the emergence both of St. Matthew and the *Didache*.

We are now beginning to ask whether the emergence of
Gospels — as apart from the material which was used in them,
much of which had a continuous life within the Church from very
early days (see e. g. I Cor. 7, 10) — was not connected with a
desire to link up the contemporary experience of the Church
with its historic beginnings in Galilee and Jerusalem, whatever
may have been the reason for this desire. If so, we should expect
to see traces of this desire in the Gospels themselves, especially
in their opening or introductory words. Curiously enough, this
is exactly what we do find.

The very first word of St. Mark is beginning Ἀρχὴ τοῦ εὐαγ-
γελίου Ἰησοῦ Χριστοῦ — the beginning of the Gospel history
centred in Jesus Christ was . . . (1, 1). St. Matthew shows that
the true beginning was further back. He does not use ἀρχή but he
uses γένεσις. His opening words (1, 1) are βίβλος γενέσεως and
although this phrase occurs in Gen. 5, 1 for "book of genealogy"
the thought of ultimate origin is certainly included in it. He says
in effect "God's redemption began not with John the Baptist,
not even with David, but with Abraham." Luke is still more definite. Many had by this time taken it in hand to draw up a
narrative of those things which had been done "even as those
who were eye-witnesses from the beginning — οἱ ἀπ᾽ ἀρχῆς
αὐτόπται — had handed over". Luke too had qualified to write,
for he had traced the course of all things ἄνωθεν and ἀκριβῶς —

to the source, and with accuracy. St. John goes further back still. Like Mark, he begins with the thought of ἀρχή — ἐν ἀρχῇ ἦν ὁ λόγος — the beginning of the εὐαγγέλιον was not in Palestine, not with Abraham, but in the eternal counsels of God, where ὁ λόγος was not a message, but one who was in the bosom of the Father, the Eternal Word, made flesh in Gospel times. (The phrase ἀπ᾽ ἀρχῆς is much used in the Johannine Epistles, which suggests that the appeal to "the beginning" was particularly valuable in times and in circles threatened with Gnosticism.)

We can now begin to piece together the evidence such as it is — and it is not very complete evidence — and work out a hypothetical sequence of events in the writing, circulation, acceptance and use of both Epistles and Gospels.

Stage one is the period between the first Easter and the writing of the first Epistles — shall we say from A. D. 30 to A. D. 50 During these twenty years the centre of gravity in the Church was Palestine and Syria and it is probable that Jewish Christianity — Hebrew and Hellenistic — dominated the scene. If an Epistle like that of St. James is at all characteristic of some of the current thoughtforms, we shall not be surprised if it was the period when the teaching of Jesus was treasured, and arranged. "Q", if it existed, would have emerged in this stage, but how far it was known outside Palestinian circles, we cannot say. It was preserved in Greek, which takes it out of the Hebraic environment, but perhaps it went little further. Some other Gospel material, e. g. the Passion stories would have taken shape now. St. Paul, at the end of the period, had the story of the Last Supper, and that of the Resurrection appearances, at his finger tips.

Stage two is the great period of Epistle writing — roughly from A. D. 50 to A. D. 70, though the *terminus ad quem* cannot be precisely stated — it could as easily be put twenty years later, and later still if every possible Epistle — e. g. II Peter — is included. This period may be thought to come to something of a climax at the end of the century with the collection and "publication" of the collected Pauline letters. We have seen that the Epistles dominated the Apostolic Fathers, and a period of strong epistolary influence from A. D. 100 to 140 would fit in with this picture.

Stage three is partly contemporaneous with stage two, but is more limited geographically. It is the period of Gospel-writing,

and can be placed in the years A.D. 65—90 if the Fourth
Gospel is not taken into account. These Gospels brought together
the Q teaching, the Passion stories, much more teaching which
had circulated in isolated sections, and many miraculous narratives, including the birth and resurrection episodes. This movement cannot have been too localised, for a Gospel like Mark became known to the authors of Matthew and Luke, and Luke
says that many had taken the task of Gospel writing in hand.
The paucity of quotations from Gospels in the Apostolic Fathers
shows however that they did not loom large in the armoury of
matter to which Christian writers and leaders resorted — except
in the writing of a book like the *Didache*, whose date is in any
case uncertain.

Stage four — which we may put from A. D. 140 to 160 — is the
period when the Gospels greatly increased in popularity and
widespread use. We can think of various reasons for this. One was
the sense that even the second generation of Christians was
rapidly disappearing. As Papias shows, about this time, it was
now a privilege to meet someone who had known a disciple. This
would make for the preservation of the apostles' "memoirs" as
Justin Martyr calls the Gospels in this period. The final destruction
of Jerusalem may have further impressed upon Christians throughout the Empire that the only sheet-anchor to link them to their
origins was in the Gospels.

Another reason was the increasing threat from Gnosticism.
While exact dates for this are hard to define, we know that some
forms of Gnostic teaching were already a problem in the sixties
of the first century, and the movement generally a major threat
by the later decades of the second century, as Irenaeus shows. It
is reasonable to guess that the middle decades of the century
were the decades of increasing danger.

The fact that Marcion placed St. Luke alongside his "aposto-
likon" showed that the Church must quickly claim the Gospels
and give them an honoured place alongside the Epistles. Some
have thought that in this sense Marcion had a canon before the
Church. Certainly his list of books is the earliest we have, but
the criticisms levelled against it by Tertullian may imply a
standard canon against which it was compared.

Stage five — say from A. D. 150 to 175 — (and I am purposely
making these phases overlap) is the period of the emergence

of a balanced canon. By the time of the Muratorian Fragment
it has reached a form not markedly different from the Canon
that we know. Subsequent changes were peripheral, not fundamental. And by this time we see the Church confidently bracket-
ing together such divergent authorities as Matthew and Paul.
The Gospels they put first. Why? Presumably because their subject matter came first in time, even if they were written later
than the Epistles. But more probably, in order to bring into
being a "New Testament" to balance the Old. The earlier volume
began with history and law, and went on to prophecy. Why should
not the New Testament begin with the Gospel history and the
New Law, and go on to prophetic apostolic comment upon it?

We do not know how soon the reading of lections from
"Epistles" and "Gospels" in that order began in the eucharistic
liturgy. We do know that in Justin Martyr's time readings were
given from the Prophets and from the Gospels (to take the usual
view of ἀπομνημονεύματα τῶν ἀποστόλων) to which Justin
refers in close proximity to the "writings" of the apostles, which
he says were read "as far as time allowed". In the Liturgy of the
Apostolic Constitutions (4th century) there were many lections, we
do not know how many. By the earliest full representatives of the
Roman Mass there were only two, the Epistle and Gospel, but
the former was often in fact a prophetic lection. It remains a
mystery why the Gospel, which comes first in the Canon, should
come last in the Liturgy. Does it mean that the order Prophet,
Epistle, Gospel goes back before the fixing of the Canonical order?
Or did they want to bring the words and works of Jesus as close
as possible to the climax of the service? Was it that the Gospel
had been part of the service from earliest days, and the Epistle an
"optional extra", read before the service, if there happened to be
one available? The fact that people stood for it, and that it was
read by a priest or deacon, suggests that they wanted to give it
the place of honour by reading it last.

I should like to conclude this paper by mentioning the special
point of view of the Fourth Gospel in connection with the
matters we have discussed. It would appear that the Fourth
Gospel presents an attempted synthesis between the typical
approach of a Gospel and an Epistle. Like a Gospel, it attaches
great importance to the historical facts of the life of the Incarnate
Lord. Like a Gospel, it gives a great deal of teaching as coming

from the lips of Jesus. But like an Epistle it speaks directly to its readers. All is set in the framework of the great credal assertions. Often a dialogue between Jesus and another — Nicodemus or Thomas — passes imperceptibly into a direct challenge to the contemporary reader. The author "had something there", if we may speak thus crudely.

For is not this still an urgent pastoral problem? We tell our people — our young people especially — that they must "follow Jesus", that they must heed His teaching, and imitate His example. But we know that the Synoptic presentation of that teaching is so firmly set in its Palestinian environment that they will not easily find the guidance they need in much of the Synoptic Gospels. The Epistles would speak to them more directly, viewing the great credal facts as in the past, as we must do. But the actual words are difficult, the arguments involved and complicated; and the spiritual experience, which is assumed in the Epistles, is non-existent, or extremely immature, in our modern hearers. So it is that the Epistle finds no echo in our present-day congregation; the Gospel, though often arresting, gracious, compelling, is not integrated into any theological framework which makes modern application possible. Is the answer to be found along the lines of the Fourth Gospel? Is this the right starting-point after all for our modern catechumens? Or should we give our own *midrash* on the Gospels as medieval priests sometimes did, and illustrate the great doctrinal assertions of the Epistles, as we go along, with the illustrative material supplied by the Gospels?

The questions are easier to ask than to answer.